LISA PINTO

Behavior Problems in Dogs

Second Edition

William E. Campbell
Dog Owner Guidance Service
487 Penny Lane
Grants Pass, Oregon 97526

Editor: Paul W. Pratt, VMD
Production Manager & Cover Design:
Elisabeth S. Stein

American Veterinary Publications, Inc.
5782 Thornwood Drive
Goleta, California 93117
© 1992

Library of Congress Catalog Card Number: 91-75740
ISBN 0-939674-36-X

Printed in the United States of America

Dedication

To my wife, Peggy.

She is still more important to me and my work than words can express.

And to the memories of Tally, the Dalmatian, and Randy, the Norwegian Elkhound, who functioned as photographic models, guinea pigs for new methods, co-residents for live-in deliquent canines, and self-controlled "bait" when used in controlling vicious dog-fighters, all without a growl or whimper, without leashes, force or punishment, all for the satisfaction of functioning within our "pack" and the rewards of praise and a few pets.

We could not have succeeded without them.

Acknowledgment

Special thanks and gratitude are owed to the following people for their contributions to my knowledge, experience, attitudes, skills and the opportunity to compile them herein with the conviction that they fill an important need: Ethologist Dare Miller, PhD, for the introduction and early guidance in the "causative" approach to problems; J. Fred Smithcors, DVM, PhD, for the initial opportunity to express new ideas to the veterinary profession; Bonnie Beaver, DVM, MSc, for broadening my understanding of veterinary attitudes and motives from those of the clinician to those of the academic, allowing, I hope, more effective communication; Al Plechner, DVM, for unselfishly sharing his work on the causes for food-induced hypersensitivities; Jim Harless, DVM, for introducing me to "choline loading," which extended and enhanced life for "Randy" and so many other geriatric dogs; Robert M. Miller, DVM (RMM), whose cartooning genius and success convinced me there is a need for humor in "unrefereed" veterinary literature; the thousands of veterinarians in hospitals and clinics who dispense my BehavioRx series of behavior problem program brochures and subscribe to the HelpLine services, proving that the methods really work; and Paul W. Pratt, VMD, publisher and editor of this work, for the opportunity to update and expand many aspects of the first edition in light of today's needs.

And, finally, to S.A. Corson, PhD, whose commitment to sharing his knowledge of hyperkinesis in dogs has saved thousands of pets from euthanasia, and their owners from needless grief.

William E. Campbell

Contents

(This page intentionally left blank)

Foreword

Thirty-two years of veterinary practice involving all kinds of animals, including housepets, horses, livestock and zoo species, taught me that behavior problems were the leading source of questions by animal owners. Unfortunately, the veterinary schools of my day did not offer any courses in animal behavior. Today, many veterinary colleges still do not include behavior in their curriculum. Those that do, offer it as an elective course or, at best, as a cursory required course.

Fifty years ago, most schools of human medicine did not deem it imperative to train physicians in basic psychiatric principles. That approach today would be archaic and unthinkable.

Bill Campbell, like I, was not formally trained in academic behavioral science. We both, with considerable time and effort, educated ourselves. I selected the horse as my primary subject. Bill chose the dog. I can, therefore, appreciate his "hands-on" experience and non-ivory-tower approach to canine behavior.

The entire scientific study of behavior is only a century old, pioneered by such workers as Freud, Jung and Pavlov. By comparison, the disciplines of anatomy and physiology have been studied for many centuries. These 3 disciplines – anatomy, physiology and behavior – form the triad of adaptation that has enabled species to survive in their environments. All 3 are genetically predetermined; but, within limits, all 3 are subject to environmental shaping and modification.

This book details these factors of shaping and modification. It is not a textbook for veterinary students. It is a guide for any person interested in the scientific methodology of correcting behavior problems in dogs. However, as a veterinarian, I see this book as a valuable information source, not only for the student of veterinary medicine, but for the practitioner who is presented daily with behavior problems that, too often, lead to the disposal and demise of what should be a beloved pet.

I urge my colleagues, therefore, not to relegate this book to the reference shelf to consult only as problems arise. Rather, it should be read leisurely and thoroughly, from cover to cover, to enhance one's understanding of our friend, the dog.

Robert M. Miller, DVM
Thousand Oaks, California

Preface

When the first edition of *Behavior Problems in Dogs* came off press, I was aghast to find that the section on our correction program for stool eating was missing, material on the clinical test for hyperkinesis was excluded, and a nasty, biting 4-year-old dog was cited as being only 4 *months* old! Other minor errors had escaped detection during a marathon proofreading session to meet the publishing deadline. Despite these problems, the book met its primary objectives: to stimulate interest in pet dog behavior problems among veterinarians, while providing methods to educate clients in practical, effective and humane remedial programs that addressed the causative factors for problems.

So, why a second edition? The 15 years since publication of the first edition have not seen marked changes in the problems faced by owners and dogs. However, my experience has been enriched by dealing with several thousand more cases than during my first 7 years of consultations and study. This has produced keener insight about client needs, leading to new techniques and important refinements in others. These have been incorporated into our BehavioRx client education brochures, dispensed for over 10 years by veterinarians, humane societies, trainers, consultants and kennels. Consultation training programs around the country have provided opportunities to improve communications with our professional clients. All of these developments form the basis for this second edition.

I have again avoided technical behavioral terminology whenever possible in favor of language that communicates clearly to readers of all types. New sections on Coprophagy (stool eating), Hyperkinetic Testing, Aggression to Owners, Introducing Babies and New Pets to Resident Dogs, Adopting Older Dogs, and Training Systems and Devices have been added. There are also important expansions on earlier concepts, plus a venture into the nonverbal thought processes of dogs.

My perspective on owners and dogs evolved from a background of industrial psychology training concerned with employee motivation (5 years); through a brief "behavioristic" period with ideas of fixing-the-dog (1 month); clinical practice with clients and dogs at the Canine Behavior Center in West Los

Angeles, guided by its founder, Dare Miller, PhD (4 years); independent practice at our Sun Valley Ranch facilities in the San Fernando Valley (9 years); consulting with veterinary practices and clientele while marketing staff and client educational materials (11 years); to the study of canine behavior and the fascinating relationships between owners and their dogs, and the behavioral ramifications of nutrition, neurophysiology and general health (24 years).

My independent studies over the years have been driven by the urgent needs of clients to solve problems, some minor, others catastrophic. This marriage of clinical reality with biobehavioral study has provided a unique opportunity to develop an *experiential,* versus an *experimental,* perspective on pet dog behavior. Though I missed the opportunity to work toward a degree through predesigned curricula limited to how animals behave among other animals or within experimental environments, I studied exhaustively all the pertinent literature, ranging back to Pavlov and E.L. Thorndike, to find data *relevant* to dogs living with people.

My studies and experiences have been rewarded by the success of the methods evolving from it, all of which avoid traditional forms of punishment, and capitalize on positive and humane treatment. They also led to a principle that is integral to these correction methods: *the quality of the emotional relationships between owners and problem dogs is the primary element that needs modification if a lasting solution is to be realized.* This principle did not derive from the literature, as there are no objective, scientific studies of owners and pet dogs. It was distilled from the combination of study and experience.

However, as with parents and children, it does not suffice to teach Mom and Dad to say or do this or that so they can communicate effectively with problem dogs. It is *how* they say and do it that counts, and the *attitude* they convey in their words and actions. Conveyed attitudes betray *emotions.* Fortunately, problem-dog owners quickly understand and implement this principle when it is pointed out and then integrated with practical, humane corrections.

On the other hand, purely behavioristic concepts struggle to fit pet dog behavior into "valid" experimental frameworks or patterns that apply between wild cousins or domestic litters. However, the pet dog develops in an environment alien to both. Training regimens may produce obedience, but the destructive dog cannot translate forced subservience into peace of mind while its inconsistent owner is away at work. Some medications and neutering may alleviate certain types of behavior, but the effects are often transitory and may risk unwanted side effects. Breeding for genetically sound temperament finds itself at odds with artificially dictated physical standards.

Because we all tend to perceive solutions to problems in light of our training and experience, it is no wonder that troubled dog owners find an increasingly confusing sea of contradictory advice from various "authorities." When this problem is addressed, cooperatively, from a multi-disciplinary perspective, a valid science concerned with pet dog behavior may become a reality. I hope this second edition will help to hasten that day.

An ancient Chinese sage once said, "There is much of man in the animal, and all of the animal in man." This work is aimed at helping all students of dog behavior realize the truth of this insight, and use it to benefit both species.

William E. Campbell
Grants Pass, Oregon

1

Problem-Prone Dogs

The parents and their 2 teenage boys stood by as their large 2-year-old German Shepherd charged me with hackles up and fangs fully bared. During pauses in his attempts to remodel me, I noticed that the owners actually looked pleased about the proceedings. This was to be the first of 6 meetings designed to help the owners solve their complaint about Brutus's behavior: destructive chewing; not of people, but furniture. Our perceptions of the dog's problems were obviously very different.

After the dog calmed down, my first interview with the clients was aimed at establishing the fundamental connection between Brutus's chewing and his aggressive overprotection of his pack, (the family). When the clients understood the dog's excitability, aggressive active defense reflexes, and his desire to act as *leader* of the group, it was clear to them that the dog's *not accepting* being left alone at home related to *not accepting* strangers. They also appreciated why their other dog, a calm, easy-going 6-year-old spayed mongrel with passive defense reflexes, had not developed any serious problems.

Brutus's problems were caused by more than his internal makeup and social tendencies. The boys had rough-housed him from puppyhood, often riling him to the point of frenzy. The entire family had been oversolicitous with their "first purebred German Shepherd." In another home, Brutus may not have developed problems; but these surroundings, combined with his innate tendencies, produced a potentially dangerous dog. Fortunately, the family was dedicated to correcting the dog's problems; all was resolved happily. However, this case points up the validity of the statement that it is the *owners* who initially define behavior problems.

Having so stated, it might seem unwise to attempt to develop profiles for problem dogs without discussing the environmental factors that influence behavioral development. However, if we understand the physiologic factors that influence the way a given dog tends to *react* to its environment, we gain invaluable insight into how problems develop, as well as what type of programs will best succeed in correcting them.

While we may not be able to use the following profiles to predict which dogs will definitely develop behavior problems, we can recognize certain types of dogs as more problem-prone than others. And, lest I seem to be dooming such dogs, I should mention that most of them respond favorably to corrective methods that avoid physical punishment while capitalizing on the dogs' innate and learned responses to positively reinforced training and social guidance.

Nervous System Types and Stress

Dogs of any breed, size or type can suffer from stress. In fact, a certain amount of stress is necessary for a healthy life. Hunger is a form of stress that motivates us to find food, a healthful activity. However, a pet dog that receives an owner's doting affection, petting and praise on demand during the weekend tends to build an insatiable "appetite" for constant social gratification.

When left alone on weekdays, the dog is frustrated by an unsolvable problem: it cannot find its *emotional food*. Whether this condition stimulates problem behavior depends on the stability of the dog's nervous system and how the animal chooses to behave in order to relieve any tension resulting from the frustration. It becomes a problem dog if that frustration is manifested by chewing up objects that smell and taste of the owner, or things that, to the dog, are *symbolic* of that person.

I have seen littermates of the same sex, one a chewer, the other well behaved, while both apparently received equally overindulgent attention from their human family members. On the other hand, I have seen the same situation in littermates living in nonindulgent homes where the stress is created by boredom or the owner's returning home late. These experiences indicate that the internal makeup of dogs influences their behavioral responses to stress.

Developmental Neurophysiology and Behavior

Each puppy is born with and develops a nervous system that is unique in many ways. Both genetic and environmental factors produce these individual variations. Some important developmental yardsticks may be applied to the canine nervous system to explain many kinds of behavior.

Production of RNA (ribonucleic acid, a vital chemical messenger in the memory process) in a pup's brain does not reach adult rates until 22 weeks of age. This helps explain why a puppy may have "accidents" during its housetraining program, or why training pups to simple "Come," "Sit" or "Stay" commands is best conducted in brief sessions no longer than 5 minutes. This may also bear on a 13- to 16-week-old pup's behavior, when it apparently does not recognize, growls at or runs from visitors with whom it had friendly previous contact.

Mammals normally born blind but reared without light until maturity develop apparently normal eyes that are "nerve blind" due to failure of the optic tract to develop normally. Stimulus deprivation of various sorts produces animals with comparatively lighter and less precisely structured brains, according to work done in Russia in the 1950s.[1]

Puppies drastically restricted from sensory stimulation in special cages from weaning until maturity failed to avoid painful burns on their noses from matches or pin pricks, while normally raised puppies quickly learned to avoid them. The deprived pups appeared to feel the pain, but did not learn to associate it with the match or the pin. Even more bizarre, these deprived puppies spent more time close to the human experimenter after being burned or pricked than before the painful stimulus. This was not the case with normally reared puppies. This work may explain why so many behavioral problems are experienced with puppies bred and reared in the restrictive environments of "puppy mills," in which litters are reared in stacked cages and then shipped to pet shops, where they spend more time in cages.

Such gross physiologic and behavioral abnormalities produced by experimentation are fortunately no longer duplicated for the sake of *science*. However, I have seen its counterpart outside the laboratory in the homes of naive, ill-advised or downright cruel dog owners. A 2-year-old male Sheltie, raised in a dark garage with a mature cat, did not know how to run and avoided all human contact except with its owner. A 5-month-old mongrel kept in a small travel crate up to 18 hours a day since 8 weeks of age as an "aid to easy housetraining" displayed precocious aggression to strangers and other dogs.

It is reasonable, to suspect that such gross perceptual deprivations and their consequences may indicate that less radical deprivation or mismanagement might produce dogs with limited ability to cope with stress, strong stimuli or a lack of stimulation when left alone. It appears that each puppy is genetically endowed with its unique nervous system makeup, but the type of *stress* it experiences may be the deciding influence on its development.

Early stimuli that produce fearful responses, especially around 8-10 weeks of age, tend to be retained by dogs.[2] Though this work was based on an electric shock applied to the pups' ears, anyone who has made the mistake of clipping their 8- to 10-week-old pup's nails and hitting the quick will appreciate its general validity.

Applying this principle to a dog's early life in a human environment, it is advisable to avoid situations that may cause pain or fear. However, mild pain, such as veterinary inoculations, need not produce fear if the owners laugh and "make jolly" during and after the treatment. It appears that puppies and adult dogs will follow the emotional and behavioral example set by their owners after a mild or severely traumatic experience. I call this the *interpretive factor*.

An example of the power of a positive, upbeat interpretive feedback occurred with our 8-week-old Dalmatian bitch, Tally.

While being taken at night in pitch darkness for her final toilet trip, she walked into our swimming pool and was heard splashing around. My wife Peggy wisely knelt by the edge of the pool and happily praised the paddling pup as I turned on the flood lights. Tally was joyously lifted out, roundly praised and dried off, then led to her original destination and cheerfully praised for eliminating. Later in life, when she was large enough to climb out at the shallow end, Tally swam almost daily. The situation might have produced a water-shy dog if Peggy had screamed, picked up the dog and reacted "normally" by cuddling Tally with a concerned, sympathetic tone of voice.

So, in considering the nature (genetics) versus nurture (environment) debate and their effects on behavior, it may be prudent to paraphrase one pioneer investigator of animal behavior, D.O. Hebb: perhaps the answer is that behavior is 100% affected by genetics and 100% by environment.

Excitability and Inhibition

"Overexcitable" describes most of the problem dogs we see, especially when they are stressed by new surroundings, strangers, other dogs, social isolation, physical restraint or stimulation, and sudden or loud noises. At the other end of the spectrum of behavioral reactivity, we see highly inhibited animals that react to stress by inaction or slow, stiff movements, sometimes catatonia and apparent depression, seeming to lose contact with environmental stimuli. Between the extremes lie the gradations of these responses. Pavlov developed the descriptions presented in Table 1.[3]

> *An excellent example of the extremes involved 2 German Shepherds, a 5-year-old spayed bitch and her sexually intact male son. The bitch had been defecating in the living room and her offspring urinating there, as well as in other areas of the house. Early in our first interview, the owners were persistently "nudged" by the dogs and were fondled about the head and ears in response. To see what might happen if the dogs were ignored, I suggested they ignore them while we continued talking. After fruitless nudging for about 5 minutes, the bitch went to a corner, lay down and licked and*

Table 1. Pavlov's classifications of nervous system types and their associated behavior.[3]

Nervous System Types	General Behavior
Excitable (extreme)	Wildly active, choleric
Excitable	Happy-go-lucky, active, sanguine
Balanced	Poised, assured
Inhibited	Reserved, stoic, phlegmatic
Inhibited (extreme)	Withdrawn, stiff, lethargic

chewed at a forepaw, another minor complaint of the owners. The young male began pacing between the office's front and back doors, whining and occasionally returning to nuzzle the owners.

This behavior usually occurred while the owners slept at night, or when the dogs were left alone. By ignoring them, even out of the context of their "home turf," we were witnessing a *symptom* of the problem. The stress of being ignored, even if the owners were not absent, stimulated the bitch to introverted behavior (self-mutilation) and stimulated the extremely excitable son toward overactivity.

Excitable vs Inhibited

Pavlov struggled with the theory that inhibited dogs had a "weaker" nervous system than normal animals, a concept largely discarded due to later findings that a combined structural-chemical interaction determines the balance of the nervous system.[4,5] Both excitability and inhibition can be heightened or abated by many synthetic drugs, as well as those extracted from living tissues. The fact that such drugs do not affect all individuals (dogs or people) in the same way supports the belief that the *balance* among internal neurochemicals may be the primary factor influencing the behavioral expression of excitability or inhibition.[6]

The individual body chemistry of animals develops and fluc-
tuates throughout life. Hormonal imbalances produce not only
structural and physiologic, but behavioral changes as well.[7]
Among the body's hormone-producing glands and controlling
organs, the emotional centers of the brain's limbic system appear
to exert considerable influence. It may be that excitability and
inhibition depend to a large degree on what has been called the
"brain, pituitary, adrenal, gonadal axis."[8] Further, not only can
drugs influence the balance among these factors, but mild or
extreme psychological stress can produce subtle and gross neurochemical imbalances.[9]

The fact that seemingly mildly stressful experiences induce
these reactions may help explain a good deal of what is generally
described as "spontaneous aggression" or the popularly labeled
"Springer rage syndrome" if we consider yet another nervous
system process called *facilitation*.[8] In this, the nervous processes
responsible for defensive behavior, such as a dog's biting, can be
sensitized but not fully activated by mildly threatening stimuli.
However, depending on the particular dog's nervous system
makeup, repeated stimulation can push the dog over the brink
and into a full-blown "rage avalanche," wherein up to several
minutes of furious behavior are necessary to exhaust the imbalance and restore equilibrium. The dog then resumes its usual
gregarious personality.

In investigating the histories of many of these cases, I found
problem dogs to be excitable or highly excitable types exhibiting
a behavior problem for which the owners have applied various
degrees and types of punishment. These included finger-in-the-
face scolding (a stimulus that can facilitate a snapping response),
muzzle-clamping with the hands, jowl-shaking, physical take-
downs, and mild to severe blows.

> *A young married couple called about their 6-month-
> old intact female Springer Spaniel that was overprotec-
> tive of its food. The dog, an eager eater, needed its
> muzzle wiped after eating twice daily, a duty that ini-
> tially fell to the wife. The Springer was excitable and
> highly oral (mouthy) in its responses to petting and the
> husband's roughhousing. The wife used a paper towel
> the first time she cleaned up the dog's muzzle and was*

shocked when the pup bared its fangs, a reflexive response to having its upper lip held. As a correction, the Springer's mouth was held shut and "No bite" was shouted, followed by milder scolding. After several of these experiences, the pup growled, which elicited even harsher scolding. This all started at about 4 1/2 months of age.

The couple then decided to "desensitize" the dog to what they perceived as food-related aggressiveness. Her food bowl was presented and she was hand-fed bits of food by the husband before being allowed to eat freely. He also started placing his hand in the bowl as the dog ate. The Springer was unwittingly being teased with food and her defensive mechanisms effectively *conditioned* to respond to action at her food bowl. She was muzzle-clamped, "No'd," slapped and jowl-shaken as corrections. She then started growling when the owners put down her food and if they stood within a few feet of her while she ate. When the clients called, the Springer had bitten the husband's hand and drawn blood during the hand-in-the-bowl ritual.

Fortunately, this sort of *negative* neurophysiologic and psychological conditioning for defensive/aggressive, *emotionally* driven responses has a *positive* counterpart. Once the owners understood their Springer's nervous system makeup and the mechanisms controlling it, they were quick to grasp corrective measures. They first fed the dog outdoors to avoid the former context of kitchen feeding. This allowed the owners and dog a cooling-off period and avoided confrontations for about a week.

At the same time, the paper towel to clean the muzzle was replaced by a soft cotton towel, as many dogs in my experience do not enjoy the texture or sound of paper. Whether this is rooted in early punishment relative to chewing up papers, or due to an innate defensive response to high-frequency sounds of rustling paper, perhaps associated with reptiles, is not certain. Roughhousing was stopped. The pup was taught to sit on command when she sought affection, and hands were withdrawn at the first sign of mouthiness. The couple was advised to apply an upbeat "jolly routine" (see Chapter 8) before and during meals and cleanups. This procedure usually takes only 1 or 2 applications before the owners see a positive result. About 6 weeks of treatment are usually required before the dog permanently adopts, or *internalizes*, the change in emotional and behavioral responses.

Though it appears to be easier to create stress in excitable dogs, I have seen inhibited types become extremely depressed, failing to wag their tails when praised and petted or happily approached for play, activities that only weeks before had produced "joyful" canine responses. However, creating such depression in inhibited types appears to require stronger, more persistent stress than is necessary to create imbalances in excitable types.

Summary

Most problem-prone dogs are excitable types, but some inhibited types also develop problems. Excitable dogs react to stress with outwardly directed activity, such as chewing, barking or digging. Inhibited types tend to direct their behavior inwardly, as with self-mutilation, excessive salivation, soft whining, loss of appetite, and depression.

While such behavioral tendencies appear to be genetically determined, the general environmental and social atmosphere and/or early emotional trauma can influence development of the nervous system, as well as emotional response tendencies throughout life, becoming important both in creating and overcoming behavior problems.

Reflexes: The Foundations of Behavior

A reflex is an *involuntary* response to a stimulus, such as the well-known knee jerk response to a tap below the kneecap, the blinking of an eye in response to a puff of air on the eyeball, or salivation when a hungry dog sees or smells food. In Pavlov's experimental work with dogs, he sounded a bell and then introduced food, which produced salivation. This was repeated until the bell's sound alone caused salivation. This experiment in *conditioned reflexes* and the resulting publicity have helped explain a great deal about canine behavior, some of it to the benefit of dogs in general.

However, it also created an unfortunate general impression that those findings, gathered from laboratory dogs in a totally artificial, unnatural environment, can be used to explain the behavior of domestic pets living in the active, often hectic human social environment. The result is that there are still people struggling to explain and solve behavior problems with treatments based on perceptions of dogs as a purely conditioned behavioral *mechanism*, without the capacity to resist or modify their stereotyped innate or learned responses.

The Polish investigator, Dr. Jerzy Konorski, commented on the scientific limitations of such *objective* experimental work.[10] After years of study at the Pavlovian Institute and the Nenki Institute in Warsaw, he warned of the unscientific temptations of applying behavioral principles developed in laboratories to dogs in a relatively free-living environment. Sadly, Konorski's words have received little attention from the popular press, and the misconception persists. However, laboratory findings are useful in explaining many aspects of canine behavior if their limitations are kept in mind, and if we reject the notion that "Dogs don't think, they merely react and behave reflexively."

Types of Reflexes

There are 3 major types of reflexes: *unconditioned reflexes* are inborn or instinctive; *Type-I conditioned reflexes* are learned and involuntary, involving mainly glandular, spinal or brainstem mechanisms; and *Type-II conditioned reflexes*, learned, voluntary motor acts.

Unconditioned Reflexes

Most unconditioned reflexes are vital for survival of individual animals and their species. Though the basic rooting reflex of sightless newborn puppies is naturally toward the mother's teat, they will blindly root for great distances toward a warm hand.[11] Shortly thereafter, as a pup's brain develops the ability to discriminate between a hand and its dam's flesh, only the nipple will be sought for food. This perceptual discrimination, the ability to *inhibit* unproductive unconditioned behavior, is one of the earliest signs of *natural conditioned learning* in puppies. Without it, a puppy might starve to death suckling on a littermate's paw. The same may be said for a pup's attraction to warmth and avoidance of cold bedding materials, including whining and yelping if left in a cold environment.

Other unconditioned reflexes, such as *starting* in response to a loud sound, appear as the puppy's sensory capabilities develop. Still others, such as eliminative, orienting, investigative, chase, active flight/fight and passive freeze defense reflexes, may all require appropriate environmental stimulation for normal expression, keeping in mind the effects of early and prolonged deprivation mentioned earlier (see Table 2).

Type-I Conditioned Reflexes

The reflexes to urinate and defecate after eating are probably the first truly conditioned reflexes. Without the mother's licking the pups' genitals and anus, elimination would not occur and the puppies would die. Urine and fecal matter are then ingested by the mother, to maintain a clean environment for her litter. In a few days the pups usually begin eliminating after eating without the mother's stimulation. At about 3 weeks of age, when the pups can see and move with some efficiency, they eliminate away from the nest area if the opportunity is available. This behavior is used to advantage by many knowledgeable breeders who move their litters to areas with outdoor access, while providing a warm environment. Then, the eat-eliminate cycle virtually pre-house-trains the pups. Because the owners must be present to feed the new pup, it is a simple matter to allow them access to the outdoor toilet area soon after eating.

In an experiment to see if a pup can learn, Scott and Fuller conditioned a leg-withdrawal response to mild electric shock with various stimuli, touch, odor, taste, sound and light.[12] Though some success was achieved as early as 14 days of age, "stable" responses were not shown until 18-21 days of age. After that age, Type-I conditioned reflexes form with dramatic speed and are well retained, especially when conditioning is done almost daily and spans 6 weeks.[4-10] This is vitally important when we consider that a dog is not consciously *deciding* to respond, but rather its *involuntary* nervous system is responding to Type-I conditioning. Another Russian, V.S. Rusinov, implanted probes in the brain of dogs. Well-retained conditioning procedures were found to produce individual, characteristic electroencephalographic wave forms. On days when conditioning sessions were not held, at the usual time for conditioning procedures, the dogs produced wave forms *typical* of those in the experimental conditioning situation, though in actuality they were in their kennels. Further work showed this biological "clock" to be accurate to within 30 seconds in a 24-hour period.[13]

This sort of experimental finding helps explain why most dog owners have seen their pets become highly active and alert when homecoming time draws near, when regular departures from home are highly emotional and when feeding times are due. Though this behavior most certainly is induced psychologically, it may be triggered by the dog's biological clock, a Type-I conditioned reflex.

Type-II Conditioned Reflexes

Type-II conditioning requires the dog to *actively* perform some movement that allows it to avoid or curtail a painful or unpleasant stimulus or set of circumstances, or to behave in a way as to be rewarded, such as with food, petting from the owner, or the mere presence of the owner.

Pavlovian research showed that if a buzzer was sounded just before a mild electric shock was applied to the foreleg of a dog, most dogs learned to raise the foreleg at the buzzer's sound alone. In this type of conditioning, the leg is raised at first as the result of a purely involuntary motor act, a defensive reflex action, a Type-I conditioned response. The dog then *learns* that the buzzer signals discomfort and then *voluntarily* raises the leg to *avoid* getting shocked, a Type-II conditioned response.

This sort of conditioning was also applied to extinguish previously learned as well as "natural" behavior. In this, the buzzer was sounded as the dog performed the unwanted behavior, and the shock applied just as or soon after the buzzer sounded. After a few applications, the dogs learned not to undertake that behavior. This sort of work forms the theoretical basis for many of the high-tech electric shock devices in use today.

In experiments on *appetitive* rather than defensive reflexes, buzzers were sounded while a cord was pulled to lift a dog's foreleg, shortly after which a morsel of food was presented. In this procedure the dog is initially *forced* to lift its leg, but quickly starts voluntarily raising it at the buzzer's sound, learning that doing so at the buzzer's signal produces food, a Type-II conditioned response to what is termed a *passive* motor movement, in that the dog does not *actively* take part in the initial leg lifting. This conditioning applies to most popular dog training systems in use, wherein the dog is physically forced to sit as a command is spoken, after which a tidbit or praise and petting are given.

It is important to mention that the Pavlovian dogs were made hungry by fasting before the conditioning. It is also important to mention that all the canine candidates for experimental schooling did not graduate, so to speak. Many were washed out because they failed to adapt to the close confinement and/or the physically restrictive harnesses of the conditioning chamber. In fact, this and other observations by Pavlov caused him to document his *freedom reflex*, which we will discuss later.

Classical conditioning procedures are often misdefined as dealing *only* with involuntary glandular and smooth muscle responses. As we have seen, this definition fits only Type-I conditioning. Type-II conditioning deals with voluntary motor responses. As we will see, to describe a dog's behavior as *purely* acquired through classical conditioning effects, or to design remedial programs based on them, may be an oversimplification of the nervous processes of an extremely complex animal, as most canine behavior derives from *operant* experience.

Operant Conditioning

E. L. Thorndike first proposed the idea of *conditioned learning* in 1911 in his work, *Animal Intelligence*.[14] His cat was placed in the confines of a small cage and released immediately when it happened to scratch itself. After release, it was replaced in the cage until it scratched again, which resumed quickly after caging, indicating the cat had *learned* that scratching led to freedom. Thorndike called this a "satisfying state of affairs," as the cat quieted down and looked quite serene after its release. This conditioning of so-called *spontaneous* (accidental) behavior came to be known as *operant* or (often) *instrumental* learning or conditioning. Rewards of food were most often used and most widely publicized through B.F. Skinner's work, *The Behavior of Organisms*.[15]

The laboratory animals mainly used by early investigators were rats, mice and pigeons. Even so, the operant method of acquiring behavioral conditioning aptly describes development of many kinds of problems in pet dogs. For instance, a puppy put in the laundry room on its first night in the new owner's home may at first whine fruitlessly, but soon elevates its vocalizing to yowls, which may bring punishment, verbal consolation or complete relief via a night in bed with someone. Behavior driven by strong *emotions* tends to be more quickly conditioned than other motivators, even hunger. So, the next time the pup is isolated in the laundry room (usually the next night), the whining may be brief, but the yowling usually starts more quickly and gets louder, as the previous night's "conditioning" tends to intensify the pup's emotional distress.

Another classic example of "accidental" operant conditioning by owners involves a different form of social gratification, such as attention in the form of petting, praise or even scolding or punishment. A pup that feels a bit lonely while in the owners' presence and approaches and nuzzles, thereupon receiving attention, often learns quickly to become a pest. If we accept that its emotional state (its motivation to seek attention) and its behavior are being reinforced, the reason for its pestering becomes apparent.

I have seen puppies who pestered almost continuously, even though they were scolded and slapped by the owners, a phenomenon described in experimental work by Scott and Fuller.[12] Though the puppy did not know it, it had been applying a classic Type-II conditioning procedure to its owners, who had naively become behavioral *subjects!* The puppy stimulates, and the owner responds and feels rewarded by the pup's affectionate behavior. Most owners also gain a visceral benefit in lowered blood pressure, at least until the puppy becomes a pest. The result of this interaction is a puppy that feels deprived without human company. When owners hear this scenario, most develop insights into the origin of their dog's problems, especially dogs that cannot be left alone without destroying things.

Reflex Conflicts, Frustration, Anxiety and Problems

To understand better the physiologic and psychological (emotional) sensitivity of dogs, we must refer again to Pavlovian research. Studies done after publication of *Conditioned Reflexes,* both in Russia and later by Konorski in Poland, received little attention in the West. This was mainly due to the isolationist political policies of Russia under communism. It is still not well known in the West that Pavlov's work was driven by his interest in human mental health. His experiments with dogs were not only aimed at understanding how the nervous system worked, but how it became imbalanced. He believed that conditioned reflexes could not only produce neuroses and psychoses, but that they also could be used to cure mental illness. Attempts to produce imbalances in experimental conditions were highly successful, and the findings are invaluable to understanding the causes of many behavior problems in dogs.

One of these is to produce *conflicts* between the excitatory and inhibitory processes of the nervous system. The second is to apply extremely strong and extraordinary stimuli. Of further importance is that imbalances were not always produced in all dogs; extremely excitable or inhibited types were most susceptible. One consistent element in this work is that the overriding forces at work on a dog are conflict and frustration because it does not know how to respond to a situation, on an involuntary glandular or a voluntary behavioral basis (Fig 1). When this principle is applied to the interactions of a pet dog with the social

Figure 1. Out of frustration, a Doberman Pinscher reacts with full-blown rage after several minutes' agitation by a mock assailant.

and structural elements in its environment, we can recognize more clearly how behavior problems develop.

Sexual Reflexes

Before leaving our discussion of reflexes, some personal observations gathered over the years may be helpful regarding a subject that has yet to be investigated seriously: the tendency of pet dogs to initiate sexual behavior and to respond to certain physical or human social stimulation with sexual arousal and/or overt sexual behavior. The following discussion is limited to observations of unintentional sexual stimulation.

I have seen and heard of deliberate sexual stimulation of a dog by people, and cases in which the owners and dogs engaged in abnormal interspecies sexual behavior, resulting in severe aggression in the dog. Such people appear to have psychiatric disorders.

Air-borne pheromones from a bitch in heat stimulate heightened libido in intact and in some castrated male dogs. However, few owners are aware that many dogs of both sexes may respond with sexual arousal to the following stimuli:

- Roughhousing.
- Rubbing or petting on the chest, between the forelegs.
- Prolonged petting or playful bumping on the neck above the shoulders, below the ears or on the throat.
- Prolonged scratching beside the base of the tail when it causes a lateral movement of the tail, in both intact and spayed bitches.
- Physical stimulation of the genital region of either sex, as during bathing.

The areas contacted during these activities may be regarded as erogenous zones, as they produce sexual arousal. They should probably be regarded as distinct from the inside of the thigh and genital areas during mutual nonsexual genital investigations between 2 dogs.

In roughhousing, a dog usually begins precopulatory clasping with the forelegs, nosebunting or mouthing, or sexual mounting with pelvic thrusts.

Most dogs respond affectionately to the petting, scratching or playful bumping mentioned, without overt sexual behavior. However, when it is prolonged, some dogs may attempt pre-copulatory "nudging," display penile erection, or even mount.

Usually the dog's responses are curtailed when the owner stops stimulating the dog. But the side effects of such handling are seen in various sorts of behavior, such as whining, renewed approaches for petting and attention, and extreme (or mild) anxiety when left alone or ignored by the owner.

In some cases it is necessary to explain the *sexual* nature of this sort of stimulation to an owner. Usually it is sufficient to point out that prolonged petting or any activity that stimulates pestering causes frustration when the dog cannot obtain the petting or other attention. Such dogs are then put on a program in which they must *learn to earn* praise and petting (see Chapter 8). When the dog seeks attention and when the owner desires to pet it, the dog is directed to "Sit." When it responds to the owner's direction to "Sit," it is praised and petted briefly (3-5 seconds). This earned-petting routine is also used to take advantage of the dog's *need to function* for the owner, which will be discussed later.

Which Reflex, What Problems?

Table 2 lists some unconditioned reflexes and their behavioral expressions that can develop into problems.

Table 3 lists problems associated with frustration of unconditioned reflexes or with normal behavior following stimulation of these reflexes.

Other reflex behaviorisms might be included in these tables, but their classification as unconditioned or learned is still not well defined. However, their impact on problem behavior development is important. They probably are best categorized within the realm of *defensive* reflexes. Specifically, these are growling, fangbaring, tail, ear and head positioning, piloerection (raising the hackles), and cringing or rolling onto the side or back.

Most dog owners are not aware of the tendency of many dogs to growl when their ear canals are massaged or even gently invaded. When this apparently unconditioned response occurs,

17

Table 2. Behavioral expression of some unconditioned reflexes.

Reflex	Behavioral Expression
Escape	Dog resists physical constraints, such as fences, harnesses, close confinement, doors and windows, as well as interference by people and other animals.
Flight	Seeks escape from harmful or threatening stimuli.
Fight	Responds aggressively toward painful or threatening stimuli, sometimes biting. Applies not only to physical pain, but also to social and territorial relationships.
Freeze	Responds to painful or threatening stimuli by freezing, stiff movement and (rarely) catalepsy.
Bite	Bites when touched unexpectedly or with perceived threat, on the trunk, neck, head or muzzle; sometimes bites at painful stimulus to the extremities, or an air puff into the ear. This is a brainstem reflex, normally inhibited by early handling.[10] Also bites at sudden intrusions into or through the visual field.[16]
Withdrawal	Withdraws limb when a paw or leg is stimulated, especially when the stimulus is unexpected, sudden, confining or painful.
Alimentary	Eliminates after eating, drinking, awakening, excitement, stress, chewing or intense sniffing. Salivates in response to or in anticipation of food.
Orientation	Alerting response to changes in the environment, especially novel, unexpected, sudden, brief, strong or very subtle changes.
Targeting	Follows the orientation reflex. The dog turns or otherwise focuses its sensory attention toward some stimulus that triggers the orienting reflex. (This is often considered part of the orientation reflex.) We list it as a separate function because it so often is interrupted by a stronger stimulus than the one triggering the preceding orientation and targeting reflex.
Investigative	The dog consciously seeks to discover and investigate the nature of novel or known stimuli that triggered the orientation and targeting reflexes. This may include visual inspection, smelling, listening, tasting (chewing, licking) or touching an object.
Chase	Chases after, and sometimes grasping with the jaws, suddenly moving or fast-moving objects, highly animated people, animals and machines. Some dogs jump on or run into such stimuli.
Positive thigmotaxis	Dog opposes physical pressure.
Balance	Attempts to retain balance.

Table 3. Reflexive behavior and associated problems.

Reflex	Related Problems
Escape	The initial stimulus is perceived by the dog as physically restricting. Responses include scratching digging, barking, chewing, pacing and jumping at or over barriers. Also included are dashing out of doors, going through windows or screens, self-mutilation, unruliness, aggressiveness, during or after confinement, fighting another family dog, or killing another animal (displaced or misplaced aggression) when frustrated.
Flight	Shyness, fear-biting (when flight is not possible), submissive urination.
Fight	Growling, fighting, biting, barking.
Freeze	Shyness, fear-biting (often after an extremely stressful stimulus is removed, such as after being held for inoculation or grooming).
Bite	Biting due to perceived threats or sudden, unexpected touch to the body, neck, head or muzzle, or when fast-moving hands or objects move unexpectedly or repeatedly into or through the visual field.
Withdrawal	Leg withdrawal makes grooming or other treatment of paws or legs difficult.
Alimentary	Excessive salivation, soiling house when excited or feeling stress, chewing as an appetitive tension reliever in stress (such as when feeding is delayed).
Orientation	Quiet, relaxed behavior, even a hypnotic state, has been noted when the orientation reflex is "extinguished" or habituated by means of a rhythmic, mild stimulus, especially touch or sound.[4]
Targeting	Hitting people with the snout or mouth when turning reflexively toward a stimulus. Often *misinterpreted* as biting, especially with small children if a scratch or bruise results.
Investigative	Lack of opportunity to exercise this reflex can lead to almost every type of problem, from "kennelosis" and catatonia to *active* tension relieving, such as chewing.
Chase	Chasing, jumping on or biting moving objects.
Positive thigmotaxis	Resisting physical manipulation, at least when the stimulus is first experienced, such as the first time a puppy's rump is pushed down for a "Sit" command. Often misinterpreted as disobedience. If the dog is punished for the response, learning may be hampered.
Balance	Overstimulation appears to be involved in many cases of car sickness.

the dog may be punished, stimulating its defensive reflexes to fight, flee or freeze. Often when the dog displays submissive growling and/or fangbaring, (the submissive "smile"), the naive owner applies harsh punishment or withdraws from the dog. In either event, serious biting problems often result, as the threatened dog displays submissive behavior but achieves no relief from the owner's threats or punishment, or the growling causes the owner to back off.

This is true of males or females, usually over 5-6 months of age, with innate or acquired *active defense reflexes* to fight or attempt to flee from threats (scolding) or physical punishment. If an uninformed owner fails to recognize the lowering of the tail, even if slight, or a subtle dip of the head as the ears are lowered rearward, and applies more severe treatment, the dog may feel threatened enough to initiate sham-aggressive displays or attack the owner.

The foregoing is especially important since the advent and publicity surrounding certain "dominance techniques," such as the *forced rollover*, the *shakedown* (elevating the dog by its jowls and shaking it) and *scruffshaking*. While these may be effective if applied properly during a puppy's primary socialization period at 5-14 weeks, they can be counterproductive at best or even disastrous at later ages, even when applied by experts. I mention this after receiving numerous calls from inexperienced, well-bitten owners who have read about, then attempted the techniques. As we will mention later, there are other, nonthreatening means of "dominating" a pet dog.

When reflexes and problems resulting from behavioral expression of reflexes or frustration are understood, it is tempting to apply *experimental* techniques to correct problems. Among these are:

- Arrange situations to stimulate the reflex to extinction (habituate them through so-called "flooding").
- Systematically increase, from very weak to very strong, the stimuli that produce the behavior, or *desensitize* the dog.
- *Countercondition* the dog by associating another stimulus that evokes incompatible response(s).
- Apply some form of *aversion* conditioning (punishment) to eradicate the behavior.

However scientific these procedures might seem, when we are faced with a pet dog, subject to numerous distractions, these methods are at best an interesting intellectual exercise, as they address only a portion of the elements that produce problem behavior. The animals used to establish these principles (rats, pigeons, cats, monkeys, dogs, etc) were functioning within an environment as free from extraneous stimuli as possible. When compared with a pet dog's intense emotional ties to its human family and territory, it is obvious that any attempt to resolve problem behavior must consider these and other elements.

For example, Pavlov's crude early conditioning chambers were plagued by extraneous stimuli, such as barking from the kennel, footsteps of workers, odors wafting through, or even minor changes in the room's setup, any of which interfered with effective conditioning of the dogs. When his laboratory and kennels were deluged and virtually destroyed by floods, it took months before many of the dogs could be used again in experiments. Pavlov even labeled these external distractions as *external inhibitors*. He also mentioned *internal inhibitors*, chief among them emotional arousal and the need to urinate.

This is not to say that we cannot use unconditioned reflexes (Types I or II), as well as operant conditioning principles, in analyzing and correcting behavior problems. However, it is apparent, especially to those with clinical experience, that they must be kept in perspective. To keep this perspective, I have always found it helpful to remember that experimental learning in animals is induced through *objective* study, wherein the experimenter is generally required to remain *outside* the procedure, and the animal is being "taught" something the *experimenter* wants it to learn. On the other hand, the pet dog is learning during most of its waking hours from highly involved, *subjective* human companions what the *dog* wants to learn. Understanding what and how the dog learns, when its motivation is driven by *internal* needs and desires, requires that we consider more than conditioned reflexes. Among additional factors are the dog's perceptual abilities and their limitations.

The Senses and Behavior Problems

Owners of problem dogs are usually aware that their dogs' senses of hearing and smell are keener than those of people. Not commonly appreciated, however, is that dogs are actually deficient in several sensory processes. Whether this leads to problems often depends on the way people interact with a dog. The following information helps explain many canine behaviorisms and reactions that owners often fail to understand or respond to inappropriately, and hence, create problems or diminish the positive quality of their pet-owner relationships. When the facts pertinent to the problem are appreciated, owner attitudes and behavior can change dramatically for the better.

Visual Perception

Dogs are nearsighted when it comes to recognizing details within a pattern, but are fairly keen at perceiving outlines. When asked to discriminate perfect circles from an egg-shaped (elliptic) outline in experimental conditions, they performed nicely.[4] But when the ellipse was gradually increased to about 8/9ths of a circle, the dog failed to recognize the difference, something most people perceive easily. If repeatedly asked to do this, the dog lost its earlier trained ability to respond to even the gross differences between circles and ellipses. This type of discrimination experiment gives some indication of a dog's extreme sensitivity to visually perceived stimuli that become inconsistent.

For instance, the owner's hand usually signals positive treatment, such as petting. When the same hand inflicts punishment or pain, the dog usually displays a momentary, often subtle, ambivalent behavior, vacillating between affectionate and defensive (submissive or *en-garde*) responses. During my first interviews with clients, this reaction is clearly seen in dogs that have been punished "by hand," so to speak. Further, when strangers reach to pet such a dog, their actions may trigger a full expression of submission or aggression, depending on the nervous makeup of the dog and its environmental history. When owners of problem dogs, or puppy owners who wish to avoid problems, understand this type of discrimination, they generally choose to apply nonpunishment techniques in handling their pets.

Most owners are not aware that their puppy's vision does not reach maturity until about 4 months of age. Until then, things appear fuzzy, which makes visual identification of objects and individuals difficult. This can cause some pups to bark or growl at family members. If punished, the pup may become confused.

Imperfect ability to distinguish various shapes may explain why some dogs become unnerved, growling at or shying from their owners, in dim light. Though they can virtually "see in the dark" as compared with people, their ability to distinguish shapes may be impaired under conditions of reduced light. So, when they are approached in low light levels by the owner, they may growl. Many owners, rather than simply clear up the mystery by speaking the dog's name, punish or back away from the pet, reinforcing the behavior. From that point, the problem behavior usually escalates and the relationship between owner and dog degenerates.

To demonstrate this canine disability to skeptical clients, I have them leave, then reenter the training area by a different door 20 feet or farther away downwind, wearing my large-brimmed cowboy hat. They are instructed to stand still and remain silent immediately after entering. Even the calmest or happy-go-lucky dogs have become unnerved, while aggressive ones have charged the owner, who is instructed to cheerfully speak the dog's name and take off the hat. I should warn that this demonstration should *not* be used if the dog has actually attacked or bitten owners or others.

Another situation occurs when someone very closely resembling an owner creates a visual dilemma, especially on the first meeting. Some dogs become unsettled and behave out of character, barking, running off or charging the person. This situation can usually be resolved by having the visitor sit quietly and allowing the dog to investigate him or her by sniffing and hearing their voice. However, if punished, taken away or physically forced to make contact with the visitor, many dogs behave worse with that person and often with all other visitors, associating them with impending punishment.

I have not seen problems directly stemming from a dog's exquisite ability to perceive movement so subtle that it would have to be magnified 10-fold for people to detect. However, I have noted something of interest about many people who, with no conscious intent or apparent provocation, tend to unnerve dogs. They often move with slow deliberation and a certain tentativeness, or have an unusual gait. Several often-bitten children in our experience have been hyperkinetic or had visual-motor problems. In a recent case, an easy-going dog who spent life as a mascot in a retail butcher shop watched casually as a mother and her first son entered, but immediately attacked her second, younger son as he walked in. The younger boy had visual-motor problems and their family dog had also bitten him. This might be explained by a sort of once bitten-twice shy syndrome in which the previously bitten person often freezes or acts suspiciously cautious (to the dog) before an attack; however, this boy did not see the dog lying in a corner before the attack. This aspect of human-canine behavior warrants further study.

Auditory Perception

Dogs have a hearing range of 20 hertz (cycles/second) up to over 50,000 hertz. We have tested over 300 dogs of various ages with a 38,000-hertz audio generator. Dogs became alert and tried to detect the source of the low-level (about 60 decibels) ultrasonic sound. This sensitivity is used in some high-tech training and behavioral devices, which will be reviewed in Chapter 15. Some ultrasonic burglar alarm systems appear to agitate certain dogs, while other dogs in the same household are not bothered. Ultrasonic alarm sensors can be replaced with microwave sensors in the event of such problems.

A dog's keen sensitivity to low-volume sound is often troublesome. Dogs can hear a faint sound at 75 feet, while a person could only detect such a sound at 17 feet. This indicates that a dog must learn to ignore myriad sounds that do not affect it, while accommodating to a veritable avalanche of sounds in a family household, such as from television, radio, stereo or other sources. However, when this sensitivity is translated to phobic behavior relative to, say, thunderstorms, it indicates that dogs may hear the thunder of an approaching storm over 50 miles away, while the local skies are still clear. If a dog has a history of becoming upset by thunder or other explosive sounds, it may become increasingly anxious as the storm nears, salivating, pacing, hiding, seeking comfort if the owner is home, or escaping.

This sensitivity may also explain why so many failures occur when "desensitizing" techniques are used, such as playing recordings of thunder at low levels. Audio speakers are not designed to produce volumes 4.4 times softer than humans can perceive. Also, storm activity is generally preceded by barometric pressure changes and variations in atmospheric ionization, elements to which dogs and some other mammals appear to be sensitive. Therefore, merely producing low-volume thunder claps may not fulfill the total *stimulus complex* required to achieve storm phobia desensitization. On the other hand, such programs are usually more successful with dogs that fear gunshots or other loud noises. However, even with storm phobias, if we can change the dog's *emotional interpretation* of such stimuli by providing a behavioral *example*, rehabilitation is generally quite successful (see Chapter 12).

An important auditory/learning tendency in dogs is to quickly develop a motor movement response to a sound stimulus when the sound is accompanied by a visual signal. In other words, dogs tend to move their head, ears, eyes or other body part in response to sound accompanied by movement. This leads to some problems if owners are not aware of this mechanism, but it facilitates training for those who use it properly.

Two examples typify common problems. The first is the human tendency to raise the hands while telling a jumping (or about to) dog, "Down!" Raising the hands not only causes reflex movement upward, but also encourages the dog to continue jumping. The usual outcome of this sort of mis-teaching is an owner who may resort to punishment, such as kneeing the dog in the chest or pushing it down, and a confused dog. Effective use of this learning tendency involves moving the hands abruptly down and/or toward the dog while saying "Down," praising it for doing so. Even more effective is to apply the movements *without speaking*, and to praise the dog's downward response. In this way the *situation* becomes the *conditioned* stimulus to stop or not start the jumping behavior.

The other problem commonly occurs when owners try to teach a pup or adult dog to "Come" as they lean or move toward the pet. Both movements visually instruct the pet to stay or retreat. Most owners end up approaching the pet and often punishing it, or giving up, convinced they have a stubborn pet. Using such visual cues as abruptly leaning or moving *away* or crouching down with one *side* of the body toward the dog (a friendly, nonconfrontational stance) and praising the first signs of approach by the dog facilitate initial learning, even in adult dogs that are resistant due to mistraining.

This sort of initial training, in which the dog is *actively* involved in performing the proper motor responses, is much faster than those that force *passive* movements through physical manipulation by the hands and/or leash. This has been demonstrated both experimentally and clinically in my own (and others') experience with dog owners.[10]

Overuse of a dog's name can create problems between owner and pet. Many owners find it necessary to say the name loudly and/or forcibly to get their pet's attention. These owners have inadvertently created the situation by saying "Tippy" while talking *about* but not *to* the dog. Then, when Tippy is spoken to, the owners must raise the volume or the sound of the stimulus. I have had clients who literally had to scream their dog's name to get its attention, many of whom have had the pet's hearing checked by their veterinarians before seeking our professional help. If the dog has been punished harshly for not responding, it is helpful to change the dog's name. In milder cases and with new puppy owners, simply using another name while talking *about* the dog, while positively reinforcing the given name with praise, succeeds quite well. Many owners choose such "pet" names as "Stupid," "Fang," "Jaws" and "Goofy," which often reflect the nature of the problem that prompted them to seek behavioral guidance.

Tactile Perception

The sense of touch probably leads to more serious problems in the relationships between people and pet dogs than any other. Though the afferent (incoming) visual, auditory and tactile nerve fibers all converge initially in the unconditioned defensive reflex brain centers, the sense of touch somehow appears to take precedence over the others in producing defensive behavior.[18] Konorski mentioned formerly docile dogs who, when simply touched at the base of the neck, would bite repeatedly after surgical removal of their cerebral cortices, the sites involved in inhibiting bite responses to stimuli.

This highly defensive response to touch seems contrary for an animal born in close physical contact with littermates, providing warmth and comfort. However, the defensive behavior apparently starts between 2 1/2 and 4 weeks of age, when the puppies begin play-fighting. At this age, the myelin sheath for the afferent nerve fibers may have developed sufficiently to allow expression of the behavior. However, control of the behavior by the "gray matter" of the brain may explain why a dozing or sleeping dog may bite spontaneously when touched or when pain is inadvertently inflicted, such as its tail being stepped on. This probably accounts for the age-old saying, "Let sleeping dogs lie."

However, when the family toddler is the target of the bite, serious problems may result, especially if the dog is severely punished immediately after the incident, while the child is present. This creates a negative association of pain and social rejection between infant and dog. The dog then usually becomes defensive, growls or tries to avoid the child when approached. Parents then may scold or further punish the dog, creating an escalating, negative social relationship between the dog and its family members.

These cases can usually be resolved when the parents understand the causes, and are willing to undertake a program to inhibit the negative, *learned* emotional association with the child, replacing it with an emotionally positive association provided by the parents' behavioral example when the child is *first* perceived by the dog. This procedure, nick-named the Jolly Routine, is described in Chapter 8. However, it should be mentioned that this type of emotional *switch conditioning* requires committed and enlighted parents who will follow both the spirit and letter of the techniques used in the program.

Pain: I mention pain under tactile discrimination because problems arising from it are usually associated with physical handling and punishment. However, as will be seen, other sources of pain also can lead to problems.

Pain thresholds appear to vary between dogs and often depend on the emotional state of the dog as well as the context in which pain is experienced. For instance, most dogs, even active-aggressive and flight types, inhibit overt defensive reflexes while undergoing veterinary examination, inoculations and treatment. The clinical context and its routine are generally established early in life, as are the dog's inhibitory behavioral responses. The same holds true for grooming procedures, nail clipping and stripping of the haircoat.

On the other hand, owners who inflict pain on the pet are not so lucky. Their home context and relationship with the dog are mainly affectionate and sensually pleasing. So, when a family member creates pain by accident or design, the dog's unconditioned defense reflexes may be expressed, as it has not "learned" to inhibit them. Therefore, we always advise owners to leave any pain-producing treatments to veterinarians and groomers. We also recommend avoiding painful physical punishment, as such punishment can lead to frustration and/or anxiety, and problems that often seem totally unrelated to the punishment.

As an example, even though a puppy may submit to being spanked or hit on the snout the first time its owner comes home to find a fecal mess or a chewed-up item, the trauma is associated with *the owner's homecoming.* In addition to inducing defensive responses to the owner, as the next homecoming approaches, the pup may become anxious because of what I call the "Jekyll and Hyde syndrome." That is, which owner is going to arrive tonight: the affectionate Dr. Jekyll or the nasty Mr. Hyde? This conflict in perceptions and the resultant anxiety can produce further *anxiety-relieving behavior,* such as more destructive chewing. Involuntary elimination may also be stimulated, producing off-schedule defecation and/or urination, the very reason the puppy may have been punished previously. Submissive urination can occur as the puppy is approached. Instead of applying *aversion* conditioning, the owner is actually *reinforcing* the unwanted behavior. This cycle also is seen in adult dogs.

Many problems arise because dogs tend to associate internal pain with the object or person occupying their attention at the moment or shortly before it occurs. Several cases involving hip dysplasia and aggression toward owners have stemmed from an incident when the owner was handling the dog or telling it to move, when the dog growled or bit at the owner. This has also been noted when dogs with painful arthritis have moved spontaneously while their attention was fixed on an owner or visitor. Many of the dogs involved have been obedient, even markedly submissive, to their owners. In most of these cases, veterinary-dispensed pain relievers and upbeat, encouraging behavior of the owners as the dogs *started* to move produced successful results.

In some cases, the dogs had been scolded or punished to the point that 6-week programs were needed for rehabilitation.

Olfactory Perception

Dogs' keen sense of smell may be involved in more problems than we realize. The odor of their owners is extremely important to most dogs when they cannot identify them by sight or the sound of their voices. We have seen the familiar scent-searching behavior, in which dogs move their snouts about as if sampling the air, during the cowboy hat visual identification test mentioned earlier. When the wind originates from behind the owner toward the dog (the owner is upwind), olfactory identification has been almost immediate, defeating the object of the test. Most dogs, even puppies, seem to strive for a whiff of the breath of people when greeting them, which can account for much of the jumping up that occurs. Sexual identification of people by sniffing the genital area is also the basis for some problems, though most dogs appear to develop the ability to assess sex at a "respectable" distance.

Other problems that may have olfactory origins appear to be tied to discrimination difficulties. I have had several cases in which the dog, male or female, has begun to avoid or growl at young girls during their first menstrual cycle. These dogs have responded well when the parents and youngster "talked jolly," bounced a ball for playtime, etc.

The odor of alcohol on an owner's or visitor's breath has unnerved some dogs, especially those who have had severe punishment, pain or unpredictable human behavior (fighting, falling down, etc) previously associated with drinking.

The residual odor of a certain perfumed soap caused one young male dog persistently to mount a family's 2-year-old child. When the soap was changed, the mounting ceased. Because of these olfactory sensitivities, I use only unscented laundry and bath soaps, and refrain from other perfumed lotions or hair sprays to avoid the possibility of looking similar and "smelling like" one of my clients.

Summary

This review of the problem-prone dog's nervous system development, types, reflexive tendencies and sensory-perceptual development and capabilities has been limited to elements that tend to lead to problems. Our experience with thousands of cases, as well as experimental laboratory work, indicates that highly reactive, *excitable* dogs are more prone to outwardly directed behavior problems, from chewing up the environment to biting visitors, while highly *inhibited* dogs tend toward inwardly directed problems, such as self-mutilation, excessive salivation and shyness. Later chapters presenting remedial programs will be divided into extroverted and introverted categories, as the problems generally involve these 2 types of pets.

We should not leave the impression that a dog of a *balanced* nervous type is impervious to stress when living in a human family. Rather, such a pet is less susceptible to the social/environmental conditions that create problems. Those social elements will be discussed next.

Social Development and Behavior Problems

It is difficult to predict if mishandling during the sensitive periods in a dog's social development will create problems. But certain social/behavioral *tendencies* can be influenced markedly, especially shyness, aggressiveness, overreactivity to certain people and other animals (either excitably or inhibitively), anxiety and phobias relating to specific environmental situations.

Sensitive Periods

The periods of behavioral sensitivity listed in Table 4 are based on previous investigations and from our clinical experience.[3,12] The most important are: the 3- to 14-week *socialization* period, during which a puppy forms its primary and secondary social relationships; the so-called *fear imprint* period, at about 8-10 weeks of age; and the *juvenile* period, at about 12-26 weeks on, up to sexual maturity. Later developmental stages overlap because these have been based on clinical rather than controlled observations.

These sensitive periods have been modified somewhat from those listed in the first edition of this book as a result of 16 more years of experience. However, the effects of mismanagement upon defensive behavior are of paramount importance. In this category we include outright aggression, overprotectiveness of food, family and property, shyness, barking at people or animals, and submissive urination.

The 8- to 10-week fear period might be an optimum time to *induce* certain avoidance behavior relative to streets (with and without traffic), electrical cords, and accepting food from strangers or diners at the table. Though the experimental evidence on which this period is based involved pain, a loud sound that startles the dog is usually quite effective in producing avoidance if the response is reinforced *positively* by the owner with upbeat, happy praise. However, the treatment must be applied until the

Table 4. Periods of behavioral sensitivity.

Age (weeks)	Period	Management Implications
3-14	Socialization (primary)	If not socialized to people, shyness or aggressiveness may occur. If taken from the litter before 5 weeks, the pup may be aggressive or shy with other dogs, and become overdependent on the owner if not allowed interaction.
6-8	Optimum socialization	Best age for transition from the litter to a human environment.
8-10	Fear	Traumatic (strong fear-producing) experiences related to pain may be permanently impressed.
12-14	Juvenile	Onset of puberty, sexual mounting. Broad socialization should be continued with *positive* social reinforcement.
14-26	Protective-aggressive	If early protective signs (barking, hackle-raising, growling) are encouraged or punished, overaggressiveness or fearfulness may develop as sexual maturity nears.
26+	Functional achievement	More forceful protective-aggressive behavior occurs. Mismanaged behavior problems become more difficult to correct. At about 36 weeks, aggressive biting may evolve into full-fledged attack behavior. Problem behaviorisms appear to reinforce themselves, making correction more difficult.

puppy avoids the unwanted behavior or objects *without* the startle stimulus, indicating that a *conditioned* avoidance response has been achieved and the puppy has *internalized* the conditioning.

> *An example of mismanagement during puberty onset involved a young couple with a 2-year-old spayed Shepherd-mix bitch who had bitten neighborhood children. When the dog got out of the car, she went to our walnut tree, backed up to it, lifted a leg and urinated on it with hackles raised, then growled as she trotted stiffly past me, tail almost erect. The dog was also aggressive toward all strangers.*
>
> *Two important elements were involved in creating the aggressiveness. From puberty the dog had been allowed to mount the owner's (the wife) legs. More subtle, but of great importance, was the wife's avowed dislike of children and an apparent fear of becoming pregnant, which was indicated by her statement, "I don't know what I'd do if I got pregnant."*

We have noted many such cases in both male and female dogs whose owners have tolerated or even encouraged sexual mounting, or have unwittingly stimulated sexual arousal. That this dog targeted children was not only due to the fact she had seen her owner (the wife) angrily chase neighborhood kids from her property, but also to the wife's *emotional* responses to them.

The correction program involved counseling the clients so they appreciated the impact of their feelings and behavior toward children in general, gaining a leadership position for them with the dog through the earned-petting program (Chapter 8), and a simple, daily ritual Come-Sit-Stay-Down routine and applying the Jolly Routine (Chapter 8) when the dog first perceived children. This brings us to another vital element in behavior problems.

Allelomimetic (Be Like/Act Like) Behavior

This genetic-behavioral term has been defined as "doing what other animals in a group do, with some degree of mutual stimulation."[12] Puppies who join a 2-legged human pack during the 3-to 14-week primary socialization period tend to "bond" with their people. On the other hand, puppies who remain solely with other dogs until 14 weeks are difficult to socialize to people. If socialization is left until later, extreme difficulty is encountered. Most such dogs display either exaggerated excitability, fearfully trying to avoid human contact (active defense reflex, flight type), or its opposite, freezing into a state of catatonia in some cases (passive defense reflex).

Many such dogs can be socialized quite successfully in a carefully managed program wherein well-socialized adult dogs or puppies are used as "bridges," providing a canine behavioral model relative to people, as well as social competition for people as a source of care-giving (epimeletic) behavior, such as petting, praise and feeding, and satisfying care-seeking (et-epimeletic) behavior. One such case is described in the Kennelosis section in Chapter 12.

It is unfortunate that a strict definition of allelomimetic behavior does not include more than merely *doing* what other animals do in a cohesive group, because it fails to consider a dog's acquisition of the *emotional* elements of the group. If we are to include these elements in analyzing and treating behavior problems, we must consider more than fearful or aggressive behavior. We must also address what *drives* such behavior, how the pet *feels* about things and how it *acquired* those feelings, such as hostility toward strangers.

One of the dog's most endearing traits is its ability to respond to our own emotional condition. It is not as important to explain all the ways dogs sense this as it is to recognize that they do respond to our emotional state, some to a greater degree than others. Just as individual wolves in a pack have different, identifiable *personalities*, so the pack as a whole has a personality of its own. Pack A's overall group personality may differ markedly from that of Pack B.[19]

This tendency to reflect the emotional state of the human group and then to respond in canine ways, chiefly toward social stimuli, was coined by Miller as the "Principle of Reflection."[16] In the pet-owner situation, I use the word "group" to include a single dog and its owner. Both the concept and the term have received little scholarly attention. The term "reflection" may be ambiguous, but the phenomenon is evident to any dog owner or professional who works with people and pets. It parallels the sociology of human groups. I prefer to call it *emotional osmosis* and have used this "dimension" of owner-dog relationships to describe and correct many serious problems, as will be seen.

On a purely behavioral level, dogs can be mimetic to varying degrees. While some may be highly motivated to dig in the garden, with or after watching their owners do so, others may not (Fig 2). I have seen a few other dogs actually resist, or move *counter* to actions of people and/or other dogs. This anti-mimetic tendency is most apparent in dominant dogs, which are considered now.

Dominant and Subordinate Behavior

Puppies as young as 3 weeks of age may show dominant behavior, putting forepaws on littermates with the tail erect, remaining still and sometimes growling. Some pups react submissively, remaining quite still or rolling onto their side. This behavior can be seen before, during or after playfighting, and completely independent of it. This sort of behavior, as well as

Figure 2. Allelomimetic behavior is often seen in people-oriented dogs. This German Shepherd is mimicking its owner's behavior of leaning against a wall.

outright fighting, which culminates with a clear-cut winner, has been interpreted and labeled variously as sorting out the *pecking order* or the pack *dominance order*. Its value to the pack has been attributed to ensuring social stability, establishing eating priorities that favor the fittest, and ensuring mating only between the *Alpha* (most dominant) male and the pack's females.

A new view of canine behavior has emerged out of these well-publicized observations. The wolf and domestic dog have come to be regarded as animals with built-in, stereotyped *submissive* behaviorisms that can and *should* be used by their human owners to control aggressive behavior through physical *dominance* techniques, such as forcefully rolling the dog over and holding it down, shaking it by the scruff of the neck or jowls, or forcing its head down.

The difficulty with these techniques is that they are based on only a portion of the reliable observations of animal behavior. For instance, among reported submissive or subordinate responses to dominant behavior by another dog and/or wolf are growling, snarling with teeth bared, hackle-raising and holding the tail upright, all of which have been popularly described as *dominant* behaviorisms.[12] As a result, when unwary owners of dogs with *active*, versus passive, defense reflexes apply these techniques, they do not recognize these other responses as submissive. Seeing them as signs of heightened aggression, corrective pressure is often increased or outright physical punishment is used. As the dog is trying to communicate submission while still preparing to protect itself from physical injury, the owner is stimulating the very behavior s/he is are trying to suppress. In other cases the owner backs off, creating a dog that has *learned* that growling curtails the owner's attempts to control it physically. Also, if either of these treatments is preceded by verbal scolding and/or threatening physical gestures, the dog often starts its own defensive displays at those cues, further convincing the owner that s/he has have a "dangerous" animal for a pet, which is not necessarily the case.

Events that precede and cause such misunderstandings are usually such problems as jumping up, chewing or soiling the house. These often have nothing to do with dominance or subordinate behaviorisms, yet the owner believes the dog must be punished. The net effect of this is a deteriorating relationship between owner and pet. If mistreatment continues, the bitten, disillusioned owner presents the dog to the local animal shelter or veterinarian for euthanasia.

This is not to say that so-called "dominance" handling cannot succeed in stimulating submissive behavior in dogs. For instance, veterinarians and other experienced professionals may often succeed with clients' dogs. However, it should be remembered that dogs relate to outsiders quite differently than to their owners. So, though a quick shakedown or a swat from a virtual stranger may subdue aggression on an examination table, that response is usually *stimulus bound*. That is, it is unique to the context and/or persons involved. An owner, whose relationship with a pet mainly involves affectionate interactions, faces an entirely different set of circumstances.

If ever an owner can use dominance techniques successfully, such as the rollover and hold-down-until-quiet method, or a quick shake by the body (not the hair, so as to avoid pain), it is with a pup under 12-14 weeks of age. The rollover technique described in my puppy selection test (Chapter 7) has been applied positively for unruliness when the pup is released after calming down, allowing the owner to stroke its head, legs and body.

Other aspects that bear on physical force and punishment as tools for managing a family dog's behavior involve the popular misrepresentation that these stem from ancestral wolf social behavior that is *rigidly* enforced. This notion is firmly contradicted by well-documented observations.[19,20] So-called Alpha males do not always mate the Alpha female. Second-rank or *Beta* males sometimes do so with no sign of apparent disapproval from the Alpha male. Nor do Alphas persistently stare at, bully or engage in dominance rituals with subordinate pack members. Such behavior is more often seen in Beta males. Mating of subordinate females is more often controlled by threatened aggression by the Alpha *female* than the male. Further, dominant/ subordinate relationships tend to be *dynamic*, changing as the breeding season approaches, when hunting is nigh, when pups are whelped, or when outsider wolves approach.

Inflicting physical or emotional punishment on subordinate members by dominant wolves, or by domestic dog dams upon their puppies, is not normal *canine* behavior. In fact, it is rarely noted. Such treatment is not conducive to harmony in a wolf pack, where life itself depends on cooperative efforts. Nor is undermining a puppy's confidence in its positive, family relationship with pack members or its dam.

At a time when physical and emotional child abuse is on the rise in our country, and children identify closely with the family dog, yet view their parents as behavioral role models, it seems less than prudent to recommend physical punishment to correct a dog's behavior problem, especially when more effective and humane methods are available.

Dog/Human Family Dominant-Submissive Behavior

Domestic puppies begin sorting out their social status at about 5 weeks of age.[12] When puppies are taken out of the litter during the primary socialization period, there is often a transfer of litter-learned behavior to the human owners. As the pup matures, it adapts its responses to its new social situation. It may become unruly and play-fight persistently with small children, while showing submission to adults who have punished it. As maturity nears and the young animal proceeds through the various periods of social behavior, such as territorial and pack protection, the dog learns to use these to satisfy its apparent need to function as part of the group. In most problem cases, it is the combination of these functional drives and the dog's ability to *manipulate* the behavior of its human companions that leads to difficulties. The following case is an example.

> *The married couple arrived with a large male Malamute that had bitten several men, both family friends and strangers. After urinating on various scent posts, he followed us into the office. When we were seated, and as I started to say something, the dog approached and snarled at me with fangs bared. The husband gruffly called him. The Malamute, tail lowered and ears backed, went to him, whining softly.*
>
> *"See? He's a baby at heart, but don't try to pet him. He nearly took a finger off my friend last week."*
>
> *The dog turned to the wife, jumped up and licked at her face. The husband pulled him off and the dog rolled onto his side.*

Here was a dog using *submissive* behavior to interact with the husband and an "up-on" *dominant* behavior with the wife. As for me, he applied aggressive dominance in an effort to intimidate me. Looking objectively at the group dynamics, it was clear that the Malamute was using most of the behavioral tools in his kit to *lead* our little group. If this aspect of problem dog behavior is kept in mind, we gain a more comprehensive picture of the *causative* elements in behavior problems. The problem dog is generally at odds with some elements of its environment due to its efforts to control its owner's social activities.

For this reason, I have found it helpful to use the terms *leader* and *subordinate* or *follower*, rather than dominant or submissive. In this way we distinguish between stereotyped behaviorisms and what a problem dog's behavior is attempting to *achieve*.

Overdependency

Along with troublesome elements growing out of the foregoing is a *dependency* factor that typifies problem dogs. Most have not matured *emotionally* beyond primary socialization. That is, they still exhibit many litter-dependent behaviorisms, usually of the care-seeking variety, licking at owners and seeking physical contact or grooming, or at least the owners' attention. As a result, if they cannot get this type of attention when they *want* it, frustration, anxiety and tensions build up, resulting in problem behavior. Typically, the overdependent dog cannot be left alone without problems, and cannot tolerate visitors, as they interfere with family interactions. Some cannot even tolerate their owners' ignoring them while reading or talking on the telephone. This mentioned, we have arrived at the crux of causes and corrections for problem behavior.

Leadership

Most problem dogs are *leader types*. That is, they behave as if they are trying to control the activities of the family or certain individuals in the group. In some cases the dogs are in conflict with their physical environment or external social elements, such as neighborhood cats, dogs, mailmen or visitors. A dog that wants to control these elements or lead the activities of its owners is destined to experience frustration.

It is valuable in analyzing behavior problems to be able to observe dogs and owners interacting in an area new to both. This exposes the relationship to the stresses of both physical and social novelties. Having spent several years going to clients' homes for counseling, I saw the flaws in these relationships demonstrated when they were off the home territory and at our Sun Valley Ranch facilities.

Leader Behavior

Leader-type dogs exhibit any or all of the following behavior, both on and off their home territory.

- Precedes owner through doors or when walking in almost *any* direction.
- Does not obey the owner's commands.
- Displays anxiety about new people or situations, either by overreacting toward or away from them.
- Interferes with the owner's interactions with other people.
- Nudges the owner persistently for physical petting.

Leader-Type Behaviorisms in New Environments

When a dog assumes a leadership role in its owner relationships, it usually exhibits behaviorisms that provide a clue. These signs suggest that the dog feels responsible for, rather than to, its owner. Some easily detected signs are listed below.

- Protectiveness of the owner.
- Nervousness (anxiety about the new area, scouting the area).
- Lack of response to the owner's direction.
- Rushes in or out of doors ahead of the owner.
- Interferes with the owner's interactions with other people in the new situation. This may involve either dominant or submissive behaviorisms.

The last category involves problem dogs that might be considered pleasant pets, but have developed a need for attention that has hampered desirable emotional maturation. It can be likened to the care-seeking behavior of the pup that whines, barks, licks, paws or in some other way encourages its owners to respond.

Such dog-owner relationships are prime examples of operant conditioning, which may persist throughout the dog's life.

In conditioning, the dog is stimulated to perform a desired behavior and is then rewarded.[3] In the experimental situation, this reward is often food, but other rewards may work as well. The next time the dog behaves properly, it is again rewarded. The following sequence of actions takes place.

Stimulus ⟶ Behavior ⟶ Reward

(reinforcement)

Once the association between stimulus and the forthcoming reward is established, the dog usually performs the behavior dependably (Fig 3).

When a leader-type pet dog is involved, the conditioning may take on the following characteristics:

Stimulus ⟶ Response ⟶ Reward

(dog nudges owner) (owner pets dog) (dog quits nudging)

This oversimplified example highlights the central theme of many problem situations between owners and their dogs. The dog is "training" its owner to provide attention at the dog's convenience. The result, in behavioral conditioning, is a social pest. The fact that dog owners often enjoy this form of behavior

Figure 3. A puppy learns to follow its human leader after a few days of training by praise and petting.

is discussed in the next chapter. Here it is important only to appreciate the dog's intense susceptibility to such social conditioning.

Summary

I have tried to present a dynamic picture of the maturing domestic dog in such a way that conclusions might be drawn concerning the appearance of critical behavioral periods and problems of either a temporary or permanent nature. One thing that appears certain is that no particular problem is necessarily exclusively related to any specific period. The roots of problem behavior may lie in a specific developmental phase, the gradual erosive effects of the environmental tenor, or some specific psychic trauma.

When dealing with a dog's specific *behavior*, we should speak in terms of dominance and submissiveness. But for purposes of clarity when speaking of the character of a dog's relationship with its owners, it may be best to use the terms *leader* and *subordinate,* or *follower*.

The "move-with" allelomimetic tendencies of problem dogs were described as either extremely mimetic or antimimetic, with independent leader types falling into the latter category.

The dog that misses its owner too much, for whatever reason, is one of the most frequently encountered problem dogs. However, independent leader types may be the most troublesome, as they are most often vicious.

Questions of leadership and responsibility arise from the dog's relationship with its owners. Though every dog has the capacity to lead in a social situation, the owners control the elements that produce problems in their pets. This may occur as a result of a series of reversed social operant conditioning procedures. The outcome is often a dog that feels responsible for, rather than to, its owners and property, especially in the case of protective-aggressive dogs. In some cases, maturation may be stilted in another way, resulting in a pet that is overdependent on its owner's presence or attentions.

All of these social developmental aspects bear on some element of a problem dog's behavior, and may cause it. For this reason, careful fact finding in all cases is required for effective solutions.

Neurotic and Psychotic Dogs

The Neurotic Dog

A neurosis may be defined as a functional nervous disorder with no sign of physical impairment. This means that to recognize a neurotic dog, we must identify some defective nervous function. This could be done in some cases through neurologic examinations, along with sophisticated urine and blood analyses. These, when combined with behavioral problems, might tend to indicate neuroses.[6,9]

Unfortunately, we are usually unable to get neurophysiologic workups and must depend on purely behavioral clues for an answer. For all practical purposes, a dog may be considered neurotic if it displays signs of a functional nervous disorder combined with behavior that is both abnormal and maladaptive for dogs in general.

But how is a functional nervous disorder described in behavioral terms? The following 4 categories of neurotic dogs are helpful.

- The dog that fails to inhibit the orienting (alerting) response to stimuli that occur repeatedly and are known to the animal to be neither harmful nor rewarding. These dogs are almost always in a state of anxiety.
- The dog that responds to novel objects, sounds, touches, movements and even odors with exaggerated defense responses. Dogs in this category often lack adequate early experience.
- The dog that fails to retain (in some cases, even to develop) either Type-I or Type-II conditioned reflexes. This cannot be applied to the dog's total behavior, but usually is pertinent to failure to form and/or retain learned associations involving defense and social behaviorisms.
- The dog that displays hyperkinesis. Signs include excessive salivation, elevated pulse and respiration, abnormally low urine output, and increased energy metabolism revealed through excessive, sometimes stereotyped activity, especially in close confinement. This is more extensively discussed in Chapters 4 and 5.

These outward signs often indicate functional nervous disorders, some of which may be caused by disease or other physical factors. However, there may be functional nervous disorders that do not fall into the definition of neurosis; they do not meet the requirements of both abnormal and maladaptive behavior.

A dog that violates its normally fastidious nature and housetraining by urinating on the front window drapes when other dogs are outside, is behaving somewhat abnormally as compared with most other dogs. But this behavior is not maladaptive because in canine terms the animal is marking its territory, a normal canine trait.

On the other hand, if in that same situation the dog were to run to its master's bed and urinate on it, we would probably say the behavior is both abnormal and maladaptive. Though possibly tension relieving, the act of urination is not normally related to the stimulus (the dogs outside).

Abnormal, maladaptive behavior can be defined as tension-relieving behavior that does not relate to the cause of tension. Such behavior does not actually relieve tensions and, in many cases, may even increase tensions in another area of the dog's life.

Examples of this behavior include urination, self-mutilation, habitual masturbation, general destructiveness, displaced aggression, and others that will be mentioned in later sections. The foregoing clues are described only to provide guidelines for defining a dog that has a functional nervous disorder and may be neurotic. These must be considered along with the total history of the dog from behavioral and medical aspects.

Neurotic states have been induced in laboratory dogs, then rehabilitated under carefully controlled circumstances.[3,15] Most of this work has been performed with an eye toward comparison with the human situation. Dogs are well suited to comparative analysis, especially on the emotional level. However, when we deal with the domestic dog we are not considering a carefully controlled environment, but rather a chaotic situation with poorly structured influences affecting the animal.

The behaviorist works with those external forces that may or may not have created a neurosis. At times this has proven adequate for rehabilitation of the pet. However, the true neurotic not only displays problem behavior, but also suffers from some neurologic problems. Whether these stem from endocrine imbalances, genetically acquired anomalies, dietary insufficiencies, brain tumor or injury, encephalitis, etc, the most rewarding results I have achieved have involved a combined veterinary-behavioral approach.

The Psychotic Dog

The line between neurotic and psychotic behavior is not well defined by psychiatrists and psychologists. However, 2 prevailing criteria can be added to the definition of a neurotic dog to describe, for our purposes, psychotic behavior. These involve circumstances in which the dog's behavior is dangerous to itself or to the welfare of others, and in which the dog appears to be unaware of the behavior during and/or very shortly thereafter its actions.

If only the first criterion were to be applied to biting or self-mutilating dogs, then they would incorrectly be considered psychotic. In fact, many people believe a biting dog should be labeled a "psycho" and destroyed forthwith, regardless of the circumstances. On the other hand, if the second standard applies, it would seem reasonable to apply the psychotic label.

The dog that appears to have withdrawn from reality or suffers episodes of withdrawal could be either psychotic or physically ill. If the behavior fits the basic neurotic model and is also in some way harmful to life or well-being, then the animal may be psychotic, if otherwise healthy.

Dogs defined as psychotic have included the following:

- Dogs that suffered "avalanches" of unreasonable rage and did not respond to external stimuli.
- Manic-depressive animals that vacillated between depression and wild activity.
- Depressed dogs that failed to respond even to powerful stimuli, such as hunger, as when dogs starve to death in the presence of food.

Such cases have been seen in pet dogs as well as laboratory animals. The rage and manic-depressive states occur mainly in excitable types, whereas depression usually occurs in those with inhibitive tendencies.

Some notable factors in the medical histories of apparently psychotic pet dogs are listed below.

- Early distemper (before 3 months).
- Prolonged severe pancreatitis (especially as pups).
- Serious parasitic infection (before 6 months).
- Severe beatings.
- Accidental injury, especially to the head.
- Accidental drug overdose.
- Prolonged corticosteroid therapy.
- Psychic trauma.

Summary

I have tried to define the neurotic and psychotic dog in terms of its behavior, relying on observation of external signs. The neurotic is described as exhibiting both abnormal (for itself or the canine species) and maladaptive behavior. Some clues may be found in an inability to develop conditioned behavior or to retain it normally.

The psychotic usually has neurotic signs coupled with behavior that is harmful to itself or others and during which the dog lacks apparent awareness of its situation. A combined approach to rehabilitation involving both veterinary and behavioral fields has yielded the best results.

Breeds and Behavior

After I reviewed 25 years of data from documented cases, owner surveys and "expert" opinions about breeds and behavior, it was apparent that statistics can be shaped and interpreted to prove almost any point. Raw statistics from nationwide surveys of more than 3600 dog owners provided statistics on only 23 of the more than 130 breeds of dogs currently recognized. We conducted the surveys between 1974 and 1985. While the results might be interpreted as statistically significant for a few behavior complaints in some of these breeds, their practical value as a guide for prospective puppy buyers is questionable.

For instance, we could say that Beagles garnered no biting complaints, but escaped their yards at double the normal rate of all breeds. However, having recently heard from 2 biting-Beagle owners, it seems unwise to present data that might be misleading, no matter how clearly we attempt to qualify such statistics. Another method, seeking opinions from professionals such as veterinarians and trainers, while an appealing concept, seems equally ill advised, as forthcoming comments are based on subjective, often second-hand judgments rather than on factual observations.

Therefore, prospective dog owners should consult the various breed atlases to select a visually appealing breed. After the initial selection, that breed can be researched for any genetic-based health/behavioral problems, and a specific breeder selected. Then the behavior test for puppy selection (see Chapter 7) can be used. It has proved invaluable as a guide to acquiring the pup best suited to the buyer's situation. In this way, puppy purchasers can base decisions on the latest data available, while making an enlightened financial and personal commitment to the new pet.

Summarizing the Problem Dog

Problem dogs have no single profile. Instead, we emerge with a montage including dogs of all breeds and sexes, with major behavioral characteristics tending toward excitability or inhibition. These tendencies may be encoded genetically or influenced during life by the environment, especially in critical early periods. External factors involved can include mishandling, poor diet, certain diseases and trauma.

The "problem dog" is defined by its owner or those who must otherwise interact with it. Perfectly normal canine behavior might be considered a problem to one owner but an asset to another. However, most problems are the result of the dog's relieving tensions created by frustration of either innate or learned behavior. Tension is relieved orally, physically or vocally, or in all 3 ways in some cases.

Each problem dog must be considered an individual "type" functioning within a sphere of environmental influences.

References

1. Stel'makh L: *Pavlov J Higher Nervous Activity* 2:216, 1958.
2. Melzak RA and Scott TH: *J Comparative Physiology Psychology* 50:155-161, 1957.
3. Fox MW: *Understanding Your Dog*. Coward, McCann & Geohegan, New York, 1972.

4. Pavlov IP: *Conditioned Reflexes.* Oxford University Press, London, 1927.

5. Rech RH and Moore KE: *An Introduction to Psychopharmacology.* Raven Press, New York, 1971.

6. Bowman RE and Datta SP: *Biochemistry of the Brain and Behavior.* Plenum Press, New York, 1970.

7. Flynn JP, in Glass DC: *Neurophysiology and Emotion.* Rockefeller Univ Press, New York, 1967.

8. Naumenko EV: *Central Regulation of the Pituitary-Adrenal Complex.* Consultants Bureau, New York, 1973.

9. Greenfield NS and Sternbach RA: *Handbook of Psychophysiology.* Holt, Rinehart, Winston, New York, 1972.

10. Konorski J: *Integrative Activity of the Brain.* Univ Chicago Press, Chicago, 1967.

11. Fox MW: *Canine Behavior.* Charles C Thomas, Springfield, IL, 1965.

12. Scott JP and Fuller JL: *Dog Behavior: The Genetic Basis.* Univ Chicago Press, Chicago, 1974.

13. Rusinov VS: *Electrophysiology of the Central Nervous System.* Consultants Bureau, New York, 1973.

14. Thorndike EL: *Animal Intelligence.* Macmillan, New York, 1911.

15. Skinner BF: *The Behavior of Organisms.* Appleton-Century, New York, 1938.

16. Miller D: *Dog Master Manual.* Canine Behavior Institute Library, Santa Monica, CA, 1987.

17. Hoerlein BF: *Canine Neurology.* Saunders, Philadelphia, 1971.

18. Abrahams VC et al: *J Physiology* 164:1-16, 1971.

19. Lopez BH: *Of Wolves and Men.* Charles Scribner's Sons, New York, 1978.

20. Allen DL: *Wolves of Minong.* Houghton Mifflin, Boston, 1979.

Helpful Reading

Delgado JR: *Physical Control of the Mind.* Harper & Row, New York, 1969.

Rosenblith WA: *Principles of Sensory Communication, A Symposium.* M.I.T. Press & John Wiley, New York, 1961.

Sokolov EN: *Perception and the Conditioned Reflex.* Pergamon Press, New York, 1963.

Papez JW: *Comparative Neurology.* Crowell, New York, 1929.

von Bekesy G: *Sensory Inhibition.* Princeton Univ Press, Princeton, NJ, 1966.

Zeigler HP and Gross CG: *Readings in Physiological Psychology. Vol 1, Neurophysiology/Sensory Processes.* Harper & Row, New York, 1969.

Pribram K: *Languages of the Brain.* Prentice-Hall, Englewood Cliffs, NJ, 1971.

Sutherland MS and Mackintosh NJ: *Mechanisms of Animal Discrimination and Learning.* Academic Press, New York, 1971.

Anderson AC and Good LS: *The Beagle as an Experimental Dog.* Iowa State Univ Press, Ames, 1970.

Clemente CD and Lindsley DB: *Brain Function, v. 5, Aggression and Defense: Neural Mechanisms and Social Patterns.* Univ Calif Press, Berkeley, 1967.

Garattini S and Sigg EB: *Biology of Aggression.* Interscience Publishers, New York, 1969.

Klosovski BN: *Excitatory and Inhibitory States of the Brain.* Israel Program for Scientific Translations, Jerusalem, 1963.

Klosovski BN: *Development of the Nervous System and Its Disturbance by Harmful Factors.* Macmillan, New York, 1963.

Zubek JP: *Sensory Deprivation.* Appleton-Century-Crofts, New York, 1969.

(This page intentionally left blank)

2

Problem Owners and Environments

After I spent 13 years practicing in the urban/suburban Los Angeles area, the past 11 years of rural living in southwestern Oregon have convinced me that big-city life takes a marked toll on both human and canine residents. The hustle-bustle, noise, frantic rushing to work and home, high crime rates and crowded schools create perceptibly more "tense" personalities among city folk, at least to this observer.

The physical and psychological benefits of daily contact with natural things are well known: hearing the wind in a forest, planting and nurturing a garden, watching a river flow, viewing panoramic sunsets, watching squirrels and chipmunks forage or play, or watching birds gather nest materials. In mankind's history, the dog was domesticated for its functional value. It hunted, warned of intruders, drove away stock predators, and even provided warmth in the bitter cold of some climates. But city life denies people the benefit of most of these canine functions, except perhaps guarding property. The dog is likewise denied its age-old group functional role.

In a city, a pet may be the only meaningful daily contact for most adults and children with the *animated* natural world. We are living in a civilization increasingly dependent on verbal skills and electronic communications. We now learn more by listening and watching than through experience. Without an opportunity to develop nonverbal communications with animals, owners tend to use human verbal and physical abilities (manipulation, force, punishment) to communicate with their dogs. Thus, the idea that the dog must be "trained" if it is to learn how to *behave* dominates the owner's perceptions of the pet. When this expectation of training is not fulfilled, both owner and dog become frustrated, and problems develop.

Dogs learn to behave according to the way people *act*, not what people say. Human *movement* and *sound* constitute our communication with dogs. On the other hand, the dog's efforts to communicate with people through movement are too often ignored or misinterpreted, creating a widening and frustrating communications gap.

The concept that dog owners should learn to interpret their pet's behavior and use movement, stance and vocal sounds to communicate and live harmoniously together may at first seem far-fetched. However, these elements play a critical role in understanding and correcting behavior problems, as will be evident.

> *A man had been shouting in an effort to calm his dog, which barked excessively when gas station attendants cleaned the windshield. He came to me at wit's end, having tried every sort of punishment to distract the yapping canine. I suggested that the owner himself clean the windshield daily for about a week, while the dog is in the car. After that week, he should sit in the car in stony silence while the attendants repeated the task. Within 2 weeks the problem resolved itself and the dog merely whined at the attendants, which was acceptable to the owner.*

Very few dog owners appreciate that shouting at a barking dog is, in fact, responding to the barking with a human version of the same behavior. Many dogs become silent because they associate the owner's tone of voice with disapproval and impending pain from punishment. However, excitable types or those with some prior traumatic experience often behave worse.

In the nonverbal world of dogs, silence signifies silence, stillness begets stillness, and action stimulates action. The fact that this apparently self-evident facet of nonverbal communication must be written or talked about to gain attention among dog owners further points up the nonverbal deficiencies of people.

Spoken language is just *noise* to dogs. It is a tribute to their intelligence that they actually learn the meaning of certain key sounds. This usually comes about through the dog's deliberate concentration and the owner's almost accidental consistency when referring to certain events or objects, such as regularly using the word "out" in such phrases as "D'ya wanna go out?" or "Tippy want out?" In these cases, the sound of the word "out" is meaningful to Tippy. The upward inflection used at the end of the sentence often indicates that it is time to get excited about something, the nature of which is revealed by the key word involved.

> *I once had a particularly critical client who debated this point about dogs and language. To prove the point, I had him repeat the sentence "Charlie one-two-three-far right?" to his Dachshund with the same upward, questioning inflection he used in asking his pet, "Charlie wanna go car ride?"*
>
> *Sure enough, Charlie responded just as if a trip in the family jalopy had been promised. As a matter of fact, Charlie responded even more excitedly to the rattle of car keys than he did to words.*

The most glaring feature of problem owners is ignorance – not stupidity, but a lack of knowledge about what makes their dogs behave as they do. I take some license in claiming that this "vacuum" of knowledge is not empty; rather, it is filled with myths and assumptions about the behavioral nature of dogs. This chapter describes some important behavioral facts about problem owners and outlines solutions to the causes of their pets' problem behavior. These elements can then be used, along with knowledge of the dog's own contribution to the problem and other environmental factors, to analyze the total problem.

Characteristics of Problem Owners

Dog owners whose problems stem mainly from personal interaction with their pets often exhibit some extreme behavioral
characteristic in that relationship. It is difficult to categorize
these extremes without giving the impression that an owner
must be "either this type or that type." As a matter of fact,
owners may fit all categories at some time. With this understood,
the following descriptions may prove helpful.

As was the case in trying to categorize problem dogs, we are
forced to oversimplify to form any classifications (Table 1). I
should restate that I have seen owners display all of these
behaviorisms with their dogs at one time or another during a
span of 6 weeks. The following cases are typical of each category.

The Domineering-Physical Owner

> *The client had a large male German Shepherd
> puppy with highly active defense reflexes. The pup
> responded to harsh punishment during the house-
> training period with snarls and actual attacks. Dur-
> ing our consultation, the dog kept going to the door
> to look out. Each time this happened the client rushed
> over, grabbed him by the scruff of the neck, slapped
> his nose and pulled him back to a forced sitting
> position by his chair.*
>
> *After about 10 of these episodes, I asked the client
> what he thought he was teaching his puppy. He
> responded by saying that he was teaching him to stay
> with him in a sitting position, rather than wander
> away. I then asked why a pup should want to stay
> with a person who grabs, slaps and pulls at him. The
> answer was typical: "Because I am supposed to be his
> master."*

It took 6 weeks to remodel this client's master-slave attitude
and convince him that his dog's individuality could be used as a
training aid. The next time the pup went to the screen door, I
had the client quietly walk over, slightly open the screen and
quickly slam it, startling the pup. I then told the owner to praise

Table 1. Characteristics of problem owners.

Owner Type	Attitude Toward Dog
Domineering-physical	Insists on total subservience and uses excessive force and/or punishment to gain obedience.
Domineering-vocal	Wants total subservience and uses vocal volume or stern tone for obedience.
Seductive	Tries to gain responses through coaxing and/or fondling the dog.
Insecure-permissive	Wants the dog's love and loyalty but avoids any form of discipline for fear of losing either or both.
Ambivalent	Mixed emotions about the animal lead to problems.
Paranoid-anthropomorphic	Endows the dog with emotional and intellectual capabilities unique to people. This type consistently misinterprets the dog's behaviorisms, and usually already "knows" all the reasons for the problem behavior.
Naive	Knows little or nothing about dogs and often follows everyone's advice, no matter how outrageous.
Logical	Uses "common-sense" methods, even in the face of undesirable results.
Intractable	Displays either extreme rigidity or elasticity of attitude in response to consultative guidance, and, therefore, cannot help solve the problem.
Children	See text on pages 70-73.

the pup quietly as he walked back to his chair. To the client's amazement, the Shepherd scurried to his side and sat down. After a few similar "treatments," the pup lay down and slept at his owner's feet for the remainder of our session.

Most domineering-physical owners are men, women and children also are sometimes involved. Children who display this behavior usually reflect autocratic or domineering parents who are physical with the children as well. Dogs that respond poorly to such owners are mainly excitable types with active defense reflexes.

Highly physical owners are usually amazed at how quickly and willingly their dogs respond to nonphysical show-and-tell methods. This motivates them to listen to advice and change their attitude about the dog. When the dog perceives its owner's changed behavior, the problem often improves immediately.

The Domineering-Vocal Owner

The "drill sergeant syndrome" may have originated during World War I (from which most obedience work stems), when the trench, sentry and communications dogs used by the German army had to be trained with shouted orders because of competing noise of artillery and small arms fire. Except in military dogs, such training is inappropriate and unnecessary. At 75 feet, most dogs can hear sounds that cannot be detected at 18 feet by people. It is well known that loud noises trigger defense reflex responses, usually of the avoidance type. When trying to gain obedience, shouting such commands as "Come," "Sit" or "Heel" is more likely to result in avoidance than compliance.

> *One client brought me a dog that, when sternly commanded to "Come," responded by rolling onto its back and emitting a virtual geyser of urine. When the client understood his dog's extreme passive defense reflex and inhibited nervous type, he switched to whispered commands. In several weeks, the dog was a willing companion whose confidence increased perceptibly each day.*

The Seductive Owner

The owner who tries to gain loyalty and obedience through constant petting, baby-talking and coaxing the problem dog is usually practicing a form of pet-oriented emotional masturbation. The owner, not the dog, gains emotional satisfaction from the behavior. This sort of owner usually has a dog that is immature and may be anything from sadistically vicious to masochistically self-mutilating.

A 2-year-old male Afghan Hound was tearing up its mistress's apartment when left alone. During our first interview, the young woman constantly fondled the hound, which responded by displaying a penile erection – a secondary complaint. When I asked if she had a boyfriend, the answer was yes, several. As a purely consultative device, I then asked how she thought any of them might act if she were to treat them in a like manner and then go off and leave them. Her coy answer was that she didn't think they would allow her to go! The point was made and she accepted the explanation that the fondling and associated baby talk were sexually arousing the dog, which was bound to be consistently frustrated.

The naive young client then asked if her dog might benefit from being bred with an Afghan bitch. Would this solve the problem? I pointed out that the problem was being caused by her own interaction with the dog and had nothing to do with intra-species sexual frustration, but was associated with inter-species frustration. Also, dogs that are sexually overstimulated by people rarely perform well with their own species. Interestingly, this last fact was a more powerful stimulus than any other in changing the client's behavior. The thought that she might be ruining her pet's chances for sexual gratification with its own kind reached her on an emotional level. The case eventually concluded successfully.

The Insecure-Permissive Owner

Through no fault of their own, many problem dog owners have never been taught any of the basics of leadership. When these people are faced with a dog that displays independence, it is perceived often as a blow to their own personal worth. These insecure-permissive owners usually overreact, either giving in to the dog's desires or becoming irate and ignoring the animal.

The word discipline is popularly accepted as involving punishment, but this definition is low on the list in most dictionaries. Pertaining to dogs, it connotes training that corrects, molds or perfects. Implicit in this definition is an overriding element of consistency, which is of prime importance in all leadership principles. Once the insecure-permissive owner understands the effects of his or her inconsistency, a program can be developed to solve the problem behavior.

> *A case that typifies this situation involved 2 children in a family, a girl of 15 and her 12-year-old brother. The boy believed that the dog, a problem chewer, was more attached to his sister than to him. In fact, this was so. Our discussion revealed that the girl spent very little time with the dog, a year-old spayed Yorkshire Terrier. The boy, however, spent a good deal of time with the Yorkie, most of it playing. The boy did not openly admit jealousy, but his behavior made it apparent. He called the dog whenever it jumped up beside his sister. This same type of jealousy often occurs between husbands and wives, and the solution is the same in principle for both types.*

With an imbalance in relationships, it is necessary to involve all of those who are part of the situation in corrective exercises. All of these people should participate in each teaching session so the dog is subjected to consistent, identical commands from everyone and begins responding consistently to each. This principle also must be applied beyond the formal training sessions. The program usually fails if one party continues to be permissive or spoils the dog, while others are stern or harsh. A middle road involving some degree of behavioral change by each person usually brings success within days or weeks.

During consultations I rarely have to point out inconsistencies to the owners. Instead, I ask them to tell me what the dog might perceive as inconsistent treatment by the various people interacting with the dog. The answers are usually amazingly accurate, as each tells me all about what the other does that is incorrect. Then, after the tempers cool off, direct criticism can be avoided merely by pointing out that the inconsistency between owners is causing the problem. We can then chart a course that requires mutual change and brings eventual success. The Yorkshire Terrier's chewing resolved in 6 weeks with this program.

The Ambivalent Owner

The comic definition of ambivalence as "watching your mother-in-law drive off a cliff in your new Rolls-Royce" does not accurately describe the ambivalence of this type of dog owner.

The ambivalent owner perceives the dog in terms of satisfying the owner's personal needs. When this standard is not reached (usually through no fault of the pet), the owner experiences ambivalence – simultaneous attraction to the dog regarding affection and responsibility for its welfare, and revulsion because of the animal's behavioral and/or physiologic shortcomings.

> *A housewife and mother had banished the family's 5-month-old St. Bernard bitch to the back yard because of its unruliness and constant slobbering, which plagues the overbred, loose-lipped specimens that seem to dominate that breed today. The young lady explained that she required the dog so her children might grow up with it. She felt responsible for the unfortunate animal but, on the other hand, the dog was not fulfilling its planned role in the family.*

The fact that anyone would assume the responsibility of adopting a puppy without considering the animal's shortcomings indicates a basic flaw in this person's attitudes about pet ownership. In most of these cases, I have succeeded in changing the owner's attitudes by pointing out basic, emotionally appealing facets of the dog's predicament. This involves asking some pivotal questions.

- *Did the dog have any choice in selecting its owner?* This helps create a basic feeling of greater responsibility on the owner's part.
- *If those who chose the puppy now find it unacceptable, how could any new adoptive owner learn to love the dog, lacking*

the value of a positive early relationship in its life? This tends to appeal to the owner's self-esteem as the one best able to help the dog.

- *Who is best equipped, when the proper tools for rehabilitation are provided, to help the dog: its lifelong owners or some strangers?* This rather logical question tends to trigger a degree of pride in most owners toward solving the problem.
- In the event the owners are also parents and contemplating euthanasia as a solution, an analogy often helps: *How will you cope if your children fail to live up to your expectations?* The answer is usually that help will be provided in any form necessary, which leads to my disclosing the relatively simpler process of helping the dog in most cases.

This procedure does not always clear up owner ambivalence, but usually provides the motivation necessary in working toward a solution.

The "Paranoid" or Anthropomorphic Owner

The psychological state of paranoid delusions, usually of a suspicious nature, describes most problem dog owners. For instance, it is far more appealing to conclude that a dog that chews up an owner's pillow is "getting even" than to consider that the animal is interacting orally with the owner's scent due to some owner-oriented frustration.

> *A 4-year-old female mongrel chewed and defecated on the owner's bed when left alone. The stools were fortunately formed and firm, and no health problem was involved. The owner thought he knew exactly why his pet was doing this awful deed: it was getting even for being left alone. But the bitch only performed the act after the owner's girlfriend had spent a night in bed with him. At these times the dog, having once tried to interfere with the couple's copulatory activity, was closed out of the bedroom.*

This sort of defecation is often seen in bitches, spayed or not. The solution to this problem was to involve both owner and girlfriend in a program that gained a strong leadership role for each of them. The dog was afforded her own bed in the room and consistently kept there, even in the lady's absence, whereas previously the dog had slept on the owner's bed. The first several "training sessions" were understandably frustrating for the couple, but thereafter an acceptable peace was established and the problem did not recur.

Many who have observed packs of wild dogs report that sexual activity by the dominant pair is not necessarily vicariously stimulating for all those dogs not participating. This does occur in certain dog-owner relationships and usually reflects an unhealthy emotional dependence upon the owner.

Paranoia is involved to some degree in most behavior problems I see. The only satisfactory solution found to date is to bring previously unknown knowledge about canine behavior to the owner's attention so a new attitude can be established, and effective changes can be implemented.

In concluding this category of paranoid owners, it would be unfair to leave the impression that any of my clients have actually had the very serious mental state of paranoia. I have used the term here only to dramatize the mild condition of thought projection common among dog owners and probably reserved exclusively for perceptions of their wayward pets.

The Naive Owner

These are normal folk from all walks of life who, through misinformation or happenstance, have found themselves with a dog that adjusts poorly to its environment. Most of these clients are naive regarding the proper upbringing of a pup, and the measures they take tend to be based on advice from popular breed books, newspaper columns, pamphlets or various types of "authorities" ranging from pet shop owners to friends who may have raised a couple of dogs. Such advice is blind to the individuality of this owner's dog. In these cases, the owner normally has no "hangups" either emotionally or intellectually; therefore, straightforward advice and explanations can usually bring about corrections. This type of problem dog owner has an open mind, quickly grasps causative factors, and readily applies necessary steps toward solutions.

The owners of a 4-year-old male Cocker Spaniel were disappointed to find that castration failed to resolve their dog's hostility toward visitors. The Cocker first started biting at about 2 years old, and had since been kept outside when guests called. However, on several occasions the dog had gotten into the house and bitten people.

The problem's cause lay in excessive teasing by a son and his friends during the first 2 years of the dog's life. With the boy now away at school, the behavior persisted. Discussion with the owners revealed that the dog had one pleasant behavioral characteristic: he immensely enjoyed anyone who would throw a ball for him, even total strangers. I suggested that all visitors be given a tennis ball (the dog's favorite type) to toss. This treatment was successful in a few weeks. The Cocker now greets each new guest with a ball and wagging tail in place of his former hostility.

This sort of behavioral therapy is always coupled with general advice to avoid pampering or other excesses during the family's daily interaction with the pet. In this case, the family was quick to understand how initial teasing, followed by isolation from guests, created in the dog a resentment of visitors that resulted in aggressiveness. No thoughts of getting rid of the pet had been entertained and no resentment toward him was apparent, as is fortunately true in most naive-owner problem situations, but rare when biting is involved.

The problem dog owner who wants to learn and has no emotional hangups can usually be assisted with minimum time and effort. However, such may not be the case with what I call the common-sense or logical owner.

The Logical Owner

Common sense used to tell us that what goes up must come down, or what was good enough for Dad is good enough for me. However, it is now becoming apparent that what goes up doesn't necessarily come down, and Dad's requirements no longer fit ours in many respects. Einstein is credited with saying that common sense results from the accumulation of our prejudices; to wit, common sense is rarely based on fact. So it is with the problem dog owner who applies methods that make sense to him but not to the dog. The result, depending on the dog involved, can be disastrous.

The client who uses common sense in the face of an undesirable response from the dog soon becomes convinced that something is wrong with the dog rather than with his approach. It can be most difficult to deal with this type of client. On a purely logical basis, the client thinks something must be done to change the dog to fit the treatment, rather than vice versa. Most often the emotional relationship between such owners and their dogs is either absent or shallow. So it is challenging to the behaviorist to discover the threads of some emotional bond and then stimulate the client to develop that relationship and gain the motivation necessary to salvage what is usually a worthwhile dog from a difficult situation.

> *A young couple with 2 children had a particularly active, spayed Dalmatian. The husband had picked the puppy and wanted a pet in the family. The wife was against it, believing that her chores with an 18-month-old son and 6-year-old daughter kept her busy enough without the added burden of raising a dog.*
>
> *When the dog was 11 months old, it was isolated in a run in the back yard due to unruliness. The Dalmatian had bitten the baby playfully with enough force to break the skin. I was then consulted to ascertain whether the pet, now 19 months old, was too "abnormal" to train not to bite the kids.*

The wife flatly stated that she had no feelings one way or the other about the dog's fate, and that her only purpose in meeting with me was to satisfy our requirement that all pivotal family members attend. The husband was passive during the early part of the meeting as the Dalmatian gaily jumped up on everyone, ran about the area and otherwise showed behavior typical of a poorly socialized dog.

The husband had no previous experience with dogs, while his wife had been raised in a rural area with old-fashioned barnyard dogs. These lived and slept with the other farm animals and never became "neurotic," as she put it, with a sideward glance at her spotted menace. She believed that the Dalmatian was simply the wrong dog for her family. The dog needed exactly what she was not prepared to give it: companionship and constant attention.

The pup had been examined by a veterinarian and found physiologically normal, so I searched for some emotional involvement between the woman and dog. The 4 questions used with the ambivalent owner did not secure anything useful. The husband desired and selected the pup, so the seeds for any emotional leverage with his wife were absent. In such cases I have found it best to try to establish some emotional interplay between the highly logical party and the dog. This usually involves demonstrating that the "misfit" really is quite tractable and will calm down and behave as the owners desire.

After explaining the highly social nature of dogs, and how the social needs of the wife's barnyard dogs had been fulfilled by the other animals on the farm, she began to appreciate her Dalmatian's isolated frustration relative to its "family." One note of agreement, even if on a purely intellectual level, may often lead to another, so I then asked if the dog might be worth admitting to the family circle if I could show that the dog was easily trainable and would calm down and become placid in our company. The answer was yes, on the condition that I could teach the family to do the same with the wayward pet.

It is not unusual for a dog such as this to learn rapidly when taught by someone with whom there is little or no emotional conflict. The Dalmatian responded in minutes, and learned to come, sit and stay on command in one of the training areas. It is normal for a dog to calm markedly after a few minutes in a learning situation, and this case was no exception. When we re-entered my office, the dog lay down and went to sleep while the owners and I finished our discussion. The husband and wife listened attentively while I proposed a program requiring adjustments by both.

I then suggested that we return to the training area and that the wife actually teach the come, sit and stay commands to her latent canine genius. When the Dalmatian responded positively to her, we witnessed a genuine change in the wife's attitude. She hugged the dog's neck when we had finished. Where there had been no emotional tie, the simple process of seeing the dog change and then participating in control of it had created the beginnings of a relationship that grew to become so strong over the following weeks that the dog was not only admitted to the family circle, but wound up sleeping in the couple's bedroom.

So the common-sense logician must often be manipulated into an emotional relationship with his or her problem dog to achieve success. It may seem unwise to admit to manipulation, in that future clients may be on guard against the technique. However, my experience indicates that most people are aware they are being influenced during these programs. In fact, at the conclusion of the case just cited, the woman involved said she believed she had been "tricked" into feeling love for a dog, a feeling she previously thought she could never have.

Since 1975 I have not found it necessary, or advisable, to do any preliminary one-on-one training with clients' dogs as described above in the Dalmatian case. Instead, I have the owners begin applying the *learn-to-earn* praise and petting ritual during our first meeting. This involves pleasantly telling the dog "Muffin, sit" when it approaches for attention, briefly petting it, then releasing it with an "all right" or "OK." This may have to be repeated many times during the first few minutes of a consultation, but most dogs calm down markedly after 3-6 such commands.

Two other exercises have been invaluable in demonstrating the trainability of a dog to dubious owners. The clients get up and head for the door as if leaving the room. When the dog *starts* to move ahead of them (and a dog almost always will), the owners abruptly turn and go to their seats. If the dog stops or turns around, it is praised quietly and beckoned back with soft hand clapping. It is petted when it reaches them. Then the procedure is repeated as many times as necessary until the dog stays back while the clients go to the door. If a secure outdoor area is at hand, this reverse-the-direction exercise can be repeated there.

Even if not, the clients are quite impressed by the fact that, *without speaking a command,* they have taught their dog to stay back from a door, something that is a general problem with most dogs. This is usually the first experience most clients have had in using the *dog's* language to communicate a desired behavior while discouraging unwanted behavior.

The second exercise requires an area at least large enough to allow clients to stand 12 or more feet apart. All must stand still with arms folded, at least 3 feet away from any wall or furniture. When the dog is not looking at the owner farthest away, that person calls, "Muffin, come." As the dog shows *any response,* even turning its head *away* from him or her, that person *instantly* crouches, sidewise to the pet, repeating happy "good dogs" while vigorously clapping hands until the dog comes, at which time the owner pets briefly and stands up abruptly. With no hesitation, the other owner repeats the process.

This back-and-forth treatment is exceptionally revealing to the behaviorist and the clients. The dog's readiness to come and its physical attitude (tail up or down, sidewise or frontal, jumping or lowering its body) indicate the way the pet feels about individual family members, which can lead to fruitful consultation discussions.

Using these procedures, rather than the behaviorist's assuming control of the dog, allows clients to make the initial "breakthrough" with their pet, and avoids the danger of the client's appearing clumsy in comparison with a professional's superior technique.

The Intractable Owner

This type of dog owner is usually one or a combination of the previous types. The intractability factor is between the consultant and client. I meet very few clients of this ilk, mainly because those who seek help have already responded favorably to their veterinarian's advice to phone for an appointment. However, years ago when our services were listed in the phone book, the number of intractables I met created a morale problem for me. These types are mainly "fix the dog" oriented and often rigidly insist that the consultant should discuss only the dog. This sort of program goes nowhere, helps no one, wastes time and effort and, more often than not, frustrates both owner and consultant.

The reason for mentioning this type of owner is to help others identify these intractables as early as possible and either avoid frustration or use a method to shake the rigidity or elasticity to the degree that further consultation may be successful. The extremes are revealed in the following cases.

The Rigid Personality: Following is a classic example of an intractable owner with a rigid personality.

The client phoned about her 2 1/2-year-old male Boxer that, from the age of 6 months, had attacked several other dogs. The victims were either small breeds or those that displayed passive or flight responses to the Boxer's first aggressive growls. This client had previously phoned for my help when the Boxer was only 8 weeks old and then again at 12 weeks of age due to aggressive responses when she punished it. At that time, nonphysical methods were suggested as an alternative, as well as at least one consultation for evaluation of the pup. Neither action was taken by the client.

Instead, the behavior was tolerated until, at 6 months of age, the dog was taken through a park obedience program, in which it placed third in its class after being "tidbit trained" between weekly park sessions by a male neighbor of the client. After the dog graduated from the park program, it began attacking other dogs that approached it when off leash. Attempts by the young lady to punish the Boxer resulted in a severely bitten hand on several occasions.

Because the dog would not tolerate punishment from the woman, a male neighbor was recruited to thrash the dog with a cane, after which the owner could take the cane and "safely" beat the shuddering animal. This punishment was administered for as long as 30 minutes after the dog had attacked or shown hostility toward other dogs. For 2 years this sort of correction was to no avail, and I was again

65

consulted by telephone. "Do you think he's too old to rehabilitate?" she asked.

In her question lies Clue #1 to a difficult case. The rigidity syndrome is clear: after 2 years spent caning an animal, most clients might logically ask, *"Is there anything more I can do?"* The intractable client, on the other hand, usually wants to know if the *dog* is too far gone to salvage.

It should also be mentioned that the Boxer suffered from a congenital heart problem. When I suggested that it would help me to speak with the client's veterinarian about this, her response was a suspicious, "What for?" (Clue #2).

Clue #3 to the extremely rigid attitude of this client popped up when I asked her what was being accomplished by the repeated thrashing of her dog, first by a neighbor and then herself. "Oh, he knows he's done wrong as soon as we go into my friend's apartment. He starts shaking and shamefully gets up on the couch to take what he *knows* is coming."

When I pointed out that dogs rarely have the ability to associate cause and effect beyond about 3 minutes, even in a single context, let alone between a park and an apartment, and that her dog was probably responding solely to the apartment context, she became defensive. "Look, I didn't call to hear what a bad dog owner I've been. I want to know if you can help my dog." (At about this point I always feel like hanging up. Instead, I pressed on.) "You contacted me for help 2 years ago. My advice was ignored on 2 instances then. Instead you chose to go the very route I suggested you avoid, that of physical training and punishment practices. Frankly, your dog sounds like a basically nice fellow. However, to help him, I must teach and work with *you*. And your attitude is such that I don't believe it is worth your money or my time in the attempt. However, you may be able to use the same system we use and succeed, and I would suggest you try."

"You mean you don't care to work with my dog?" (Clue #4. That classic response was the clincher.)

"No, I do not mean that I don't care to work with your dog. What I said is that I do not believe I could be successful working with and teaching *you*, not your dog."

"Oh." (Pause) "You don't want me to call you anymore?

"Oh, please phone and let me know your progress."

"Okay. Goodbye."

"Goodbye."

Though I did not expect to hear from this young lady again, she did call again. The passage of time seems to make it easier for clients who have been somewhat rebuffed to soften their attitudes and again try to solve a serious behavioral problem.

This case is not typical regarding the ominous overtones involved in treatment of the pet. The owner's rigid personality, defensive, contradictory and downright aggressive in some instances, can be involved in even the simplest housetraining problems. In most cases, the client's personality is an integral part of the problem. In a few it is not.

As more and more professionals have become involved in consulting on pet behavior problems, many problem clients may seek out other sources of assistance, having learned from the first rebuff that a change in attitude is required to succeed. The rigid types have one redeeming factor: they clearly indicate exactly where and how you stand with them.

The Elastic Personality: If you have ever met someone who agrees with every idea or opinion you express and rarely interjects ideas of his or her own, then you need no further description of the dog owner with an elastic personality. Because it is difficult to gain frank feedback from these owners regarding their true reactions to factors in the case and to adjustments that may be recommended in the corrective program, success with their problem dog can be elusive.

"You just tell me what to do and I'll do it," is the type of statement that usually sets the tone of these consultations. Elastics usually express agreement during face-to-face consultation so as to avoid confrontation with the consultant. This often extends to the dog, with disastrous results. Working with excessively agreeable clients is both difficult and rewarding. The difficulty lies in drawing out their true feelings and actual behavior toward their dog. The rewards stem from not only salvaging the future for the pet, but helping bring genuine insight to the sometimes socially inhibited client. A case in point indicates the deep-seated, latent and strongly monitored resistant and often violent "second self" masked by a facade of agreeableness in many dog owners with elastic personalities.

A bachelor in his late twenties complained of his dog's destructive chewing while he was away from his apartment. Our first telephone conversation indicated he was deeply troubled about the problem. After relating in detail the considerable expense involved in refurnishing the rented apartment and his affection for the pet, he expressed a willingness to do anything necessary to solve the problem.

He showed up an hour early for his appointment. After patiently waiting, he was shown into the office with Rex, his exceedingly excitable but pleasant year-old male Terrier mix. He tried to prevent the dog from jumping up on me by commanding him to come and sit by his side. This elicited only more excitement from the gregarious little dog. When I petted and quieted him with distractions, the dog relaxed markedly but responded with a penile erection as well.

This brought the client's complaint that the dog's sexual display was a constant source of embarrassment. It seems the dog usually tried to mount anyone new to him, especially women. I asked what was normally done to control his canine Lothario's amorous advances and was told that the only successful method was to place the dog in the bathroom. Spanking, hitting, even kicking had not abated the sexual behavior, nor had punishment at the scene of destructiveness produced results.

Inquiries as to whether the dog showed sexual aggressiveness toward the client revealed that if an arm hung over the side of a chair or a leg extended forward, the dog immediately mounted the limb. What was done about this? Rex was pushed away and scolded; this was effective until the next opportunity to mount presented itself.

The first consultation concluded after my suggestions to ignore Rex and pet or praise only after response to commands or following corrections. The client was attentive and solemnly nodded in understanding and agreement. However, I believed that somehow I had not been told the entire story. There seemed to be missing elements that might contribute to the hypersexuality of the little dog, as well as its apparent hysterical excitement when left alone.

During the following week my answering machine recorded the following 25-second message:

"This is (client). Well, I'm trying to keep calm. (Heavy emotional, tremulous breathing.) I'm sitting here in the midst of a shambles. He has destroyed a chair now, completely! The carpet is a jigsaw puzzle and he's shit all over the place. (Tearfully) And now, he's eating the shit! This is it! (Hangs up)"

Needless to say, this call required my immediate attention, and was well worth delaying my next appointment. The conversation required listening for several minutes to the vivid description of the client's now decimated apartment and awaiting the inevitable tension relief afforded by this outburst.

When the client was ready to answer some questions about the intervening interaction between himself and Rex, I discovered that no more than 50% of the suggestions made during the first consultation were understood and only 25% of those put into practice. All the nodding had been the client's way of avoiding critical comment or avoiding the embarrassment of admitting he had not understood my advice.

During my efforts to uncover more descriptions of previous events, the client confessed that, 2 months previously, after coming home and finding the carpet ripped, he had picked up Rex and thrown the dog *full force* against the wall.

The little dog lay motionless for a few minutes, during which the client cried and attempted to comfort him. In fact, after the pet was again sensible, the guilt-ridden man spent many hours cuddling him, trying to express his remorse.

Interestingly, the following day when left alone, Rex did no damage in the apartment at all. However, the second day after the trauma, the dog wreaked havoc never equalled before or since. This is not uncommon in behavioral outbursts; response is often repressed for 1-4 days before erupting.

Our next meeting turned up another significant fact about the interplay between Rex and the owner, which tended to confirm my niggling hunch that missing links were still involved. The client was attempting to give me just the amount of information he thought I might require to be of help, but avoided telling me of events that might adversely affect my opinion of him. He finally revealed that at bedtime the dog was allowed or, rather, tenaciously insisted on licking the owner's feet meticulously for no less than 45 minutes. With this information, the dog's sexual disorientation began to come into perspective.

Though I have had clients who admitted to permitting their pets to cleanse their genitalia as an extension of this syndrome, it appeared that Rex had not done so with the owner. However, persistent and generalized mounting of strangers indicated a possibility that the dog may have at some time been permitted to achieve orgasm.

During the following week, Rex displayed signs of epilepsy, exhibiting what appeared to be grand mal seizures. The dog responded to anticonvulsive therapy. Brain damage probably resulted when its head struck the wall. Combined medical/behavioral therapy produced acceptable temporary results in Rex.

The dog was finally euthanized. Several behavioral regressions and a prolonged grand mal seizure sealed this fate. Autopsy was refused due to the client's deep spiritual convictions against the practice. The client was advised against getting another dog immediately so as to avoid a new pet's becoming the object of guilt feelings. Quick replacement of a pet that has died prematurely often results in overindulgence of the new animal. The owner tries to make up for the apparent or imagined injustices suffered by the deceased pet. This tends to occur with owners of any personality type.

Children

The role of children in pet dog problems deserves a book by itself. It is virtually impossible to build a categorical picture of children in this regard within the limited space available here.

Children and pets are too intricately interwoven into the total family picture to allow analysis as individuals. However, it is possible to list some of the *behavior* children display that can cause or aggravate behavioral problems in the family dog or even with other people's pets (Table 2). Many of these contributory behaviorisms are common to adults. I will not attempt to go into detail here as to why some of the more bizarre of these acts occur or how they are dealt with in programs of rehabilitation. That is discussed in later chapters.

About half of these child behaviorisms are quite innocent. Once the parents become aware of their contribution to a problem, things are normally brought under control within a few days or weeks, depending on the severity of the problem. However, if the parents do not represent effective authority figures to the children, rehabilitation is often difficult and prolonged,

Table 2. The role of children in pet behavior problems.

Child's Behavior	Pet's Response
Pulling ears, tail, hair (usually children under 4 years).	Growling, snapping, biting (especially in excitable dogs).
Hitting with hands or objects.	Growling, biting, submissiveness in pups.
Teasing, especially pups, to achieve rage responses.	Viciousness.
Encouraging aggressiveness toward outsiders.	Biting, viciousness, bicycle chasing.
Stimulating jealousy between dogs in the family.	Fighting.
Prompting the dog to attack other dogs or cats.	Fighting, killing small animals, viciousness.
Tidbitting.	Begging, sometimes biting when food is withheld.
Playing tug-o'-war.	Chewing problems.
Screaming.	Biting, especially in highly excitable types.
Scolding.	Growling, biting, especially in leader types.
Sexually stimulating the dog, especially male pups.	Mounting, bossiness, urinating in the house, biting other children or strangers who interact with the child.
Unruly household behavior.	Unruliness.
Inter-child fighting.	Aggressiveness, biting.

sometimes requiring qualified child-parent guidance as well as canine behavioral guidance.

Cases involving deliberate, mischievous stimulation, sadistic tendencies, jealousy of the dog, and sexual experimentation or disorientation require extremely sensitive consultations that must often be preceded by private telephone consultation with the parents to ensure a neutral emotional atmosphere during the fact-finding stages. Parents should not remain passive, but should display genuine interest and understanding for the child's behavior, especially in the areas of aggressive and sexual problems. If the child or children believe that telling the truth may result in their punishment, effective communication can be stifled.

Most prepubertal children respond openly to an outsider's questions about how they get along with their dogs, much the same as they discuss their siblings. However, from puberty on, children tend to conceal, evade questions of, or outright lie about atypical interaction with the pet. If the dog's behavior blatantly indicates sexual experimentation, for example, and the child is obviously avoiding any frank discussion of personal involvement, it is sometimes effective to cite, as examples, situations that have come up in similar cases. Though the child may not participate in the discussion by mentioning his or her own role with the problem dog, the mere *discussion* of it can stimulate an adjustment by the child that is reflected in the dog's improved behavior during subsequent meetings. The obtuse nature of this method of child consultation usually fits family situations in which one or both of the parents are autocratic and tend toward extreme punishment measures. Unfortunately, these circumstances usually prevail when communication between the parents and children is poor.

One helpful aspect of treating the problem dog as an integral part of the family is that cooperation between family members is necessary to ensure the success of the rehabilitation program. This facilitates interaction among the parents, children and dog once a week under supervision, and on a daily basis at home. The combined training and consultation approach helps create a healthy rapport among all parties, based on methods of nonphysical stimulus-response-reward that are so effective in human therapy. Further, all family members begin treating the dog uniformly, the lack of which is often one of the initial causes of problem behavior.

The nonverbal basis of relationships between children and their dogs has been written about masterfully by several authors and needs no further explanation here. I should mention, however, that I have found it helpful to talk over this aspect with both the children and parents involved in behavioral programs. Once understood, the subtle language of movement, stance and unspoken attitude can bring about behavior corrections more quickly than any other method I have experienced.

Specific cases involving children are discussed in later chapters and demonstrate the values of dog ownership within the family.

Environmental Factors

Lying beyond the direct influence of the people who own and live with a problem dog are factors that affect the animal continually or occasionally. These elements often cause problems even though the dog has a healthy relationship with its family. These factors are discussed in detail under the separate problems in later chapters. However, a listing of some of the more important structural, social and other types of problem-stimuli will be helpful here (Table 3).

Whether or not these factors are the source of a problem depends mostly on the dog's individual nervous and behavioral type. These will be discussed in the cases cited later. The partial listing in Table 3 includes factors that may lie outside the direct control of the owners, but may contribute to various types of behavior problems.

Summary

If you believe I have neglected some classic types of owners, such as jealous types (people who cannot bear to see their pets show affection toward others), perfect parents (those who believe they have done everything properly for the dog and cannot accept advice), etc, it is true. However, these will be covered in later chapters in cases related directly to certain problems.

Whether the problem dog owner is domineering-physical, paranoid or permissive, or has other traits encountered in this chapter, the behaviorist always faces the same human relations task in solving problems: to recognize the owner's contributions to the problems, the dog's type and history, and other environmental factors involved; and then to use these facts toward understanding the problem's causes. Thereafter the challenge lies in developing a program individually suited to each situation and recommending changes that ultimately will stimulate desirable behavioral adjustments in the problem dog.

Table 3. Environmental factors related to problem behavior.

Structural Factors

Fences and other barriers	Tethers
Picture windows	Swimming pools
Noisy doors, gates, mail slot covers	Carpets containing urine odors

Social Factors

Howling or barking dogs in the area	Service station attendants, car hops, etc
Neighboring or stray dogs	Sirens
Bitches in heat	Autos backfiring
Silence, monotony	Noisy neighborhoods
Outsiders or friends who accidentally or deliberately tease the dog	Birds, squirrels, other animals on or near property
Sibling rivalry between dogs in the family	Gardeners or others who work around homes
Hostile episodes witnessed by the dog	Mail carriers, meter readers, etc

Other Factors

Ultrasonic alarms and other devices	Rain, thunderstorms, cold, heat, wind, earthquake, snow, sleet, etc
Darkness	Diet or nutritional problems
Health problems	Cameras, flash units, mirrors
Things that go bump in the night	

The key factor in solving any problem is *the dog's owners,* who are the only ones with the power to change their own behavior toward the dog, and the dog's environment. A deeper insight into the emotional fabric and intellectual outlook of owners is critical in producing satisfactory results.

Helpful Reading

McGuigan FJ and Schoonover RA: *The Psychophysiology of Thinking.* Academic Press, New York, 1973.

Pavlov IP: *Conditioned Reflexes.* Oxford Univ Press, London, 1927.

Leavitt HJ: *Managerial Psychology.* Univ Chicago Press, Chicago, 1964.

Barnett L: *The Universe and Dr. Einstein.* Wm Morrow, New York, 1948.

Broadbent D: *Perception and Communication.* Pergamon Press, New York, 1958.

Coch L: Overcoming resistance to change. *J Human Relations,* 1:512-532.

Jung C: *Psychological Types.* Kegan Paul, New York, 1938.

Slater E: *Patterns of Marriage.* Cassell, London, 1951.

Tagiuri R et al: *Person, Perception and Interpersonal Behavior.* Stanford Univ Press, Stanford, CA, 1958.

Bingham W: Halo, valid and invalid. *J Applied Psychology,* 1939.

Strodtbeck F: Husband-wife interaction over revealed differences. *J Am Social Review* 16:468-473, 1951.

Tindall R: The use of silence as a technique in counselling. *J Clinical Psychology 3,* 1947.

Porter EH Jr: *An Introduction to Therapeutic Counseling.* Houghton Mifflin, Boston, 1950.

Heiman M: The relationship between man and dog. *Psychoanalytical Quarterly* 25:568-585, 1956.

Burke WF: Children's thoughts, reactions and feelings toward pet dogs. *J Genetic Psychology* 10:489, 1903.

Bossard J: The mental hygiene of owning a dog. *Mental Hygiene* 28:408-413, 1944.

(This page intentionally left blank)

3

Analyzing Problem Behavior

When clients seek professional help for behavior problems in their dog, their primary attention tends to be focused on the dog. This is to be expected. It is also to be expected that the owner is emotionally upset to some degree.

The first phone inquiry I ever received was from a near-hysterical young lady. Her neutered male Italian Greyhound had awakened her by urinating on her head. Her sobbing description of that morning's mini-drama was convincing evidence that my new career in canine behavior would, of necessity, be client centered.

Her call effectively modified any ideas I had about "reconditioning" the dog. It was obvious the little Greyhound's fate was at the owner's mercy and depended on my ability to convince her of the *cause* of the problem, then to motivate her to make adjustments in her attitudes and actions. Only then would the dog feel secure about its relationship with the owner and no longer feel the need to "mark" her.

This case, as in most, required more than simply acquiring the information for problem analysis through an interview, then propounding the elements of a cut-and-dried remedial program. It was necessary to find out *other times* the dog urinated in the house, *what* was the general living situation of client and dog, etc. In this case, the dog usually slept on the client's bed, but was shut out when her fiance spent the night, "because we don't want the dog in there."

A successful program involved weaning the overdependent dog by having it earn its praise and brief pettings from both the owner and her fiance, having them engage in upbeat play with the dog, giving the dog its own bed on the bedroom floor, and instituting another housetraining program.

Not all cases are so extreme. But if an ethical service is to be rendered, a professional behaviorist/counselor must indicate understanding of the client's emotional state through an attitude that genuinely communicates empathy, personal interest, a sincere desire to help, and a nonjudgmental, professional consideration for the client's role in the problem. These qualities are the hallmark of successful counselors in all fields involving personal relationships, whether with people or pets. Without them, clients tend to reveal only the superficial details of life with their dogs, while omitting or glossing over important details.

Each of us knows from personal experience that we resist sharing our true feelings with others, even trained professionals, if we perceive them as objectively indifferent, personally judgmental or insincerely sympathetic. So, while we will discuss gathering facts, framing questions and analyzing case information in this chapter, we will also talk about keeping the interviews client centered at the same time.

The following case is an excellent example of obtaining the facts and recording them in a useful form.

The Jumper

The client was a young pregnant woman who phoned because her 2-year-old male Shepherd-mix, Barney, jumped on her almost constantly when she stood in his presence. A friend had told her to bring her knee up into the dog's stomach or chest to solve the problem. She told me she wasn't strong enough, nor did she have the emotional constitution for this type of treatment.

"Isn't there another way I can get him to stop it? If he doesn't quit, I'm afraid we'll have to get rid of him, and I don't want to do that."

I asked what steps she had taken to keep the dog down. "I've scolded him and put him out in the yard, but my husband has beaten him to the point that I have actually cried for the poor dog."

"Tell me how your dog acts both when your husband beats him and when you scold and put him out."

"Well, he only growls at me, but he really snarls at Ralph. I think they will have a real fight one day, and I can't have that around the baby. How will Barney react to my baby?"

A few simple questions revealed the true depth of the problem: the dog was displaying emerging aggressive defensive behavior that was aggravated by inconsistent treatment.

What Information Is Needed?

Through the years I have developed a written "fact sheet" that elicits important information about almost every type of problem (Fig 1). In using it, I am forced to ask the questions necessary to do a professional job, and to avoid making snap judgments when recommending remedies. The case of Barney, detailed in Figure 1, gained a new perspective when the following facts were revealed.

- The dog, an excitable type, had been a pest in the house from 8 weeks of age, and had to be put out because of chewing and housesoiling.
- No formal training efforts had ever been made, and the couple disagreed on how to discipline the pet. The wife tended to scold, while the husband preferred spanking. Beating started at 10 weeks when the pup snarled while being spanked.
- Since 14 weeks, the dog had been put out when visitors arrived, and now stood at the sliding glass doors, barking viciously whenever guests were in the house.
- The owners were deeply concerned about whether or not the dog would harm the new baby when it arrived.

Figure 1. Fact sheet used to gather information in cases of problem behavior.

Behavior Fact Sheet

Date __10/12/74__ Time __3:45__ to __4:00__ Breed __SHEP MIX__ (M) F N Age __2 YRS.__

Client __MARY KARNAK (RALPH)__ Dog __BARNEY__

Address __17439 PONCE ST__ City __CANOGA PARK__ State __CA__ Zip __91364__

Problem:
- ✔ Housesoils
- ___ Chews
- ___ Digs
- ✔ Jumps up
- ✔ Unruly
- ___ Barks
- ✔ Aggressive
- (✔) Bites
- ___ Fights
- ___ Runs away
- ✔ No obey
- ___ Howls
- ___ Shy
- ___ Pica
- ___ Coprophagia

Other: __Unruly with guests: vicious, barks — was put out at 14 weeks__

Problem notes: __particularly unruly with owner when she is alone with pet — jumps on client — dog possible biter in stress — poor behavior since a puppy__
(Age noted-locale-situation-frequency-etc.)

Corrections to date: __Scold (mary) - Spank/beat (ralph) - put out (both)__

Dog's reactions: __growls at her — snarls at him__

Age dog obtained: __8 weeks__ From: __Newspaper ad__ Price: __$15.—__

Litter behavior: __not seen__

Housetraining method: __Scold/spank__ Other training: __Sits for treats__

Where sleep? __Bedroom floor__ In house other times? __Yes — all over__

Bathed? __NO__ Brushed? __seldom__ Play periods? __Seldom (dog is unruly)__
(where?)

Last vet. check: __at 1½ years__ Purpose __DHL__ Outcome __OK__
(Who - how)

_____ Other: __Roundworms at 8 weeks ε 5 months__

Diet __Kibble__ Daily feeds: (1) 2 3 Who feeds? __client__

Quantity __12 cups__ Supplements __tidbits, scraps__

Family data: (M) S D Children __presently 3 mos pregnant__ Other __—__

Occupation(s): __client = homemaker ; spouse = marriage counselor__

Other pets? __None__

Recommendations: __Feed 2x daily ½ chicken + 2 cups meal + Vitamin Don't punish! Teach to come, go, stay — use SRX for jumping Keep inside - act "jolly" with visitors 2x daily - get pet door!__

Case outcome: __Excellent — No problems after 5th week__ Date __11/31/74__

Notes: __Both owners attitudes excellent after consultation__

Send aid literature? __YES — Biting case study__

Recommendations in this case involved far more than a simple knee in the chest. If the wife had tried this, judging from the dog's behavior, she might have been bitten. The animal was extremely dominant and overprotective toward her. The husband was given only cursory and aloof attention. Except for approaching me once and growling menacingly, the dog ignored me almost completely.

Rehabilitation required a complete basic training program, a housetraining regimen, and reintegration of the dog into family life, including when guests came to call. Specific recommendations included:

- Feed twice rather than once daily.
- Switch from predominantly carbohydrate to a high-protein diet of chicken meat and byproducts, together with dry food. Double the dietary B-complex vitamin content (see Chapter 5).
- Stop scolding and all forms of punishment.
- Teach basic command responses and use nonphysical correction for jumping up.
- Keep the dog in the house as much as possible.
- Apply the Jolly Routine (see Chapter 7) for 2 visitors daily (owners actively and happily greet guests with the dog present).
- Install a dog door.

During the 6-week program the dog improved steadily until, at the fifth week, both owners were confident of the dog's behavior at all times.

Important Information

The relevance of certain facts concerning a problem dog may seem elusive when viewed out of context. However, when considered in relation to each other, a behavioral profile emerges. The behavioral implications of the following questions may shed light on the problem.

- Is the breed known to be prone to the problem complained of (for example, excitable, aggressive)?

- Is the problem sex related, such as a male dog's over-protectiveness or sexual aggressiveness toward women? Is the dog neutered? If so, was this related to a change in behavior?

- Is the dog now in, or did the malbehavior begin during one of the known behavioral transition periods? For example, Fear Imprint at 8-10 weeks; Sexual Aggression at 12-14 weeks; Territorial and Group Protectiveness at 22-28 weeks; Functional (meaningful job-like behavior) at 36-56 weeks; Protection (trained function) at 90 weeks and older.

- Facts about the age at which the dog was obtained are important. If taken from the litter before 5 1/2 weeks, the dog may tend toward overdependent shyness. If taken after the age of optimum socialization (after 6-8 weeks), the dog may tend toward aggressiveness if not correctly handled.

- From whom was the dog obtained? This may reveal a caged or petshop background in the litter. The price of the dog gives insight as to the owner's perception of monetary value in the consideration of treatment, but this is not always indicative.

- The dog's litter behavior may indicate basic behavioral tendencies, such as dominance, submissiveness, etc.

- Housetraining procedures, especially if during the Fear Imprint period, may explain some exaggerated behavioral reactions. Questions about other training and the success ratio in any efforts made to date.

- Where the dog sleeps and its in-house activities allow some evaluation of social interaction within the family.

- Health information and its impact on behavior are of prime importance in analyzing a problem (see Chapter 4). The diet, feeding practices (see Chapter 5), and who actually feeds the dog also are important.

- Knowledge of family structure can help determine who should be involved in consultations and remedial programs. Children over 10 years of age usually do well in consultations with their parents and the dog.

- The owners' occupations may suggest their general orientation. For example, a salesman may differ in outlook and, therefore, would require a different consultative approach than, say, an attorney. Though not specifically true, occupations often reflect social orientations and logic patterns.

- Involvement of other pets may be important in some cases.

Asking the Right Questions

Age, Quantities, Statistics

Numerous ambiguities are built into our spoken language, not only by the words, but by the way we use them. For instance, when we ask someone how old the dog was when they acquired it, only about 1 in 4 clients provides an accurate answer. Almost 75% of the clients say, "He was just a puppy."

This tells us little, as many owners think dogs are pups until they are over 6 months old. For this reason, when asking questions that require specific information, it is a good idea to frame questions so that we at least minimize general answers.

Here are a few examples that tie into the Behavior Fact Sheet (Fig 1).

Age: "When was Tippy born?" This is a direct way to determine a pet's age, as it elicits a fact from which we can deduce the dog's exact age.

On the other hand, "How old is Tippy?" can lead us astray or even require more questions, as the client can answer, "Oh, I guess he's about 2 years old." This guess can be as much as a year off in some cases. To determine which developmental stage the dog is in, or was in when a problem was first noticed, we need more than guesses.

Another good question to determine age is, "When is Tippy's birthday?" This may have to be followed by, "And what year?" to get the right age.

Quantities: Questions about dates and amounts, that is, *quantity questions*, are most effectively posed so that the client must answer with specific numbers. For instance, if you know that a dry diet is fed, "How much do you feed Tippy?" is a poor question. A better question would be, "How many cups of dry food do you feed per meal?", as it causes the client to think in terms of a specific quantity and usually avoids such ambiguous answers as, "Oh, about half a bowl."

Statistics: Questions seeking statistical facts are posed properly when they make the client think in terms of the *measures* we need for them. At the same time, it is wise to avoid leading questions that suggest an answer. These suggest that the client must contradict us if they answer otherwise. For example, "From what you've said, Tippy must be about 3 years old now. Is that correct?"

This leads the owner to answer "Yes" or "No." "Yes" is nice and agreeable with our assumption, whereas "No" requires the client to contradict the assumption. Either one is less than desirable. Though there is nothing wrong with asking if the animal is neutered, this principle of questioning is most valuable when applied to gaining operational information, which is our next category.

Operational Information

Operational descriptions are the backbone of effective fact finding. During initial contacts, most clients are anxious to relate, in extreme detail, what the *pet* did. This is vital information. However, equally vital is a complete description of what *those around* the pet did, before, during and after each behavioral episode. This is the area in which open-ended, nonleading questions are invaluable.

For instance, the client says the dogs fought today. To find out what ended the fight, we might ask, "How did you break it up?" This is a poor question because it assumes that the client broke up the fight and implies that the client *should have* intervened. The implicit bias in the question could obscure what really happened. It is an excellent question if the client has said he *did* break it up, but not a wise preliminary question. A better one is, "To get a picture of what happened, tell me what everyone did before, during and after the fight."

Even if this elicits more than we may want to know, it provides useful operational facts. Such facts are necessary to formulate a clear picture of the events and environment related to the problem.

These questioning techniques concern areas of the Behavior Fact Sheet (Fig 1) that relate to behavior, versus dates, ages, weights, etc. Other facts that can be most useful, though not mentioned on the sheet, concern emotions.

Emotional Facts

Clients convey a great deal about their feelings by their tone of voice and the words they use to describe things. In client-centered counseling, these facts are of central importance because they are tools for motivating owners toward solutions.

During the initial fact-finding interview, behaviorists must bear in mind that clients do not contact us just because they think we can help. This is only the intellectual portion of the picture. As mentioned previously, most seek professional help because they are emotionally upset. This is their motivation.

This is also why many initial contacts with clients contain all the trappings of a grievance interview about the pet. The client feels any of the full range of emotions and may even display some of them. At this stage, it may seem a waste of time to listen to what appears to be irrational, often unrelated elements of a problem. However, the fact that the client mentions them makes them relevant. So we must ascribe importance to this information. We may have to ask questions that assure the client that we are interested in them, and that also elicits other information.

The client may say, "When I got home and saw pieces of that pillow strewn all over the house, I could have killed the little bastard." Or, "When I saw that pillow torn to shreds, I wanted to sit down and cry."

These statements tell us a great deal about the client's *feelings* at the time of homecoming, but nothing about what they *did*. Two elements of counseling must be applied to each statement: (1) The client needs to know that we understand their feelings, through our responses, such as, "I can appreciate that," or "That's understandable"; and (2) We must know what the client *did* about their feelings of mayhem or despair. The client often describes his or her actions without any rationalizing (or downright deception) if you have effectively communicated your empathy, as shown in element #1. An open-ended, nonleading, followup question is called for, such as, "So, how did you handle the situation?" or "What did you do then?"

If we are lucky enough to develop an idea of the client's general behavior and attitude, all's well. More often, however, we'll get an earful about the dog's behavior, which is also useful information, of course. It is unwise to call the client's attention to this natural tendency to focus on the pet. Instead, we should merely rephrase the query about what the client did, after acknowledging the dog's behavioral response. For example, "I can see how you felt. What were you doing then?"

This accomplishes 2 things: It provides operational descriptions of what happened, and it helps establish an initial degree of rapport between counselor and client.

Information on a client's emotional responses sometimes is difficult to elicit. Some people try not to reveal their true feelings about other people, pets, situations and (especially) themselves. Though it is not a pet behaviorist's role to "probe the client's psychic depths," it is important to let them know that you understand their feelings about the misbehaving animal. To communicate this to the client, I have found it effective to present the following facts and a brief case history.

- About 99% of the interaction between people and their pets is emotional. There is very little intellectual exchange between them.
- If animals were not sensitive to our feelings, we probably would not have them as pets.
- When pets feel insecure about their relationship with us, they become frustrated and anxious.
- Behavior problems develop because the pet is trying to relieve tension produced by frustration and anxiety.

One of the most striking examples of this was a lady whose Yorkie had started urinating in the house. He was a year-old male. She acquired him "as a replacement" shortly after her older Poodle had died.

However, the Yorkie was not as warm and affectionate as her previous dog. Also, the lady remarried shortly after getting the dog, and the husband also found the Yorkie a less than desirable pet. The lady insisted on enrolling in a program, saying that the dog needed more housetraining and some behavioral modification. Further, she stated that if we could not clear up the problem, she would just have to "get rid of him."

I mentioned the emotional points outlined above and told her that until they made a decision to keep the Yorkie, "no matter how long it might take to correct the urination problem," we could not ethically take her case. She got very upset, saying that she could not sacrifice her carpets and furniture to a dog's "psychological hangups."

I expressed understanding for her feelings, but then suggested she discuss the points we had made with her husband. She got furious, saying I was not acting in the best interests of the dog and was not ethical, and that she would find someone who was.

A few days later she called to make an appointment. The urination had stopped! Asked what happened, she said she and her husband had decided to keep the Yorkie "no matter what." I offered my congratulations, but asked why she still wanted to enroll in a program. She explained that they wanted to rename the Yorkie and believed they could use some help with a couple of basic commands and "things in general." The dog was also a chewer, and this vice had actually led to the idea of getting rid of the dog in the first place. The program to eliminate the chewing went exceptionally well.

Simply stated, the principle of this story is, when clients change their attitudes toward their dog from one of ambivalence between rejection and conditional ownership, to an attitude of unconditional acceptance of the animal, the dog's behavior begins improving almost immediately.

Unless the owner makes that commitment, it is extremely difficult to eliminate any behavior problems. Unfortunately, not all clients reveal their intentions during the initial contact, so it is a good idea to ask them what courses of action they have considered.

This case helps illustrate 2 points. The first is about human emotions and pet behavior. The second is that we must tell the client something about our method of working and ethical standards.

It is apparent that the initial fact-finding contact with clients entails more than simply filling out a form. This nondirective style of initial fact finding may require moving to various parts of the form, making cryptic notes, maybe even explaining that notes are being made. This tells the client we are interested, that details are important, that we are professional, and that our services will be complete.

This technique also helps avoid what I call the "OFF syndrome": the Officious Form Filler. The public is generally fed up with "officials" who solicit information in monotonous, disinterested tones, asking questions in rigid order.

We should also avoid sounding "busy" or making the client feel rushed. If we really are too busy for the interview, this should be stated and an interview conducted when things can be undertaken with no time constraints.

The Useless Echo

Another distraction and waste of time, especially in the statistical fact-finding phase, is the habit of repeating what is being noted. This "echoing" goes like this: "How old is Tippy?" "He's about 6 years now." "About 6 years?"

Not only are these poor questions, but they waste time by reinforcing an inadequate answer.

Another example involves emotional facts: "When I saw the mess in the house, I whaled the tar out of him." "Whaled the tar out of him."

This "echo" might not have been so poorly used if it had a questioning intonation. Asked as a question, it fits into the category of a "mirror," which lets the client know we heard correctly, but indicates that we need to know of what "whaling the tar out of him" consisted.

A better response would have been to acknowledge that the client is upset, and then seek operational information: "It must have been upsetting to you. Exactly how did you punish him?"

The Useful Mirror

It is always a good policy to avoid echoing. But the "mirror" statement performs a needed function in fact finding. Used properly, it not only lets the client know that what he said has been understood, but can cause him to delve farther in that area.

"I've had Pugs all my life and never had any problems to speak of. But this one is different."

"He just doesn't fit the mold, eh?"

"Right! He won't take a spanking. He even growls when we scold him."

"That must be frustrating."

"Frustrating! It's maddening! Frank said he's going to take a baseball bat to him the next time he tries to bite him."

"A baseball bat! How did you react to that?"

This interview uncovered a great deal of contention among the husband, wife and their two children, most of it concerning a feisty, aggressive little Pug. A highly successful corrective program followed.

It is important to note that the "mirror" statement does not just parrot back words to the client. It acknowledges emotions in many instances, such as, "That must be frustrating." This can open up a discussion of the *real* problem: the way the wife, husband and kids felt about the Pug. When they understood the various behavioral responses of dogs, they began working together nicely.

The Dangers of "Halo"

In any interviewing or counseling work we meet people with whom we quickly establish a high degree of rapport, for whom we hold a great deal of respect, or whose personality and/or professional achievements we hold in high esteem. With such clients we naturally become especially sensitive to their feelings, particularly during counseling sessions. We find ourselves nodding to acknowledge everything the client says, creating the impression that we agree. Instead of asking for details of a personal nature, or an emotional commitment to a course of action, this "halo" surrounding the interaction can cause us to assume that the client understands things without our having to look for feedback or bring out misunderstandings.

This kind of halo exerts itself as a common aura of agreement around both the counselor and client. The halo can be a problem with all sorts of clients whose personalities seem to fit nicely with my idea of what a pet owner ought to be. Often, after a counseling session, a review of my notes shows that we had a congenial chat, but little useful information was produced. The clients were excellent listeners, we nodded a great deal, and we "halo-ed" beautifully.

I mention this so that it will be recognized. I don't know of any technique to prevent it except to stick to one's professional guns and follow the principles of effective interviewing.

When the professional principles for obtaining facts are applied with warmth, empathy and genuine caring, we not only elicit the full range of required information, but we also forge the atmosphere for a successful client-counselor relationship, and then can develop an effective correction program.

A Framework for the Facts

Obtaining facts is one thing, but putting these facts within a framework that reveals causes and indicates remedies is best accomplished according to the specific problem. Dividing a behavior problem into its elements requires labelling: Is the behavior orally, vocally or physically oriented? Is it aimed outward (extroverted) or inward (introverted)? Table 1 helps in this classification.

Note that several of the behaviorisms appear on both sides of Table 1. This feature requires another step in classifying problem types, delineating the actual situation(s) in which the dog displays the behavior. For this reason, extra notes are needed in cataloging behavioral facts. It becomes necessary to learn when the behavior was first noticed (dog's age, the situation, locale) and how often it occurs.

These elements may be used to define the behavioral framework. The following example is from one of my cases:

- *Problem:* Digging (extroverted behavior). Dog digs near back door of house and at side gates.
- *When first noticed?* Dogs was 4 months old (now is 7 months), and after being put outside when it pestered guests.
- *How often?* Now digs whenever left alone in yard.

This scenario is so typical of digging cases that it has become classic in canine misbehavior. The cause is isolation frustration.

The problem became so vexing that the owners telephoned their veterinarian to ask how to find a new home for their pet. When I was brought into the case, the main problem perceived by the

Table 1. Classification of various types of problem behavior.

Behavior	Extroverted	Introverted
Oral	Biting Chewing destructively Licking at people Nipping at people Stealing food Pica (eating nonfood items)	Sucking holes in materials Chewing of a gnawing nature Licking self Self-mutilation Coprophagia (eating stools) Pica Teething/chewing
Vocal	Barking (at things) Howling (response to sirens or dogs) Growling (at non-threatening stimulus) Snarling (at non-threatening stimulus)	Barking (at nothing apparent) Howling (at nothing apparent) Whining Squealing Growling (when threatened) Snarling (when threatened)
Somatic	Aggressiveness (herding, bumping) Car chasing Dashing out of doors Digging Fence jumping (to roam) Fighting (instigator) Housesoiling Jumping up on people Killing animals Leash pulling (forward) Running away Scratching Sexual mounting Unruliness Disobedience Masturbation	 Car sickness Digging (cooling holes) Fence jumping (to get indoors) Fighting (only when severely threatened) Housesoiling Leash straining (backward) Running away Scratching (especially on nonbarrier objects, such as pillows, etc) Self-mutilation with paws Shy, stiff movement Sympathy, lameness Stubbornness Disobedience Masturbation

clients was the digging. They lost sight of the origins of the behavior, that is, the dog had been excluded from socializing due to unruliness with guests and had, in highly stressful circumstances (isolation), relieved its tensions through vigorous digging. This was the beginning of a conditioned response to dig when isolated in the yard.

The stimulus (social isolation) had been repeated almost daily for months. The owners had reached the point of exasperation, having tried all the traditional deterrents and punishments. The fact finding and problem analysis made sense to them, and they were ready for a cause-oriented remedy.

The Individual Dog

The behavior of any dog is the result of both external and internal forces acting upon it. For this reason, it is vital to obtain "operational" descriptions of its behavior from the clients and, if possible, make your own personal observations. It is not useful to settle for an owner's statement that the dog "acted sorry" after biting a family child. We need to know what was happening to the dog when it "acted sorry" and what the dog *did* to indicate it. A good question is, "Tell me exactly what you and the others did after the biting. Can you describe what Peppy actually did?"

In this way we learn what the client *saw*, rather than how s/he *interpreted* the events. Such operational descriptions allow us to interpret Peppy's contrite behavior, which is usually submissive behavior in response to scolding, punishment or threatening gestures toward the dog.

Chapter 4 discusses the effects of the physiologic state of the problem dog. However, we must emphasize here the need for complete information on the animal's medical/health history, diet, litter environment, treatment during critical periods, current and past living and sleeping conditions, and general behavior during day-to-day life with the family. Without this information, we risk misinterpreting a problem as solely "behavioral," when it actually may stem from physiologic factors.

4

Physiology and Behavior

Of the thousands of dog breeders to whom I have spoken over the years, only a few have claimed that there is any financial profit in the endeavor. "A labor of love" or "devotion to improvement of the breed" is most commonly cited as their motivation. Notwithstanding the soaring prices charged for purebred pups these days, it is apparent that there are considerable expenses involved in a reputable breeding program. The nutritional and medical costs of managing an ethical breeding program can run into hundreds, even thousands of dollars per litter. In exchange for this, the reputable breeder may gain the satisfaction of placing pets with responsible owners who will benefit from a tractable, well-mannered family companion or working dog.

Despite the honorable aims of most dog breeders to improve a particular breed, some breeds are branded as vicious, spooky, fear biters, untrainable, high strung or unpredictable. The reasons may be Western Civilization's preoccupation with physical attributes, as well as sensationalism propagated by the mass media.

Animal totems are of ancient origin as family and/or tribal symbols. This aspect of human social behavior seems to persist today in dog breeding, as breeders display their animals in dog shows and on signs for kennels and on teeshirts. However, these canine totems are suddenly thrust into popularity by the media (definitely a for-profit business). This instant popularity of a breed creates a *demand*. And it is up to dog breeders to meet the demand in either of 2 ways: increase output, at the expense of quality control, or retain quality and raise prices. The second would seem the prudent course to follow. However, it is obviously not the popular choice, as there are very few "limited editions" among dog breeds.

High-volume breeding programs reduce the quality of any breed, as the ever-widening gene pool deteriorates from genetic mutations and poor judgment in mate selection.

While instant breed popularity is provided by the media, advertisers and others who profit by promoting dog ownership, ironically this popularity is fueled by the only group capable of setting and controlling responsible breeding practices: dog breeders. With this in mind, the following information is presented to assist conscientious breeders improve the behavioral quality of tomorrow's dogs, as well as canine-human relationships.

Genetic Behavioral Links

Genetic Vulnerability

In the early stages of mankind's social interactions with canines, *controlled* breeding was practiced with an eye to several functions the dogs were to perform. These functions concerned the dogs' usefulness to the human social group, in exchange for which the dogs were fed and otherwise cared for.

Functional breeding objectives have been gradually displaced by anatomic and cosmetic aims since the advent of dog shows. In these canine beauty contests, there are no standards concerning a Setter's ability to scent birds or a Terrier's ability to pursue game underground. The primary concern is how well the animal's appearance and gait measure up in the eyes of the judge, who may never have even hunted with dogs. Curiously, the American Kennel Club's breed groupings still retain functional titles.

Perhaps it is the dog's prolific genetic variability, making it possible to create lasting mutations in only a few generations, that accounts for the popularity of artificial selection. Its genetic structure of 78 chromosomes, intended by nature as an adaptive function for survival of the species, may well lead to extinction if current standards persist. With few exceptions, it is now generally agreed by those who study physiologic and behavioral genetics, today's breeding practices may threaten the continued popularity of *Canis familiaris* as a household pet.

Genetic-Endocrine Implications

A convincing body of clinical evidence indicates that either naive or deliberate breeding of physiologically inferior dogs is producing offspring with serious endocrine imbalances. These are reflected in autoimmune deficiencies that produce skin, coat, digestive and other ailments. In people, endocrine imbalances can cause many types of emotional disturbances, such as mood swings, spontaneous aggression, depression, hyperactivity and personality changes. Though no scientifically controlled studies devoted purely to this aspect of canine behavior have been performed yet, such a study is warranted.

Dogs displaying mood swings, a low threshold for aggressiveness, spontaneous aggression, hyperactivity, depression, stereotyped pacing, hypersensitivity to touch, or other abnormal responses to the typical aspects of family life should be referred to their veterinarians for a complete analysis of endocrine and immune system function.[1] When imbalances have been clinically evident, remedial programs have been largely successful when combined with appropriate veterinary treatment. Most of these cases have involved inadequate thyroid function, or hypothyroidism.

While improper breeding practices can lead to behavioral problems, such problems have been successfully treated. However, for the few that have benefited from veterinary/behavioral treatment, many more have gone untreated.

Breeding and Whelping

Breeding Responsibility and Principles

Fortunately, there is now a physio-behavioral screening program that may help minimize suffering by both dogs and their owners stemming from unwise breeding practices. With this in mind, the following procedures and practices are recommended.

- *Select a sire and dam at least 2 years of age.* Both must be free of physical defects and obvious behavioral deficits, such as hyperactivity, aggressiveness, shyness, excessive excitability or inhibition, or hyperreactivity to sound or movements.

- *Investigate the parentage and grandparentage of the sire and dam for health and behavioral problems.* If negative factors are found, do not breed the descendants.

- *Investigate the environmental history of the sire's and dam's parents and grandparents.* If they are from strictly kennel environments or puppy mills, do not breed them.

- *Have blood samples analyzed.* This analysis should be performed by a veterinary diagnostic laboratory. The bitch must *not* be in estrus at the time of blood testing. Two samples of blood are withdrawn. The first is analyzed to determine the complete blood count, and *resting* plasma cortisol, estrogen, T_3, T_4, IgA, IgM and IgG levels.[1] The bitch is then given ACTH, and a second blood sample is withdrawn for a plasma cortisol level determination.

- *Do not breed the bitch if the blood analysis uncovers abnormalities.*

- *Have the sire's semen analyzed by a qualified veterinary reproduction laboratory.*

- *Do not breed the bitch more than once every 2 years.*

This procedure is more elaborate and expensive than a simple semen analysis, but it helps to assure reputable breeders that they are preventing further spread of heritable problems that may plague their breeds.

Behavioral/Environmental Effects

The environment in which a pregnant bitch lives can influence not only the bitch, but also her unborn puppies. In a study of brain development in puppies, bitches that were made "nervous" whelped pups with poor brain-cell differentiation, which was often reflected in abnormal behavioral development.[2]

The evidence suggests that a pregnant bitch should enjoy the opportunity to move about and engage in normal canine and/or human social relationships. Close confinement, social isolation, or excessive noise or activity can induce stress that may result in puppies with physiologic or behavioral abnormalities.

In addition to this freedom to engage in normal social conditions, a bitch also needs the opportunity to retire to a quiet, undisturbed area as whelping approaches. A partially enclosed whelping box about 1 1/2 times as wide as the bitch's length should be placed in a room always accessible to her. If this is done during the first 3-4 weeks of pregnancy, it largely eliminates the risk of the bitch's selecting an inappropriate area, such as a closet, in which to whelp.

To increase the appeal of the whelping box, a den-like atmosphere can be provided by overturning a large cardboard carton on the box, with an entry cut large enough to allow her access without having to crouch to enter. This temporary setup can be removed as needed for cleaning, and discarded after birth of the puppies. Some breeders believe that placing the bitch's water bowl in the whelping room and feeding her there help curtail the pre-whelping "searching" behavior displayed by some bitches.

Many successful breeders report that the floor of the whelping box is best lined by carpet, such as a remnant obtained from a carpet store. However, it is important to ensure that the carpet and its backing contain no toxic chemicals. The carpet floor of the whelping box is comfortable and gives the puppies early experience with the material they will encounter in their new homes.

Whelping

If whelping is to be supervised, and it should be, the room's light should be only bright enough to allow observers to monitor the births.

During whelping, human intervention should be minimized, and practiced only by an experienced "midwife" who knows how to recognize and handle emergency situations. If children are to be present, they should be prepared by a graphic verbal description, or preferably, a video of what to expect. This will help avoid a child's screaming during parturition, which has been known to arrest the process in some bitches.

Neonatal Transitional Period

During the first 3 weeks, the dam is best left undisturbed, except for once- or twice-daily inspection of the puppies to make sure they are well. This is best done after the dam has nursed the puppies and cleaned up their urine and fecal evacuations. Each pup should be picked up gently for examination, which requires about 30 seconds.

Socialization Period

As the 4- to 5-week weaning period approaches, the dam will leave the puppies increasingly more often. Gentle daily handling of the puppies should be continued. When solid food is provided for the puppies, the dam will begin to curtail her cleanup activity. This is the optimum time to provide the pups a means of leaving the nest area *immediately* after eating to defecate and urinate, preferably outdoors. If the pups are not allowed outdoors, they should at least have access to a "natural," non-household type of surface. This helps precondition them to avoid evacuating indoors or on common household surfaces.

When the puppies have been weaned completely, they should be fed 3 times daily. The number and time of defecations should be noted. Most animals defecate shortly after eating, so the pups can be easily escorted to their toilet area after each meal. The new owners can then be provided with the feeding (and defecation) schedule for quick and effective housetraining in the new home.

Another preconditioning practice can help avoid chewing problems. A commercial puppy chew bone should be provided at the first signs of chewing activity. Once again, these should have an odor and composition different from household materials.

Continued socialization to people should be practiced after 5 weeks and continued through the time of placement in the new owners' homes. The puppies should be picked up (even large breeds), restrained on a table, rolled over and inspected, massaged (especially on the back, up to and including the skull), and felt on the abdomen. The eyes, teeth and ears should be periodically inspected and their paws gently handled until they relax and accept it. In addition to the breeder's immediate family, this should be done, if possible, by other well-coached children and teens. This gives each puppy early physical and olfactory (smell) experience with the full spectrum of its eventual social contacts with people.

As a further socialization aid, many breeders integrate the foregoing program with the Behavior Test for Puppy Selection, presented in Chapter 7.

Selecting Buyers

The most successful breeders, in terms of personal satisfaction, are those who screen their buyers with some fairly demanding standards. Most of these breeders select their buyers *before breeding the dam*. This is done by advertising the breeding before the bitch is bred. The prospective buyers are then interviewed personally or by telephone. When possible, the buyers' homes are visited to ensure that the social and physical environment meets the breeder's standards. If not, photographs of the home are solicited and a telephone chat with family members is conducted. I know one breeder who asks for a videotape of the house, yard and family members before committing to sell a puppy.

The best indicator for predicting future behavior of a dog owner is past behavior. People and conditions best *avoided* include:

- People who have gotten rid of a dog because of "inconvenience" created by a behavior problem, moving, a change in family status (new child, divorce, etc), excessive shedding, grooming requirements, etc.
- People who complain about veterinary expenses, feeding costs, etc.
- People who have never trained a pet.
- People who kept former dogs outdoors, especially for "protection."
- People who state that past pets became overly aggressive toward family members, outsiders or other dogs.
- Families showing signs of friction relating to how the puppy is to be raised.

- Assignment of feeding and care to one child in a multi-child household, or to a single child that is too young or too disinterested to care for the puppy.
- Evident hostility between family members, whether or not related to raising of the puppy.
- Signs of alcohol or drug abuse.
- Unstable economic conditions.

This sort of screening may appear strict and time consuming. However, if the puppy's welfare is held as the most important element in selecting buyers, discerning breeders have found it well worth the effort. The benefits are low puppy return rates, high-quality future referrals, and the peace of mind derived from fulfilling a professional responsibility.

Considerations for New Puppy Owners

A new puppy represents all the owner's hopes for a fine, intelligent pet. But the owner also has his or her prejudices and opinions about how to train the pup. Most owners rely on their own past experience, friendly (if not accurate) advice, popular breed books, and, rarely, facts for guidance in shaping their dog's personality. Many pups develop into acceptable adults despite adverse owner handling and care, which is a tribute to their psychic resilience. However, hundreds of thousands of others are returned to their breeder, given away to unsuspecting new owners, deliberately dropped off in new neighborhoods or in the wilderness, or taken to the local pound for probable euthanasia.

A dog's personality is characterized by the behavior displayed as a result of learning. Learning is that which is absorbed and retained from a dog's interaction with its environment. A dog's brain matures by the age of 22 weeks. Therefore, early puppy experience affecting adult behavioral tendencies is more easily controlled and its benefits more quickly recognized than with children. Every puppy owner should be aware of this rapid development so as to ensure careful early treatment.

Does Health Affect Personality?

Most puppy owners I counsel are aware that certain diseases in dogs are communicable to people, such as transmission of roundworms to children. But few know that parasitic, viral, mycotic, protozoal, bacterial or metabolic diseases can affect the dog's brain and learning.[4] This information usually succeeds in gaining the owner's appreciation for immediate veterinary attention for a pup that seems unable to learn. That a dull coat might signal a dull mind or behavioral problems seems pretty "far out" to many, but our experiences indicate this to be more than coincidental.

> *A 14-week-old male Irish Wolfhound appeared to have trouble remembering commands. Fecal analysis revealed a roundworm infection. Proper treatment eliminated the roundworms and also helped create what the pup's owner called "the smartest dog I ever saw!" The client is now an avid proponent of regular health checks.*

What Type of Puppy Is It?

Every owner can benefit from an evaluation of their new puppy from both physical and behavioral standpoints. Most clients lean heavily on their veterinarian for this. How the pup behaves while receiving vaccinations may indicate some defense reflex tendencies. Unfortunately, this test does not relate well to the handling and treatment an animal will experience in its home environment.

A few moments spent testing the pup's reactions to elevation, immobilization, and touching its back and shoulders may reveal its responses to human social dominance and provide reference for special owner handling procedures (Figs 1-3). This is important with pups whose responses appear either extremely aggressive or submissive. Neither type of pup is likely to respond favorably to physical punishment, harsh scolding or social isolation, especially during the 8- to 10-week fear imprint stage.[5] The evaluation procedure is also helpful in overcoming myths about breed behavior that tend to cloud an owner's awareness of his puppy's unique individuality.

Perception, Pain and Personality

The idea that puppies need to feel pain or experience fear in order to learn persists widely today despite research evidence to

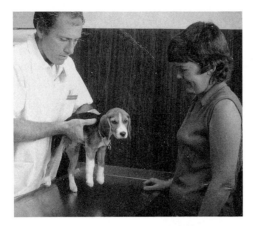

Figure 1. A veterinarian demonstrates the elevation dominance test. This pup struggled for a few seconds, and then settled down, accepting its position of helplessness. This is a sanguine but fairly balanced reaction.

Figure 2. The same puppy as in Figure 1 struggles when inverted, but soon becomes calm again. A highly excitable pup would continue struggling and perhaps even bite, indicating active defense reflexes. With such animals, special handling instructions would be in order.

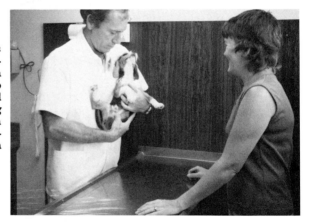

Figure 3. Petting of the shoulders, an act of social dominance, is accepted by this pup. The animal showed no biting or other antagonistic response. Such a calm response indicates excellent social adaptation.

the contrary. This often leads to ego-crushing physical punishment and the trauma of social isolation. The result may be a guilt-ridden owner applying such punishments during the pup's most impressionable age, between 5 and 16 weeks.

Unfortunately, punishment can rarely be administered quickly enough relative to the pup's misbehavior, or with proper consistency. Consequently, the owner, who should appear to the pup as a model of consistency, is perceived by the pet as unreliable. The owner's homecoming times produce ambivalent behavior as the pup vacillates between joy and hypersubmissive "shamed" actions. Most of my clients are quick to appreciate that their puppy is responding to them, rather than to the fact that a pair of shoes has been chewed up in the bedroom. This is also coupled with the onset of client complaints that their puppy will not come when called, which is understandable when one considers that the pup has received punishment inconsistently from hands that also try to express tenderness through petting.

Puppies that learn that human hands and actions may be dependably associated with pleasure rather than pain seldom exhibit punishment side effects, such as hand-shyness, submissive urination or overaggression. Training systems relying on social reward produce more healthy and stable behavior than those emphasizing punishment. This is especially true in pups with highly excitable or inhibitable nervous systems. Accentuating the positive and eliminating the negative in puppy training may require more patience than expeditious punishment, but the benefits usually outweigh the disadvantages in the long run.

The puppy owner will be better equipped to influence his pet's behavior if he understands the behavioral effects of health, nervous type and consistency in handling. Therefore, the veterinarian who spends a few extra minutes to explain these factors will help to prevent early fear imprints and resultant behavior problems that often prompt owners to get rid of their pets.

Veterinary Care and Related Problems

Every veterinary practice has a distinct "personality" that influences its clientele and their pets. From the first call for an appointment, to the contact with receptionists, technicians and doctors, personal impressions are made that influence the way the client anticipates their dog's treatment. If the reception staff appears relaxed and friendly, and greets clients warmly, taking a moment to explain the forthcoming treatment, clients tend to relax. On the other hand, when the staff appears rushed and harried, or cool and officious, clients tend to respond in kind.

While observing the ambience of hundreds of veterinary practices, I have also noted its effects on clients' dogs. When the staff has a positive attitude, the pets tend to relax. Conversely, when the staff projects a negative attitude, dogs appear tense. Whether this tension erupts into problems on the treatment table depends on the dog's ability to adapt to the stress involved. In other words, the general mood of a veterinary practice can profoundly affect the behavior of dogs under treatment.

After an owner purchases a pup or adult dog, the veterinarian is usually the first professional consulted. This affords a prime opportunity to educate clients about the owner's role in preventing or correcting behavior problems, as well as matters of physical health. Many veterinary practitioners now offer "puppy kindergarten classes," which bring several owner-families and pups together for 6 weekly meetings at the clinic. During such meetings, pups are given the chance to socialize with other dogs, adults and children. A veterinary staff member, knowledgeable in behavioral development, can discuss emerging problems and offer effective remedial advice.

In addition, brochures are available to educate dog owners on various aspects of behavior and behavior problems. These brochures address virtually the entire spectrum of behavior problems encountered in dogs from puppyhood to old age.[14,15] Some behavior consultants offer telephone consultations.

An increasing number of veterinarians find that taking a few additional minutes themselves to speak with clients about behavior problems in their dog pays off in increased goodwill, client retention and referrals. This allows the practitioner to evaluate the problems holistically.

The skills necessary for effective fact finding in behavior problem cases are not highly sophisticated. Nor is consulting with owners to motivate them to recognize all of the causative factors, including their own contribution. Dog owners rarely mismanage their pets with malicious intent. It usually is done through ignorance of the effects of their own feelings and behavior on the dog. Behavior consultants need not attempt psychotherapy of their human clients, trying to improve their self-image and bring about personality changes. Rather, the pet behavior consultant's role is to understand the client's situation, properly diagnose the problem, and then educate the client concerning the diagnosis and treatment program. This counseling function may readily be fulfilled by any clinical veterinarian who takes the time to study and practice it. Where the pressures of a busy practice preclude it, the principles and techniques already detailed, coupled with those to follow, will allow the veterinarian to select other competent professionals working with behavior problems to form an ethical diagnostic and treatment team.

At a time when veterinarians are becoming increasingly sensitive to meeting the emotional needs of a client whose pet has just died, it would appear equally appropriate to provide services and information that consider the total needs of clients and their living, though errant, pet dogs.

Creating Positive Treatment Associations

A very early discovery about canine learning is the dog's tendency to generalize responses to strong stimuli.[2] That is, a dog may respond similarly in similar circumstances. For example, if the animal reacts violently to a particularly stressful event, it may become violent whenever it experiences a similar event. Therefore, as the first stranger to place the dog in a stressful situation, the veterinarian can do all strangers (to the dog) a great service by carefully manipulating several factors surrounding the pet's experience.

Every experienced veterinarian knows that most dogs tolerate treatment well; these dogs generally have an inhibitable type of nervous system and/or passive defense reflexes. However, the excitable and/or active defense reflex types that do not tolerate treatment can be a threat to the personal safety of those who must handle them. How can a veterinarian and staff members spot potential problem dogs and avoid the behavioral consequences of stimulus generalization? The solution lies in the veterinarian's ability to control both his or her own handling of the pet, and the client's behavior relative to treatment.

That dogs, and even people, can learn to tolerate painful stimuli is well known.[3] If a painful stimulus is reinforced quickly with one that is strongly pleasant, the expected defense reactions are replaced by responses appropriate to the pleasant stimulus. Several veterinarians I know have put this principle into practice by sticking a doggy treat into their patient's mouth immediately after inoculations or treatment. This helps immediately replace a noxious stimulus (pain) with a positive stimulus (pleasant taste). Though not 100% effective, it has proved helpful.

However, the strongest forces acting on the pup or older dog commence well before treatment, and continue to affect the animal long afterward. These forces are social, and they are controlled for the most part by the pet's owner. For this reason, the owner's overall attitude toward the pup, its health, and veterinary care must be considered the primary determination in how a dog responds to veterinary treatment.

Emotion and Treatment

When an owner goes to a veterinary hospital with a dog that has just been hit by a car, the emotional prelude to treatment is usually steeped in concern, if not outright hysteria. Few clients have the insight to control their emotions in such situations, adopting the calm approach of a trained technician. In these cases it is generally wisest for the veterinarian to treat the injured pet without the owner present, thereby avoiding further emotional stimuli and their influence on the dog.

On the other hand, a dog or puppy experiencing its first visit for routine veterinary care can be conditioned to perceive the entire procedure as one of pleasure when properly handled by the owner. If, during the trip to and arrival at the hospital, waiting in the reception area, meeting the staff and veterinarian, during and (especially) following treatment, the owner is careful to display only happy behavior toward the pet and the external circumstances, the experience will be positive and socially rewarding for the dog. This behavioral routine is not easy for owners predisposed to overly sympathetic reactions toward the pet. However, when the importance of their exemplary behavior is explained, they usually comply.

Other aspects of small animal practice can affect an owner's emotional state and, thence, the dog or puppy involved. I do not wish to propose techniques for improvement of veterinary services, only to suggest that the emotional tenor of the owner does influence the behavior of dogs. Many helpful articles have appeared in veterinary publications on the specifics of client relations, staff procedures and training, etc. A pertinent observation in this context is that staff members tend to reflect the attitudes of the on-duty veterinarian. So, a positive, cheerful approach by the "chief" would seem to keynote the mood of the entire veterinary service.

Table Trauma

The transition from tail-wagging good humor to hysterics that takes place when certain dogs are lifted onto the veterinary treatment table may appear to be spontaneous. However, dogs usually acquire this unfortunate reaction as a result of several traumatic experiences on the table.

> *An excellent example is Randy, a 2-year-old male Norwegian Elkhound. Randy had a history of recurring roundworm infection and had been to the veterinarian several times for treatment. At 18 months I took him to a local veterinary clinic and mentioned to the veterinarian on duty that there was further evidence of roundworms. In the examination room, I lifted Randy onto the table and scratched his chest while he was given an injection to prevent vomiting. It had been our experience that dogs would next be placed in a holding cage for a while before administration of medication. In this instance, however, the doctor left the room for a moment and returned with a large capsule of deworming medication, saying, "Hold him while I try to get this down him."*
>
> *The doctor used a hammerlock while I restrained Randy's body. Within 15 seconds the following events*

occurred: Randy screamed; the dog's anal sacs were expressed; the dog urinated; and his rear claws dug into my ribs, leaving deep scratches. A second smaller capsule caused a similar reaction.

Randy was then taken away to a holding cage and released after about 7 hours, his general good nature seemingly intact. I asked the veterinarian if perhaps we should have waited a while before forcing the capsules down the dog's throat.

"We usually do," he said, "But he seemed so easy-going that I thought we could get away with it."

Three months later Randy acquired what appeared to be a fungal infection on his chin. He was taken to a different veterinary clinic. The first "table trauma" was explained to the new veterinarian, and it was suggested that if the dog were examined on the floor, the procedure would probably be uneventful. This was agreed. However, while the doctor turned to wash his hands, 2 assistants entered the room, jerked Randy up onto the table, and attempted to place him on his back. The predictable occurred: Randy screamed and tried to bite; his anal sacs were expressed; and he urinated and defecated. The veterinarian quickly looked at Randy's chin and diagnosed fungal infection as a likely possibility. Everyone later agreed that examination on the floor would have been less troublesome.

The next trip to the veterinarian was for routine vaccinations. Randy was taken to his regular doctor, known to be an expert handler of dogs. On entering the treatment room, the dog became unruly. Hackles erect and fangs bared at anyone who tried to approach him, Randy slipped his collar and retreated to the waiting room. He calmed down in a few minutes and was taken home without treatment. The formerly sanguine Randy now requires special handling for treatment.

Fortunately, table trauma is rare. It is usually the culmination of several stressful experiences associated with the examination table, and does not involve dogs that are naturally fractious when treated. At the first signs of untoward reactions, treatment might better be conducted on the floor. Though restraint is usually necessary in advanced cases, the severity of the dog's reactions may be reduced to the point that treatment can be achieved without giving tranquilizers.

I should point out that the entire unfortunate experience with Randy was my fault. I violated a basic principle that every dog owner should respect implicitly: Always take a dog to the veterinarian who knows and has treated the animal in the past. Except in unavoidable emergencies, a dog should be taken to familiar surroundings to be handled and treated by those who have gained favorable responses and calm behavior from the pet. In Randy's case, I needed only to rearrange my schedule slightly in order to get him to his regular doctor, but shortsightedly failed to do so. On the other hand, the personnel contributing to the problem could have minimized the effects of this misjudgment by spending a few moments getting to know the animal and relieving its heightened tension in the new situation.

Rehabilitating the table-traumatized animal is possible but time consuming. Tranquilization before the trip to the hospital is followed by examination or inoculation on the floor, with gentle restraint provided by the owners. The owners should not be present if they contribute to the animal's anxiety.

Table trauma is only one example of the various types of stimulus-bound fractiousness that may occur. Fortunately, only about 5-10% of dogs require special handling during visits to the veterinarian. Their recalcitrance can relate to the owner, waiting room, holding cage, examination room, leash, veterinarian or staff, or even the scents of the clinical setting. Whatever stimuli or combinations of stimuli are involved, an adjustment in procedure to avoid these stimuli seems wise.

How far can the veterinarian adjust treatment procedures to accommodate a fractious patient? This is up to the individual, of course. However, upon arriving at one veterinary hospital, I saw the veterinarian, instruments in hand, preparing to examine a large German Shepherd in the parking lot. The examination proceeded uneventfully. I later learned that the dog routinely transformed into a savage beast if examined in the hospital.

Diseases, Treatments and Behavior

Very few behavior problems have been caused by a disease or medical treatment. Generally, it is the owner's management of the dog that determines whether a problem may develop. Unfortunately, mismanagement can create problems that persist following recovery of the pet from its medical problem. There are notable exceptions to this, especially in treatments involving hormonal therapy, castration or ovariohysterectomy, and a few other disorders of unknown cause.

Since the first edition of this book, veterinary interest in animal behavior has increased dramatically. Though many articles have appeared in journals and books regarding behavior problems and therapy, mainly from academic sources, problems associated with diseases have yet to be addressed in detail. So, while the following conditions and cases must be regarded as "anecdotal," they nevertheless are derived from clinical cases that involved many practicing veterinarians and me.

This information is not intended to recommend or refute any type of medical treatment, though the diagnostic and treatment regimens for hyperkinesis are reported among clinical case histories, as such information is not reported elsewhere in the veterinary literature, to my knowledge. Otherwise, it seems appropriate for a dog behavior specialist to relate data that can assist veterinarians in educating clients on behavioral problems possibly related to diseases and treatment.

Home Care During Illness

Owners generally are not aware that dogs usually tolerate physical discomfort quite well. People identify emotionally so closely with their dogs that they often shower them with attention and affection after veterinary treatment. This is especially true if home nursing care is necessary. If this is carried out with optimistic good nature, I have rarely seen problems associated with illness. However, problems can arise when owners convey their anxieties or pity through tone of voice and actions. This was dramatically demonstrated in 2 cases I handled years ago.

A poorly managed 2-year-old male Great Dane was vicious toward any other dog. At about 3 months of age, the dog broke its toe and required close confinement for some weeks. The owners showed extreme concern, and daily placed the pup's pen at a front, full-length window. There, it was exposed to the constant frustration of seeing the family and other children playing with neighborhood dogs.

When the dog whined or otherwise showed anxiety, it was patted for reassurance and verbally reassured. The toe healed nicely, but the reinforced anxiety behavior erupted into an attack on the first neighborhood dog encountered thereafter.

When we first saw the dog at our facility, its energies were directed at escaping so as to get to a neighbor's dog he had seen from the owner's car (Fig 4). He broke through our sturdy front wooden gate and ran across the road in full-blown rage. Fortunately, cyclone fencing protected the neighbor's German Shorthaired Pointer. I literally had to drag the Great Dane back to our

Figure 4. An aggressive Great Dane seeks to attack a Dalmatian on the opposite side of a fence. The Great Dane became aggressive after a period of prolonged confinement, during which it was frustrated by viewing other unconfined dogs.

office, where he spent 90 minutes pacing from door to door. Unfortunately, the Dane was later killed on a busy boulevard while chasing a neighborhood stray after a household door was inadvertently left open.

In contrast, one of the most happy-go-lucky dogs I ever met was a 3-legged, 1 1/2-year-old Malamute whose foreleg had been amputated at 10 weeks of age. The owners said they treated the puppy as if it were normal on the advice of their veterinarian. Though raised in a 2-story house, the puppy was never carried anywhere or picked up when it fell or faltered. The behavior complaint concerned chewing when left alone; the dog responded well to a standard remedial program. However, had the owners mismanaged the puppy's emotional development, I might have met my first aggressive 3-legged dog.

Home care for dogs recovering from distemper has produced more problems than any other situation, probably because of the pathetic symptoms such dogs have. The most effective tools for avoiding creation of behavioral problems during home care are probably advice from the veterinary staff, coupled with a type-written sheet detailing what must be done and how the treatment should be rendered, and pointing out the benefits of a cheerful (versus sympathetic) attitude.

Parasitism

"Don't all puppies have worms?" The client, whose 11-week-old Terrier was literally shivering from malnutrition associated with roundworm infection, was taken aback to learn that the condition required immediate veterinary attention. When the woman bought the pup, she was assured that it had been dewormed. She did not know that more than one deworming might be needed, nor that a vaccination against distemper, hepatitis and leptospirosis was necessary.

Most problems related to internal parasitism involve an owner who is ignorant of the adverse effects of digestive malfunction, yet still expects a young dog to control its loose stools, be successfully housetrained, and learn more complicated lessons of domestication. When the animal does not respond acceptably, the owner may react by isolating, punishing or rejecting the pet socially. In some cases, the sympathy syndrome mentioned previously may develop. Any or all of these reactions can and do occur when family members are interacting with the animal. The resulting confusion and mismanagement of the pet often produce a wide spectrum of behavioral maladjustments. The following problems may be noted in dogs with internal parasites.

- Housesoiling (due to loose stools).
- Shyness (due to harsh punishment).
- Biting when scolded or physically punished.
- Chewing, digging, barking, whining, unruliness (due to isolation as punishment).
- Stool eating (possibly due to a fecal fixation resulting from excessive punishment relative to stools).

Flea infestation has led to ostracism of some pets. Most dog owners only try to get rid of fleas on the dog. They buy a flea collar or flea spray, but do nothing about the fleas infesting the dog's regular sleeping and resting areas. The result is that the dog continues to be infested and is eventually banished to the yard. The problems associated with such social isolation then may evolve.

Ear mite infestation led to isolation-based problems in 2 dogs I saw, both involving destructive chewing. "His constant scratching just drives us nuts," was the statement made by each owner when asked why the dog was shut away. I pointed out the rather obvious ear odor commonly associated with ear mites, and refused to handle the behavioral problem until the ear problem was cleared up. Veterinary treatment ended the scratching problem, and subsequent behavioral corrections were successful.

Mycotic and Protozoal Infections

Among these diseases I have noted only 2 cases of owner-induced problems. Both concerned pups that were not responding

113

to housetraining at the normal pace. The animals had coccidiosis, which was associated with loose stools and impaired learning ability (perhaps due to nutritional side effects). These in turn stimulated excessive punishment, resulting in submissive urination in one dog and stress biting in the other. Both dogs responded well to combined medical/behavioral treatment.

Hypermetria

I have observed 3 dogs with hypermetria. The dogs tended to bump into objects, invariably submerged their noses when drinking, and displayed an exaggerated forethrow of the front limbs when walking. One of these dogs, a 2-year-old male Shepherd mix, was abnormally hostile and seemed to be devoid of long-term memory. That is, it had to be retaught simple lessons every day. The dog's hostility toward me was overcome if I remained motionless and allowed it to approach me at leisure. However, if the dog lay down to nap for a few minutes, it would awaken with all its original hostility. Unfortunately, this dog was euthanized and no postmortem examination was performed.

It is interesting that all 3 animals displaying signs of hypermetria had histories of heavy roundworm or tapeworm infections as puppies. Two dogs responded well to nonphysical training techniques as part of a program to overcome the basic complaints of general unruliness. Progress was slower than in most cases.

Impaired Hearing

A 6-month-old female Dalmatian was enrolled in a residential program at our facility. Her hearing was adequate for training when an ultrasonic device was used, but the dog failed to respond to spoken commands unless she saw the person speaking. For example, if I approached the dog from behind and called her name, her attention (orienting reflex) and movement would be toward the direction she was already facing. Repeating her name (usually twice) would usually catch the dog's attention.

The animal was under treatment for a mild ear infection (otitis externa), but otherwise appeared to be in excellent health.

Behavior complaints were of jumping up on people, chewing plants and household articles, and general unruliness.

After 5 days of intensive conditioning, both to commands and to corrective procedures, the Dalmatian behaved calmly and would respond well to commands spoken in a loud voice. When reunited with the owners, the dog regressed. Though prepared for this possibility, the owners seemed unable to cope with the physiologic condition and did not follow through with the behavioral program.

Seizures

> *A client telephoned me to make an appointment for a consultation about his German Shorthaired Pointer. The dog, a male about 2 years old, had a history of several seizures and anticonvulsant medication apparently had not been effective. The dog had been growing increasingly excitable. As the owner explained to me, "The problem really isn't so much the seizures as Harry's unruliness and disobedience." He had tried all modes of punishment imaginable, to no avail. Scolding, hitting and confinement in the back yard only seemed to make the dog more "hyper." Could I help?*
>
> *"Sure thing," I responded. "Take your dog back to your veterinarian and allow him to perform the diagnostic procedures he recommends to find out what is causing the seizures. In the meantime, keep the dog inside the house as much as possible. Don't pamper him, but let him adjust to living with people again. (The dog had been forced to live outside for 18 months due to unruliness.)*

The case was similar to several I had handled in the past. The owner really wanted to believe that his dog did not suffer from epilepsy, and had not administered the anticonvulsant as prescribed because a seizure had occurred 2 days after starting treatment. He did not give the drug time to prove itself.

Most dog owners follow veterinary advice in cases of epilepsy. However, if there is an associated behavior problem, some situations may require close cooperation between the behavioral consultant and veterinarian. Ultimately, such problems may be treated at the veterinary clinic, if both medical treatment and behavioral counseling are included in the total service. This type of approach is used by a few behavior-oriented veterinarians. The reason it is not practiced more widely may be due to a general lack of recognition of when it is needed.

Behavioral consultation should be considered as an adjunct to medical treatment when the owner expresses guilt about not bringing the pet in for treatment earlier. To offset the possibility of owner sympathy affecting the long-term behavioral aspects of the case, the owner should be reassured that, under the circumstances, he or she has performed properly and that a nonemotional approach to rehabilitation would be most productive.

> *Some dogs have seizures in emotional or exciting circumstances. I had a case involving an excitable and pampered Cocker Spaniel that, after being treated for epilepsy, continued to display seizures whenever it was ignored. The most recent seizure occurred when the family gathered around the piano for a song session. The dog watched the proceedings for a few minutes, and then began to jerk spasmodically, fell onto its side, and lost consciousness for about 15 seconds. The singing ceased, and the dog recovered quickly to the petting and attention of family members.*

In such cases, the owners should establish a leadership pattern, wherein the dog responds to the owner, if only to obey simple commands to sit, stay or come. Fondling and excessive sympathetic reactions should be discontinued. Praise is reserved for favorable responses to owner control.

A seizure may be a conditioned response to a certain stimulus, and a dog may learn to display seizures in order to gain sympathy. Whether the seizures are caused by epilepsy or some other condition must be determined by medical tests. When this has been properly diagnosed, control of environmental reactions can alleviate and avoid associated behavior problems.

Endocrine-Related Behavior Problems

Behavioral neuroendocrinology is still in its infancy. Experimental use of dogs is being severely reduced and more strictly governed for humane reasons. For this reason, if any useful information about dog behavior and hormonal conditions is to be gathered, it may soon be available only through clinical observations.

The Role of Hormones

It is generally recognized that proper endocrine balance is necessary for normal physical development. The complications created by functional abnormalities of the pituitary, adrenals, gonads, thyroid, pancreas, liver, and perhaps even the tiny pineal gland are documented, and most veterinarians are alert to the signs of endocrine dysfunction.[5] However, the fact that specialists are emerging in the field suggests a need for even more careful attention to certain aspects of hormone treatment.

The hormone environment affects nervous function in many subtle ways. The master control of endocrine balance lies mainly in the "emotional center(s)" of the brain, and is itself controlled by the feedback obtained in the various axes between and among the endocrine centers.[6] It is becoming apparent that experience can affect and be affected by hormones. At the clinical level, this knowledge has been helpful in dealing with some behavior problems. For example, in aggressive bitches that display male behaviorisms (leg lifting and sexual mounting), antiandrogen treatment of the dog, in conjunction with behavioral guidance for the owners, often produce good results. The physiologic problem of endocrine dysfunction may require lifelong treatment, but associated behavior problems tend to clear up to the point where the pet can function acceptably.

Hormone Therapy

Many veterinarians with behavioral interests have begun to cautiously use hormones for controlling certain behavior problems, particularly hypersexuality and aggressiveness. Combined with enlightened behavioral guidance, this seems likely to be a rewarding approach, especially when the only alternative is euthanasia for the errant pet.

Current research into the effects of hormones is done primarily with laboratory animals (rodents), so it is important to guard against interspecies generalizations. Because clinical measurements of hormone-induced behavior variations are vague and imprecise, careful behavior records should be kept. Too often a pet's behavior goes unobserved or is poorly recalled, making any attempt to reach meaningful conclusions very difficult at best.

Behavior problems may arise when hormones (particularly corticosteroids) are used in treatment of certain diseases, such as skin conditions. Corticosteroids have lowered the thresholds of excitability in laboratory animals.[7] Some investigation of the effects of these agents in dogs appears warranted.

Polydipsia (excessive water consumption) and polyuria (excessive urination) following corticosteroid administration for inflammatory problems are common. During the summers I receive many calls from clients whose pets have received corticosteroids for hot spots and other skin conditions. These dogs uncharacteristically violate their house manners when confined for any time. This indicates, at least statistically, that clients should be more often forewarned of this common side effect of corticosteroids, as many of these callers have inadvisedly punished and/or confined the hapless pet to a cage or travel crate to correct the "behavior problem." In several cases involving punishment, additional problems have been noted, such as aggression or submissive urination.

In the clinical situation, it may be useful to determine whether a dog is on the brink of some behavior problem. Some problems that may be exacerbated by corticosteroid use include aggressiveness, excitability during isolation, submissive urination in stress, and tendencies toward excessive vocal and/or physical tension-relieving activity.

Much of the research involving corticosteroids and behavior I have encountered indicates that a behavioral price is paid for relief of physiologic problems.[7] This is not to say that corticosteroids create problems; they usually do far more good than harm. However, latent behavioral problems may be pushed over the threshold by some of these agents. Therefore, a behavioral profile of each dog given corticosteroids might be beneficial in the long run. The owner should report to the veterinarian any specific or general behavioral changes. A record would indicate the degree of coincidence (if any) between administration of corticosteroids and behavior changes. Given enough cases, perhaps through pooling data, some useful information could be compiled.

In specific cases where a problem does erupt or an existing one becomes worse, it would be useful for the veterinarian to do blood and urine tests to ascertain whether levels of various hormones or their metabolites fall within normal ranges. If imbalances are evident, remedial treatment or alternative drugs might be used, with behavioral guidance.

Psychoactive Drug Effects

Various psychoactive drugs, such as chlorpromazine, phenothiazine, reserpine and imipramine, can affect the hormonal balance of animals and may be associated with behavioral reactions.[8] A veterinarian is best qualified to decide whether administration of these drugs may alter endocrine function to the detriment of a pet dog's behavior. For instance, the fact that chlorpromazine may induce lactation or suppress growth hormone may be irrelevant in one type of situation but highly significant in another, such as false pregnancy.

On one hand, the behaviorist must be in a position, when attempting to analyze a behavior problem, to communicate with the veterinarian effectively regarding past drug treatment. On the other, the veterinarian, who is attuned to the possible hormonal shifts and behavioral changes resulting from use of psychoactive agents, is in the unique position of monitoring the effect of these drugs. In the event the drug produces undesirable hormonal-type side effects, further investigation may indicate the need for substitute or supplemental medications.

Thyroid Dysfunction

The most common behavioral change associated with thyroid dysfunction has been mood swings. The owner finds the dog less tolerant of children, other dogs, scolding and/or punishment. This usually leads to lower thresholds of aggressive behavior when the dog is stressed. Some of the conditions associated with onset of the problems have been neutering, acute or prolonged corticosteroid therapy, and allergies. In many cases involving purebred dogs, certain breed lines appear predisposed to such problems.

Cushing's Syndrome and Aggression

A 7 1/2-year-old male Wirehaired Fox Terrier was presented because he viciously attacked the telephone whenever it rang. Any loud or sudden noise produced extreme excitability and trembling. The dog had started chewing on doors when left alone in the owner's apartment.

The dog was rather full-bodied, but underdeveloped in the hips and chest. His hair was soft and puppy-like, rather than typically wiry. On arriving at our facility, he went immediately to a tree and urinated, trembling so violently that he nearly lost his balance. He then proceeded to my office door and stood, expectantly watching it, even though his owners and I were outside in the courtyard.

"He's looking for your telephone," the owner said. "He wants to attack it if it rings."

I called and the dog came happily, sniffed at me and then dutifully returned to his sentry post outside the door. I suggested that we go into the office and dial the office number from an extension.

It took only a minute or so for the dog to locate the telephone on the desk, after which he sat and alertly waited. When the phone rang, the dog leaped at the coiled receiver cord, pulled the instrument onto the floor and proceeded to snarl and bite at it, even though the ringing had ceased. The owners parted the dog and its hate-object, and the dog returned to his former position to await Round 2.

"How long have you been putting up with this?" I asked.

"If you can believe it, for 7 years, along with his constant scratching," the wife replied.

At 6 months of age the dog had begun scratching and was given a daily oral dose of cortisone. This helped somewhat. When the dog was 4 years old, the owners were advised that castration might alleviate aggression toward the phone. This was done, but no improvement was noted. Years previously, the couple had resorted to plug-in telephones that were disconnected when the pet was left at home alone. At about 5 years of age, prednisolone was prescribed in place of cortisone to minimize physical side effects that were becoming rather obvious. However, the behavioral problems continued and the case was finally referred to me.

During our consultation, the phone rang several times. Ultrasonic distractions and scolding did not allay the dog's assaults on the phone, nor did physical punishment by the owner prevent further attacks. The dog was apparently unable to inhibit this behavior.

I explained to the client some of the known long-term effects of corticosteroid therapy on behavior, and suggested that without veterinary help, behavioral modification would be a waste of time, effort and money. I referred the dog to a veterinary endocrinologist, whose tests revealed a dangerously high blood lipid content, hypocalcemia and severely depressed endogenous adrenocortical hormone levels. Treatment is expected to require considerable time. Behavioral therapy should be possible when the animal is able to perform motor acts without trembling, indicating some restoration of inhibitory nervous function.

Hypersexuality, Aggressiveness and Dermatitis

A 9-year-old male Airedale Terrier had recurring dermatitis since 7 months of age. Early treatment with antihistamines and topicals proved successful, but cortisone alleviated the signs and was used during acute episodes that occurred 2-3 times a year.

The dog showed signs of hostility each day when the husband returned home from work. At these times, the Airedale would growl for a few minutes, then allow the owner to stroke him on the head and back, and begin growling again. Similar "pet me and then I'll menace you" behavior was exhibited toward the wife and others who petted the dog. He also growled whenever disturbed while lying around the house. The couple had obtained a female Airedale several years previously, but the male bullied the bitch so viciously that a new home was found for her. Recently another Airedale bitch was bought, with the idea of breeding them. However, the same type of aggression was displayed by the male. The behavior complaints brought to me were of the male's biting the bitch, the female's defecating in the house, and both dogs' urinating inside.

When they arrived at our facility, the dogs methodically sniffed the area and urinated on scent posts. The male constantly nuzzled and licked the bitch's genitals, though she was not in heat. The bitch was pleasant and clownish, and attempted to jump up on me. The male ignored me, but interposed himself between me and either the bitch or the wife. The male was obviously a leader type and extremely bossy.

Our consultation revealed that the wife was highly sympathetic toward the male, petting and cooing to him when he showed signs of hostility. This stopped the growling, but only for a few moments. The male was increasingly hostile in the confines of my office, so I asked the owner to stop petting and praising the animal. After several minutes the dog lay down and went to sleep.

The female paced the room from door to door as if she wanted to leave. This hyperactive behavior appeared to upset the owner, who called the bitch to her side gruffly and scolded her, commanding her to Sit and Stay. The bitch obeyed for about 30 seconds each time, after which the pacing and whining resumed. In a few more minutes, one of the causes for the male's attacks became apparent; he began growling whenever the bitch came near. He appeared to pick up on the owner's exasperation with the bitch and took over the role of a scolding leader.

The advice given in this case was that the male be put through his previously learned obedience exercises twice daily and praised only after obeying commands. Otherwise he was to be ignored. The bitch, which had never received formal training, was started on an off-leash program, with the same general daily treatment recommended for the male. The owner's reaction to this advice was mixed. She thought she and her husband would have considerable difficulty carrying it out, having been solicitous with the male for so many years. However, it was attempted.

Within 3 days, the aggression toward the female subsided. However, the urination by both and the bitch's defecation did not decline. Because a degree of competition was apparent in their urinating habits, I suggested that a complete housetraining program should be started at home, teaching each dog to perform its toilet duties only in one area of the yard. This was intermittently successful until the bitch came into heat, then both dogs regressed to their former behavior, and the male developed prostatitis.

I consulted the owner's veterinarian about the problem because the male dog always seemed to be hypersexual. We discussed the possibility of giving the dog stilbestrol (a female hormone) to suppress possible hyperandrogenism. This was tried with dramatic results. The dog ceased his attacks on the bitch and became less hostile generally. Spaying the bitch had no calming effect. She did stop urine marking, but still defecated in the house about once a week.

After 6 weeks, stilbestrol use was discontinued and the male retained a good deal of the mellowness acquired during the treatment period. Several weeks later the owners reported that the dogs were now acceptable in their general behavior.

Castration

Many dog owners are vehemently opposed to castration of males. In the above case of the Airedale, the owners believed that castration was to be avoided as a kindness to the pet, even though the animal's sex hormones appeared to be a major cause of behavior problems. However, they were easily motivated to spay their female pet. Perhaps a major reason why owners object to castrating a male pet is that the castrate displays visual evidence of its deprived masculinity. If this is the case, perhaps the time for cosmetic testicular implants has arrived.

I have found that most owners become less resistant to castration when they understand the role of testicular androgens in their dog's behavior. The fact that secondary sex characteristics are not profoundly affected by castration is reassuring to those who fear that castration might feminize their dogs. Many are also reassured to learn that the adrenal cortex produces gonadal steroids and tends to take up the "slack" created by castration. In behavioral terms relevant to the owner's concern, this means that castration of a mature dog will not cause it to revert to puppy behaviorisms, become sissified, or run from a burglar.

> *One owner called to complain that her 9-year-old Sydney Silky Terrier was engaging in marathon copulation with her 1 1/2-year-old Silky bitch, then in heat. The client's fear was that the dog might die of a heart attack due to the furiousness of his sexual activities. I asked if she had considered castration and was told that this had been performed when the dog was 2 years old in an effort to stop his leg-lifting in the house (which had not abated). I advised the client to have the bitch spayed at a time recommended by her veterinarian. This was done and at least the sexual problem was solved. Correction of the household urination required a 6-week behavior program.*

When supported by remedial behavior programs, castration may help alleviate habitual running away or roaming, fighting (other males), house urination and sexual mounting. Preexisting problems that may persist or become intensified after castration without behavioral programs include aggression toward owners, children or outsiders, fighting with bitches, and fecal housesoiling.

My 4-year-old male Norwegian Elkhound was castrated to save the lovely ivy that covered our front wall. An aggressive type, he was responding to the neighbor's dogs, who daily urinated against the outside of the wall. Before castration he had never displayed spontaneous aggression, though he had become defensively aggressive on the veterinary exam table after 2 unfortunate experiences.

About 2 weeks after castration, he snarled at and drove away our blind Dalmatian when she walked into him while he was eating. This had happened numerous times before, at which time the Elkhound simply paused and moved out of the way. From 4 months of age he had always been submissive to the spayed Dalmatian. He was not scolded or punished for his "attack." There were no further episodes. However, the next evening my wife thought she heard a car engine running. Turning around, she saw Randy under the dining room table, teeth bared and growling. She clapped her hands and said good-naturedly, "Hey, Randy, whatcha doing?" His demeanor changed instantly and he got up, walking toward her with tail wagging.

We consulted a veterinary friend, then in the department of nuclear medicine at UCLA. After the behavior was described, his first question was, "When did you have him neutered?" The dog was tested and found to be hypothyroid. Thyroid hormone replacement therapy resolved the behavior problem.

Since that time, when postcastration personality changes are reported, we refer the clients for a complete veterinary examination before instituting behavioral programs. The number reporting back with hypothyroidism or other hormonal imbalances is too significant to ignore.

Spaying

Ovariohysterectomy in females has appeared to contribute to only 2 types of behavior problems. Persistent immature submissive wetting has been noted if surgery has been performed as early as 5 months of age. Some early-spayed dogs develop an abnormal degree of masculinity. In cases involving submissive wetting, affected dogs did not appear to be generally less submissive following hormone (stilbestrol) therapy, but the urination disappeared or was minimized. In the masculine females, urination and aggressiveness were the predominant complaints. A combined stilbestrol and behavioral program produced acceptable results in these animals.

Just why the lack of ovarian hormones contributes to submissive wetting or some masculinizing in females is a subject for speculation. It might be that early ovariohysterectomy is somehow related to impaired sphincter control, and that lack of ovarian estrogens, which are antagonistic to androgens, allows an androgenic type of masculinizing to occur. Whatever the cause, the problems do not erupt immediately after spaying. Therefore, environmental factors also may be involved.

I have limited my investigations to environmental factors that may be associated with these problems. That is, where physical punishment appears to be associated with submissive wetting, I have recommended that the punishment be stopped and a more positive remedial program be undertaken. When there appears to be no environmental cause and hormone imbalance may be a factor, the case is referred to a veterinarian. In the case of masculinized and aggressive females, rehabilitation has always required off-leash teaching of command responses, as well as controlled exposure to those things and situations that evoke aggressiveness.

In summing up the problems in early-spayed bitches, hormonal imbalance may be associated with the onset of problem behavior, and hormone therapy under veterinary supervision appears to be helpful in many cases.

Cryptorchidism

Sex hormones exert vital developmental influences during specific periods before and after birth.[5,6,9] I have seen precocious puberty, excessive sexual aggression, and hostile aggression in several pups under 5 months of age. Some of these animals had 1 or 2 undescended testicles. Whether there is a relationship between these conditions and the behavior problem is not certain. Once the behavior begins, environmental reactions become part of the problem. The condition itself is considered genetic in origin. I have yet to see the results of a blood and/or urine analysis in such animals. However, all of them have responded well to proper behavioral guidance.

Aggression Associated With Occipital Aplasia

A 2-year-old male Lhasa Apso displayed aggression when approached by owners after it was accidentally stepped on several times. The dog was also overprotective of toys and food, and persistently attempted to mount the owner's legs. Ophthalmologic examination revealed a lack of focal vision, caused by occipital aplasia.

The dog responded well to the earned praise and petting program, coupled with Jolly Routines (see Chapter 8) when approached.

Shyness Associated With Juvenile Cataracts

A 9-month-old male mixed-breed dog actively avoided all contact with people other than his owner. When the dog's juvenile cataracts were corrected, the dog's behavior became normal.

Influence of Pheromones

Pheromones are chemical substances secreted by an animal that influence the behavior of other animals of the same species. Unlike other hormones, which are secreted internally to regulate an animal's internal environment, pheromones are secreted externally and influence other animals, typically by smell.[10,11] In this regard, pheromones may play a very important role in animal behavior.

Studies in insects, which produce pheromones in various specialized glands, indicate that these substances are used in communication.[10,11] In dogs, pheromones may influence group integration and may be a factor in fighting and general aggressiveness. There is speculation that dogs release pheromones in urine and feces, and perhaps through exhaled breath and the foot pads (Fig 5). This would tend to explain why aggressive,

Figure 5. Scratching the ground after urination may spread pheromones, thus marking the dog's territory.

127

fighting dogs are often compulsive urine sniffers and urine markers, and why they become less aggressive when sniffing and urine marking are not allowed by their owners.

There are significant exceptions to these generalizations. Some dogs need no priming whatever to fight or attack other dogs (most do however). Where there is an olfactory (sniffing) prelude to aggressive behavior, it is reasonable to speculate that pheromones may play a role.

Pheromones may act as a trigger or primer for certain types of behavior. The trigger pheromone produces an immediate change in behavior of the animal smelling it. The primer pheromone alters long-term physiologic conditions so that the recipient's behavior can subsequently be influenced by specific accessory stimuli.[11]

> *A possible example of behavioral effects in dogs is provided by a 2-year-old male Husky that had been in several fights away from his own property. The animal was taken on regular evening walks in the neighborhood, and was allowed to sniff and urinate at will.*
>
> *One afternoon the Husky escaped from the yard into the street, where a female and 3 male dogs were congregated. One of these males, a Collie, urinated daily along the street. The Husky's approach to the dogs was witnessed by his owners. The dog approached the group and sniffed the female, and then a male. No hostility was shown. However, when the Husky sniffed the Collie, he instantly attacked it.*

This case is typical of many wherein a dog appears to sense, by smell, another dog that may be perceived as a threat. Also typical among some vicious biting dogs is an apparent need to brand a strange territory with their own pheromones before launching an attack. I have also seen this take place even when the biting dogs were on their home territory.

The remedial program includes restricting urination of the problem dog to a single area of its own yard. This tends to lower the aggressiveness, as well as diminish the incidence of household urination.

Attack behavior on a predatory level has been stopped by severing the olfactory (smell) nerves. It is also well-known practice in the dog show world to insert strong-smelling agents into the nasal passages as a deterrent to fighting and hypersexuality.

Research into the effects of pheromones may provide answers to many puzzling canine behaviorisms.

Hyperkinesis

Anyone who has worked extensively with dogs has occasionally been confronted by a raging, vicious beast, the handling of which has required a heavy-duty tranquilizer and several assistants. In many instances, such behavior cannot be explained by improper handling or cruelty and neglect by owners. When it seems that nothing can be done, the dog is written off as "just plain mean" and relegated to the end of a chain or destroyed as a menace to the neighborhood. More recently, such excitable and vicious behavior has been identified in some dogs as hyperkinesis, which in children has been under study for 40 years, and which can be effectively treated medically.

Signs

Signs associated with hyperkinesis in dogs are usually displayed when the dog is stressed by close confinement and/or social isolation. Signs include rapid heart rate and respiration, excessive salivation, a high metabolic rate and reduced urine output.[12] The major difficulty in identifying the syndrome, however, is that there is no apparent cause. Clinical signs may be evident in dogs that are normal under other circumstances. Moreover, dogs identified as hyperkinetic do not always exhibit a precise behavior pattern.

Diagnosis

Despite variations, clinical signs can give the veterinarian diagnostic clues in distinguishing the hyperreactive from the hyperkinetic pet. Some initial clues may come from the pet owner. In my experience, complaints fall into the following categories: the dog cannot sit still, even for a minute; it never becomes accustomed to everyday situations; it cannot learn anything (often an obedience school failure); and it salivates constantly and always seems excited or nervous.

Many dogs living in stressful environments may be stimulated toward hyperreactivity. An amphetamine response test can differentiate hyperreactivity from hyperkinesis. The seemingly paradoxic calming effect of amphetamines on hyperkinetic and even violent children and adults has been put to use for many years. In veterinary cases, amphetamines have given positive results in about 75% of the dogs tested.

Treatment

The first controlled studies of hyperkinesis in dogs were an outgrowth of a long-term attempt to develop animal models of psychopathology. Dogs were chosen for these studies for several reasons, primarily because there were so many breeds available. This allowed an evaluation of genetic strains in certain breeds. Also, dogs are the only domestic animal with a variety of emotional responses comparable to those seen in people; they worry about things not essential to their survival.

In studies designed to evaluate responses to stress, some dogs did not respond to Pavlovian conditioning. Positive reinforcement, negative reinforcement and tranquilization were all tried, but nothing did a bit of good.

Typically such dogs would be eliminated from the study, but because the researchers were interested in the interaction of genetics and psychological environment, they were curious about dogs that appeared unwilling to be studied. Eventually the researcher decided they were dealing with the equivalent of a hyperkinetic child. On that basis, amphetamines were given, and the tentative diagnosis proved correct.

The first model of hyperkinesis in a dog was Jackson, a Cocker-Beagle mix whose usual response to any approach was to snap, snarl, growl or, if possible, bite (Fig 6). Many experienced, gentle dog handlers were bitten, until eventually laboratory personnel refused to approach the dog. Jackson responded the same to other dogs. He viciously attacked any dog without hesitation, even friendly and docile animals. He refused to submit to Pavlovian conditioning, and destroyed laboratory equipment in his rages.

Because depressants were not effective against Jackson's abnormally hyperactive and vicious behavior, it was suspected that hyperkinesis may have been involved. On this assumption, the dog was given amphetamine orally at 1 mg/kg. Within 2 hours, Jackson's personality changed to complete docility (Fig 7). He whimpered as if he wanted to be petted. When petting was stopped, he begged for more. He became nonviolent, even sub-

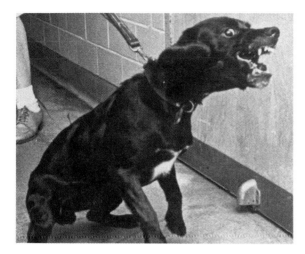

Figure 6. Jackson, a hyperkinetic dog, showed extreme aggression to any approach.

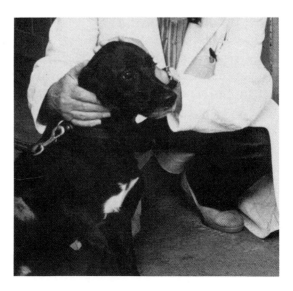

Figure 7. Within 2 hours of oral amphetamine administration, Jackson became docile and friendly.

missive, toward the same dog he had attacked earlier. Jackson appeared to be perplexed and unsure of what to do.

When placed in the Pavlovian experimental stand after medication, Jackson responded normally and learned rapidly, indicating that his previous failure was not a result of mental retardation, but rather a secondary effect of his behavior problem. After 6 weeks of drug-facilitated psychosocial therapy, medication could be withdrawn without reappearance of aggression, but hyperkinesis reappeared in low-threat situations. Aggression was apparently trained out by the drug-facilitated social interaction and conditioning experiments, indicating that what is learned under the influence of amphetamines is retained later.

After 2 more months of psychosocial therapy using amphetamines, Jackson's unmedicated hyperkinesis was also reduced. Because he was between 1 1/2 and 2 years old at the time of the experiments, maturation could have been associated with the cure; however, 6 older hyperkinetic dogs did not outgrow their abnormal behavior patterns.

Both dextroamphetamine and methamphetamine at moderate dosages alleviated Jackson's aggression, but resolving hyperkinesis required 4 times as much of the latter drug. There were similar variations in drug response in other hyperkinetic dogs. The effective dosage usually ranged from 0.5 to 1 mg/kg, but several dogs did not respond to 3 and 4 mg/kg.

Undesirable side effects of amphetamine treatment included stereotyped behavior and eating disturbances, particularly in slow eaters. Stereotypy was sometimes manifested as circling, running in place, hopping and head wagging, particularly when large doses of amphetamines were given. Eating disturbances were generally characterized by an approach-avoidance conflict; the dogs seemed unable to approach or finish eating food. Such reactions emphasize the need for careful clinical judgment when administering amphetamines.

This study demonstrated that it is possible to permanently eliminate apparently uncontrollable aggression in a hyperkinetic dog. Jackson has since remained a well-behaved dog. The drug therapy probably did not cure the violence; this simply made it possible to develop a positive relationship with the dog.

It transformed Jackson from an animal one could not pet, into an animal that appeared to realize that petting may be nicer than biting people.

Mechanism of Drug Action

The petting and training given hyperkinetic animals under the influence of drugs made it possible to establish new patterns of behavior. These involve new transmitter mechanisms opening new synapses in the nervous system which, once established, beome permanent.

Most animals responded to amphetamine-facilitated therapy. The few that did not subsequently responded to methylphenidate (Ritalin) or phenytoin (Dilantin). This suggests that different neurotransmitter mechanisms are involved. It has been hypothesized that hyperkinetic dogs suffer from a lack of neurotransmitters in inhibitory centers of the brain. Amphetamines act by either releasing neurotransmitters (phenylnorepinephrine, l-dopamine) or by preventing neurotransmitters from reentering the nerve endings at synapses. In hyperkinetic dogs, these particular neurotransmitters may be lacking only in the inhibitory centers.

If the appropriate amount of amphetamine is used, these transmitters are released, supplying inhibitory mechanisms. The primary deficit is not hyperkinesis, but inability to inhibit appropriately. Learning involves an interplay between inhibition and excitation.

Clinical Test for Hyperkinesis

The preliminary clinical test for hyperkinesis was recommended by Dr. Samuel Corson, who performed the early investigations at Ohio State University's Department of Bio-Psychiatry.[13]

1. The heart and respiratory rates are measured with the dog in mild physical restraint, such as being held. In hyperkinetic dogs, these rates usually are much higher than normal.

2. Methylphenidate (Ritalin) is given at an oral dosage of 0.2 mg/kg for nonaggressive dogs, and at 1 mg/kg for fractious, aggressive dogs. Both dosages are considered within the moderate therapeutic range.

3. The dog is placed in a quiet holding area for 75-90 minutes.

4. The heart and respiratory rates are then measured again, as in Step 1, but preferably in a different exam room by different staff, to avoid any influence of accommodation.

5. A reduction in posttreatment heart and respiratory rates of 15% or more suggests that the dog is hyperkinetic.

6. The dosage should be doubled until an optimum is found; that is, the dosage produces normally calm behavior. This can be done by the owners, with daily veterinary consultation. A dose is given each morning and afternoon, and sometimes before stressful events. *The drug is always used in conjunction with a remedial behavior program.*

7. When the behavioral goals are achieved, the drug dosage is either gradually reduced until it is completely withdrawn, or drug use may be immediately stopped following veterinary examination.

8. The remedial behavior program is continued for at least 6 weeks after medication is withdrawn.

In dogs we have treated, behavioral adjustments have been well retained after withdrawal of the medication. However, mild hyperkinetic fidgeting has reappeared in 3 dogs. Though the following discussions mention dextroamphetamine as the drug used, Ritalin is the main medication currently used.

Clinical Cases of Hyperkinesis

Through veterinarians in the Los Angeles area, we have managed a number of cases of hyperkinesis. Of 16 animals, all of which came into the program from owners who wanted to get rid of them, 10 were less than 2 years old. Satisfactory results were obtained in 7 of these 10, and in 3 of the 6 older dogs.

If any program with hyperkinetic dogs is to be successful, the owner should be informed by the veterinarian of all aspects of the treatment program. The owner should also be made aware that treatment does not require lifelong medication, and that the treatment regimen is minimized.

Medical treatment does not work a miracle. Rather, *what the owner does with the dog* really makes the difference. We have not yet encountered a dog that responded like Jackson. The reason for this is probably that the owner's home environment is not as tightly controlled as that in a research institute. However, owners who have put their dogs through drug-facilitated therapy state that their pets behave acceptably. The following cases are typical.

Case 1: A 2-year-old spayed Labrador-Setter mix was hyperactive and had to be tranquilized for treatment or bathing. The owners complained of constant unruliness, fence jumping and failure to respond to commands or punishment (Fig 8). They had found Val in their neighborhood and brought her into their home, where she got along well with their 8-year-old Boxer. Five weeks of daily off-leash training did not improve the dog's behavior, and ultrasonic conditioning was only transiently effective when used for commands or distraction from misbehavior. After 6 weeks the dog was tested for amphetamine response by a veterinarian and was diagnosed as hyperkinetic.

The dog was given 10 mg of dextroamphetamine orally twice daily, with a 7-hour interval between doses. Training sessions then produced stable conditioning and good retention. After 7 days, some regression to hyperactivity and salivation occurred, and the dose was reduced to 5 mg. Improvement in behavior was reported by the owners (Fig 9). Four weeks later, the dog ap-

Figure 8. A hyperkinetic Labrador-Setter mix displays typical unruly behavior.

peared to be accommodating to the drug and was switched to ephedrine (25 mg/45 lb). At the seventh week, medication was withdrawn, with no adverse signs. Command responses, formerly impossible to obtain, are now said to be excellent. Some initial unruliness with visitors is still noted, but is controllable. The owners originally were considering getting rid of the dog, but now find Val an acceptable pet worth keeping.

Case 2: A 7-month-old female Golden Retriever displayed unruliness, poor conditioning, no retention to commands or response to discipline, and excessive paw licking (Fig 10). Tranquilizers appeared to aggravate the condition. Hyperkinesis was suspected, and amphetamine response tests proved positive.

Dextroamphetamine, given orally (7.5 mg) at 5-hour intervals, significantly reduced spontaneous physical activity (Fig 11). Commands and misbehavior inhibition, using an ultrasonic device, were taught by the owner. After 6 weeks of this program, behavioral goals were attained and medication was then withdrawn. During the following days, the clients noted some heightened excitability, after which the dog settled nicely. The owners now express satisfaction with the dog's behavior.

Case 3: A 7-year-old male German Shepherd had bitten several small children and a man. Each incident occurred relative to a barrier, either at a door or when the dog was tethered. The dog

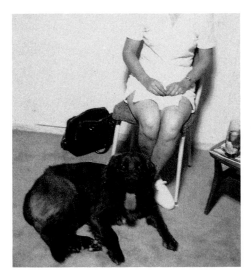

Figure 9. The hyperkinetic dog in Figure 8 became much more calm after treatment with dextroamphetamine and behavioral training.

Figure 10. A hyperkinetic Golden Retriever was overly active.

also urinated on walls and draperies. Neighbors complained of constant barking when the dog was placed in a 6 x 12-foot run as a safety precaution. Hyperkinetic signs displayed included constant physical activity, hyperpnea and excessive salivation (Fig 12).

Figure 11. The dog in Figure 10 poses quietly for a photograph after treatment with dextro-amphetamine and behavioral training.

Response to dextroamphetamine confirmed hyperkinesis. Treatment with 10 mg/75 lb twice daily at 8-hour intervals proved effective. The first dose improved barking and overt viciousness (Fig 13). The dog was exposed to children, on and off leash, and remained calm. The only exception was a previously bitten girl, toward whom the dog showed aggression when the girl was at the front door. It is pertinent that this child displayed aggression toward the family children, often hitting them.

Urination in the house was corrected by the third day through application of ultrasonic inhibition when the dog sniffed upright articles, walls or drapes. The dog now allows the client's brother to pet him and appears friendly in response. Though the client did not test the dog relative to the girl previously bitten at the doorway, its behavior was said to be vastly improved several weeks following withdrawal of the drug.

Figure 12. A hyperkinetic German Shepherd lunged at strangers before treatment.

Figure 13. The dog in Figure 12 became much less aggressive after dextroamphetamine treatment.

Case 4: A 1-year-old male Golden Retriever displayed hyper-kinetic signs. The client complained of no response to commands, unruliness, digging in the garden, and sexual mounting of female family members. Standard leash training and punishment seemed to stimulate the dog to heightened activity. The dog was good natured and very friendly.

A dextroamphetamine dosage of 0.1 mg/lb was effective. An 11-week program of off-leash command response conditioning and malbehavior correction was successful. Anorexia at the morning feeding was evident for several days after use of the medication was begun, but this resolved. Several weeks after withdrawal of medication, the dog continued to display marked calmness and is now acceptable in social situations.

Summary

From genetic manipulation to medical treatment, the delicate interplay between the physiologic condition and behavior of a pet dog needs a great deal more study. Even so, much is already known from clinical and scientific findings.

As in any newly developing field, there will be conflicting opinions regarding the efficacy of any regimen of behavioral therapy, especially when it involves physiology and several disciplines of study and practice. This is not a new phenomenon. Nor is it unhealthy, except when criticism lacks empirical or scientific foundations.

References

1. Plechner AJ and Zucker M: *Pet Allergies.* Very Healthy Enterprises, Inglewood, CA, 1986.
2. Wyrwica W: *Mechanisms of Conditioned Behavior.* Charles C Thomas, Springfield, IL, 1972.
3. Pavlov IP: *Conditioned Reflexes.* Oxford Univ Press, London, 1927.
4. Dumenko VN: *Electrophysiology of the Central Nervous System.* Consultant Bureau, New York, 1970.
5. Ganong and Martini: *Neuroendocrinology.* Vol 2. Academic Press, New York, 1966.
6. Naumenko EV: *Central Control of the Pituitary-Adrenal Complex.* Consultant Bureau, 1973.
7. Sawyer CH and Gorski RA: *Steroid Hormones and Brain Function.* Univ California Press, Berkeley, 1971.
8. Valzelli L: *Psychopharmacology.* Spectrum Publishers, Flushing, NY, 1973.
9. Krushinskii LV: *Animal Behavior.* Consultant Bureau, 1973.
10. Scott JP: *Animal Behavior.* Univ Chicago Press, 1972.
11. Wilson EO, in: *Animal Engineering.* Freeman Co, San Francisco, 1974.

12. Corson SA *et al: Centennial Symposium on Huntington's Chorea.* Raven Press, New York, 1973.
13. Corson SA: Personal communication.
14. Dunbar I and Bohenkamp G: *Behavior Booklets.* James and Kenneth, 2140 Shattuck Ave, Berkeley, CA.
15. Campbell WE: *BehavioRx Client Education Brochure Series.* PO Box 1658, Grants Pass, OR 97526, 1991.

5

Nutrition and Behavior

The old adage, "You are what you eat," needs modification in light of recent investigations into the behavioral effects of both natural and synthetic elements in a dog's diet. Better stated, and tailored to canine nutrition, it might read, "Today's dog is the result of the way its genetic predisposition responds to the diet."

From hyperactivity to lick granulomas, nutritional diagnoses and management techniques are now at the disposal of every veterinarian with the desire to take advantage of them. It is not my purpose to detail the clinical procedures that may implicate nutritional hypersensitivities in a behavior problem. However, the literature relative to the regimen will be cited.

Information on nutritional supplementation and detoxifying diets will also be cited. Cases will be described to illustrate the effects of today's holistic approach to canine behavioral therapy.

General Feeding Practices

People eat when they want to or when hungry. Their dogs eat when their owners feed them, except for those whose owners allow access to food at all times. This constant availability of food works well with some animals, but can lead to catastrophic obesity, unhygienic conditions or housesoiling in other dogs.

Whenever any of these problems is evident, it is wise to switch the dog to scheduled feedings.

Hunger Tension

Most pet dogs are fed once daily. It is interesting to note that most dogs actually switch themselves to once-a-day feedings by turning up their noses at either the morning or evening meal somewhere between 6 months and 1 1/2 years of age. Most owners are quick to interpret this behavior as a clue that the pet needs only 1 meal a day. What is probably happening, though, is that the dog has reached the point of going off growth nutrient requirements and is entering the maintenance stage. In many dogs, maintenance requirements equal a little more than half of dietary requirements to sustain growth. So the owner naively starts a feeding program that leaves the dog with an unaccustomed empty stomach for approximately 14-18 hours a day. The result can be called "hunger tension."

Dogs generally digest food in their stomachs for longer periods than do people, probably because canine saliva has no discernible digestive enzyme function. It makes sense that the dog's gastric juices may require more time to sufficiently break down food before it enters the upper intestine. Even so, it is not hard to imagine the consequences of cutting an accustomed 2 feedings down to 1 per day. The dog has been conditioned over several months to expect and enjoy 2 meals, and suddenly 1 is withheld.

Most dogs adjust to the change, though many owners tell me they give their once-a-day eaters tidbits around the time of their former feeding; and many dogs simply do not require feedings twice daily. Others, especially excitable types, often develop related oral behavior problems, such as chewing, stealing food or begging at the table.

The reason some animals require only 1 meal and some others 2 meals a day is mainly due to the rate at which they metabolize nutrients. Once-a-day eaters are probably what can be termed "slow oxidizers," while those requiring 2 meals a day are "fast oxidizers" – the hayburners. Other elements of the environment can bear on the situation as well. The amount of exercise a dog undertakes spontaneously, or is stimulated to undertake, affects food intake. For these reasons, I always recommend 2 meals a day in problem cases involving an active type of dog, especially one with an excitable nervous system. This requires feeding half the once-daily ration twice daily.

Feeding Times

Dogs have relatively few highlights in their daily lives as city pets. They wake up in the morning and take their first trip outside to investigate the odors of any night invaders. They may be left alone by their owners, barking at the mailman or other potential intruders. They urinate or defecate in a favorite spot. And they *eat*. It is no wonder that monotony and boredom are the greatest sources of tension in behavior problems.

Feeding times can play a significant role in problem behavior. If these are too near either the regular departure or arrival times of the owners, any change in the schedule because of unexpected delays or early departures can upset the routine, which can upset the dog. This is especially true when feedings are given immediately after the owner's arrival at home in the afternoon or evening. If the owner is late, the dog is doubly troubled. The emotional ritual of the greeting is frustrated and the gastric schedule of the animal is violated.

Therefore, even though this practice may not appear as clearly part of the problem, it may be worthwhile to schedule feedings at least an hour before the owner's departure and an hour after homecoming on regular workdays. The same feeding time is used on weekends, at least until the problem is cleared up. This may affect the social schedules of some owners, but the results are worth the effort.

Variety in the Diet

Changing the type of food to satisfy our own misguided feeling that "Fido needs variety to be happy" risks creating intestinal chaos in a dog. The intestines maintain a bacterial population that helps digest a given diet. When the diet is continually changed, the bacterial population may be unable to adjust to the new ingredients. Diarrhea or loose stools often result, and flatulence can be a problem. Because dogs are easily affected by intestinal upsets, becoming too easily overexcited or even lethargic in some cases, problem dogs are best fed a steady diet that supplies their nutritional requirements.

When a change in the diet is required, it is best to introduce the new diet gradually, adding the new food in increments of 25% of total diet volume over a 4-day period. This schedule allows the pet's intestinal bacteria to accommodate to the new food without the shock of instant changeover. Loose stools and general psychological reactions (such as outright refusal of the 100% new ration) are avoided, together with their potential behavioral consequences of housesoiling, food-begging, or chewing caused by hunger tension.

Particularly sensitive dogs, especially those with a history of gastritis, may temporarily have loose stools after a diet change, even with this gradual approach. However, it has been beneficial in these cases to persevere with the changeover rather than revert to the old diet. If the looseness persists, veterinary attention should be sought.

Between-meal tidbits are fun to give, and dogs are grateful for a tasty morsel, but this is a luxury we must avoid if a problem exists. I remember a fellow who lost his hearing aid to his dog's chewing problem. We discovered that during the evening the owner had been eating some corn chips and delighting his Irish Setter with an occasional nibble. At bedtime the owner took off his hearing aid with salty fingers, only to awaken later to the sound of a $300 crunch as the Setter satisfied its well-teased taste buds. If tidbitting were practiced consistently daily, it might not contribute to problems. However, it rarely happens on schedule, so it becomes another forbidden practice in problem behavior cases.

How Much to Feed?

How much should a dog be fed? This question is no longer properly answered with the "pound of food per 50 pounds of body weight" rule of thumb. The huge variety of commercial dog foods available today requires that we ask, "What kind of food?" Is it dry, soft-moist or canned? In any case, the quantity fed should produce firm and well-formed feces. Any tendency of the stools to become loose indicates overfeeding in a healthy dog. Conversely, a stool so dry that it appears to have a chalky coating indicates underfeeding. The quantity fed should be increased or decreased by 10% in such cases.

In growing puppies, I recommend feeding for formed stools. Further, the *number* of feedings should be the same as the number of bowel movements per day. This practice tends to attune the input frequency with the metabolic rate of the pup. It also results in up to 6 feedings per day for some pups, which is often inconvenient for owners. Most owners agree that this feeding schedule is not quite as inconvenient as an unhouse-trained puppy, however, and they choose the limited high-frequency feeding as the lesser problem.

Pregnant or lactating bitches with puppies require especially large quantities of high-quality protein. The old wives' suggestion of "eating for 2" tends to carry over into feeding of pregnant bitches. The uninformed breeder often merely offers 2-4 times as much of the bitch's standard diet. The trouble with this practice is that the huge quantity of a commercial diet usually results in some degree of obesity if the bitch actually eats it.

This tendency toward obesity stems from the fact that many popular diets are usually significantly higher in carbohydrate than in protein. If the pregnant bitch does not metabolize the vastly increased carbohydrate intake, she usually gets fat. This can lead to a number of problems, such as sick or stillborn pups, or prolonged labor.

Pregnant and lactating bitches (up to 4 weeks postpartum), as well as their pups, require increased amounts of a high-protein diet. It might be more sensible to meet this need by supplementing, rather than loading them with more of the usual diet. Addition of raw liver, cooked eggs, milk, dicalcium phosphate and an oil containing vitamins A and D, in addition to a daily general vitamin supplement, satisfies the special dietary requirements of mother and offspring, and avoids overfeeding with its possible side effects of loose stools and obesity.

Quality of the Diet

If a problem dog shows normal levels of excitability and is in robust health, a nutritional problem may not be involved. However, when environmental factors cannot be implicated as the sole source of a problem, nutritional and other health factors deserve immediate attention. Examples of this are the bitch who lives for months with family children and then abruptly starts snapping at them, or the formerly easy-going dog who suddenly exhibits phobic behavior before and/or during storms or when cars backfire.

In general, if a dog develops personality changes, sudden bursts of activity, avoidance of formerly appealing people or situations, hypersensitivity to sounds, light or touch, and for which no compelling environmental-behavioral cause is apparent, the animal is a candidate for a complete physical examination and nutritional evaluation, and a combination medical/nutritional/behavioral program.

Considering that the pet food industry grew from a commercial desire to use the waste of manufactured human foods, mainly cereal by-products, it is not surprising that most commercial dog foods contain relatively high ratios of carbohydrate to protein, usually in the range of 50:22 or above. Recent generations of domestic dogs have evolved while eating relatively high-carbohydrate diets. Until recently, the idea that this may have produced animals more susceptible to nutritional hypersensitivities was either ignored or even disclaimed by some animal nutritionists. However, these attitudes are changing, mainly due to pioneering clinical work and a commercial awakening to the growing market for specialized diets. While most pet owners feed for economy, a growing number are becoming quality conscious.

So many new specialized diets are appearing yearly that a review of them would be immediately obsolete. However, certain principles should be followed when feeding hyperreactive (not hyperkinetic) dogs. These principles apply only to healthy animals, with no predisposition to kidney problems.

Feeding Hyper-Reactive Dogs

- Replace chlorinated or fluoridated water with unsoftened well or spring water, or distilled water.
- Eliminate all foods and treats containing artificial coloring, flavoring, preservatives or processed sugars.
- Feed a diet containing about 55% protein, 35% carbohydrate and 10% animal fat. The best sources for protein and

fat are ground lamb or ground whole chicken necks. Whole-grain rice is the best source of carbohydrate.

- Supplement the diet daily with a vitamin-mineral supplement, plus 500-1000 mg of niacinamide (nicotinamide).

Using this approach, many overactive dogs have calmed down to become normal, enjoyable pets. However, specific nutritional therapy may be required in the event certain dietary elements produce allergic reactions.

Artificial Additives

Dramatic improvement was reported in almost half of a group of hyperkinetic children when all artificial dietary elements were removed from their daily food intake.[1] When the children were again allowed to eat a hotdog and cola diet, the hyperkinetic syndrome returned. An FDA official confirmed the US Government's concern about the detrimental effects of artificial flavorings and coloring on human health.

This news is far from scientific proof that certain individuals, whether children or dogs, may be allergic to some artificial food elements, but I have noticed that some dogs become more calm when fed the previously mentioned 75% animal protein/25% commercial kibble diet. Perhaps this has nothing to do with the artificiality factor being lower in this diet. It may be the higher protein content that accounts for lower excitability.

Protein, Brain Function and Behavior

In a carefully controlled study, protein-starved animals were studied to evaluate the effects of protein depletion on various organs.[2] Examination of the brain revealed only a 14% average protein loss, as compared with gross depletion (27-65% or more) in other organs. Researchers concluded that, because it directs hunting/food-seeking behavior, the brain may have naturally evolved to be less susceptible to protein starvation. The animal can still find food if the liver or heart is failing, but not when the brain falters.

Protein-starved experimental animals exhibited no serious learning deficits regarding responses to aversive (shock) stimuli or maze problems involving food reward. However, the animals did have a lower threshold for electroconvulsive shock, that is, they convulsed at lower voltages than normal animals. The researchers tentatively concluded that a protein depletion of up to 14% in the mammalian brain does not appreciably affect learning, but slightly reduces excitability thresholds. This study raises interesting questions about the effects of protein, carbohydrate and fat ratios on the general level of excitability in mammals, particularly in problem dogs, most of which are excitable. However, there is a lack of such nutrition-behavior studies using dogs.

Studies on rats indicate that carbohydrate-rich diets can significantly increase levels of serotonin in the brain.[3] Serotonin (5-hydroxytryptamine) is an essential but still poorly understood chemical neurotransmitter found in greatest concentrations in the raphe nuclei of the medulla oblongata, which has a role in determining the general level of excitability. I do not wish to speculate on the role of serotonin in canine behavior. What is pertinent is that the ratios between carbohydrate, protein and fat intake may produce both immediate and long-term changes in the amount of some neurotransmitters in the brain. It now remains to relate this to certain dietary effects on behavior.

Stress Diets

Conditions that can create stress include surgery, pregnancy, lactation, demodectic mange, nonspecific dermatitis, and many other diseases. Canine nutrition manuals emphasize feeding stressed dogs a relatively high-protein diet, with moderate amounts of fat and high-quality carbohydrate. Such a diet is expressed by the following dry weight percentages: 46% carbohydrate (maximum), 29% protein (minimum), and 10% fat (minimum).[2]

The carbohydrate to protein ratio in the example is obviously not representative of a *strictly* high-protein diet, but the protein level is high relative to the amount of other ingredients. Unfortunately, it may be difficult to determine the ratio of dry weight components, as most commercial dog food manufacturers do not state the percentage of carbohydrate in their products.

The nonspecific excitability of rats, ascertained by measuring the rats' general investigatory activity, susceptibility to noxious stimuli and libido, was lowered by a diet high in protein (60% protein-calories), and low in carbohydrate-calories (27%), with fat-calories at 13%. Working with proper controls and using animals bred as either excitable or inhibitable, general levels of excitability could actually be manipulated with diet changes.[2] Increased potassium in the diet further calmed excitable types if a high-protein, low-carbohydrate diet was fed. This sort of dietary adjustment requires a healthy animal, of course, but more investigation by canine nutritionists and behaviorists may be fruitful in terms of maintaining less excitable and hence less problematic dogs.

One difficulty in assessing dietary effects on dog behavior lies in the fact that several days to several weeks are required before changes are discernible. Because my work involves external behavioral controls as well as dietary adjustment, I have been unable to accurately assess dietary effects alone. However, we do note some changes in excitable animals when diets are adjusted by feeding higher protein and lower carbohydrate levels:

- Conditioning to commands and signals is better retained.
- The dogs appear less hyperresponsive to incidental stimuli from the environment, such as other dogs barking or cars backfiring.

We have supplemented these diets with vitamin B-complex in most cases. The well-known detrimental effects on the nervous system and behavior in cases of thiamin and niacin deficiencies are often revealed in poorly conditioned reflex formation before they become clinically apparent. Therefore, it is good "insurance" when working with problem dogs to give a B-complex supplement even though they appear healthy.

High-carbohydrate, low-protein diets have not been used in our programs extensively because clients rarely complain that the problem dog is lethargic. Therefore, there is rarely a need for a pep-up diet. We may have to wait for an objective analysis of how diet affects human behavior before such information can be applied to dogs and their behavioral quirks. In the meantime, these guidelines may help control possible aggravating effects of an improper diet.

Food Allergies

When hypersensitivity to nutritional elements is suspected, an elimination diet can be used to determine the offending element(s).[4] This is a veterinary diagnostic procedure and, as such, is beyond the intended scope of this book.

Senility

Many older dogs seem to "forget" their housetraining rules. This may be a sign of senility. Some older dogs appear not to recognize their owners or other familiar people. Studies with elderly people indicate that dietary supplementation with choline often produces dramatic improvements in patients with progressive memory loss.[5-8]

I was fortunate to meet Dr. S.J. Harless during a staff-training program at his clinic in Omaha, and become aware of his work with geriatric dogs and cats. Our own Norwegian Elkhound had become lethargic and appeared to have "forgotten" some simple command responses. Because Dr. Harless had extensive clinical experience with choline supplementation, we began supplementing Randy's daily diet. Within 4 days the dog was literally puppyish. At the time, he had been on a hypoallergenic diet for several years and had no health problems requiring medication. Therefore, the rejuvenation process could only be credited to the supplement. Since that time, we have consulted with many clients whose veterinarians also have prescribed such supplements with beneficial results.

References

1. Feingold BF: *Why Your Child Is Hyperkinetic.* Random House, New York, 1974.
2. Lat J, in Kare MR: *The Chemical Senses and Nutrition.* Johns Hopkins Univ Press, Baltimore, 1967.
3. Fernstrom JD and Wurtman RJ: *Science,* Feb, 1974.
4. Plechner AJ and Zucker M: *Pet Allergies.* Very Healthy Enterprises, Inglewood, CA, 1986.
5. Goodman LS and Gilman AG: *The Pharmacological Basis of Therapeutics.* 6th ed. Macmillan, New York, 1980.
6. Wurtman RJ: Nutrients that modify brain function. *Scientific American,* 1982.
7. Rosenburg GS and Davis KL: The use of cholinergic precursors in neuropsychiatric diseases. *Am J Clinical Nutrition,* Oct, 1982.
8. Harless SJ and Turbes CC: Choline loading: specific dietary supplementation for modifying neurologic and behavioral disorders in dogs and cats. *Vet Med/Small Animal Clinician,* Aug, 1982.

6

Correcting Problem Behavior: Introduction

The next few pages describe how dogs perceive the world around them, and how dogs apparently think. We will not theorize about where and how information is stored in the brain, nor the processes involved in recalling it. These mechanisms remain almost as mysterious today as when Karl Lashley, the pioneer of investigations into the subject, said after 30 years' work: "I sometimes feel in reviewing the evidence on the localization of the memory trace, that the necessary conclusion is that learning is just not possible."

In spite of this, we can theorize what dogs and people experience during the process of thinking. This is central to understanding the development and treatment of behavior problems in dogs. Once this concept is understood, correctional programs emphasizing positive procedures and avoiding physical or psychological negatives can be appreciated for more than their humane aspects. The reasons these methods are effective will become evident.

How Do Dogs Think?

People generally find it difficult to think like a dog. Most dog owners assume their pets think like people, ascribing to them mental abilities far beyond what they actually possess.

Because dogs do not use words to communicate, we can assume that they do not use words to think about their daily activities or to remember experiences, people, objects or their environment. For example, a chewing dog who was severely whipped by its owner at homecoming yesterday does not think today, "George is due home in a few minutes. I wonder if I'll get a whipping today!" More likely, the dog may recall "images" of yesterday's experience. Despite this difference, the anatomy and other functional aspects of human and canine brains are remarkably similar.

Dogs have been used in comparative behavioral studies to better understand human neurophysiologic processes, mostly in Russia and Poland. Western scientists have tended to favor primates, cats and rodents. Studies published by Pavlov, and later by Konorski, have provided valuable insight into many functions of the human brain. Because dogs were their research models, a great deal was also revealed about how dogs perceive the world, learn from their experiences and "think." The following observations are of great interest.

Significant Observations

In many of his dogs, Konorski noted events he described as "hallucinations." These involved the visual, tactile, auditory and gustatory/olfaction senses.

Visual: A dog was conditioned to salivate upon exposure to a flickering light while food was simultaneously offered. Thereafter, during pauses between presentations of the light, the dog would spontaneously react with salivation and turn its head, as if actually seeing the food.

Tactile: A dog was trained to lift a foreleg and place it on a feeder tray in response to a tactile stimulus on that leg. During pauses, the dog would often spontaneously place its foreleg on the box, though no stimulus had been given.

Auditory: A dog trained to lift its foreleg at the sound of a buzzer would spontaneously turn toward the buzzer's location during pauses, and lift its leg, as if the buzzer had actually sounded.

Gustatory/Olfactory: Dogs trained to respond to various types of stimuli that signaled introduction of a mild acid into their mouth reacted to the conditioned stimulus with the same vigorous mouthing and salivation elicited by the acid itself. In this case, no reactions were noted between trials.

Konorski suggested that conditioned stimuli can produce not only a particular trained *behavior* (motor movement), but also a *mental image* of the original unconditioned stimulus that produced the behavior. The term "mental image" is not limited to a *visual* picture of the original unconditioned stimulus, but to its *total sensory effect*, such as odor, flavor, tactile effect and sound.

This is especially significant when considered along with work by Rusinov, who performed electroencephalographic examinations on dogs. By accident, the equipment was not shut off one weekend, and recorded readings from a dog in its kennel. During the weekend, the dog's brain emitted wave forms almost identical to those recorded during conditioning sessions. It was as if the dog were mentally reliving its weekday experiences.

Perceptions and Mental Images

These findings provide insight into canine thought processes. Most of us can envision, say, a loved one, even with our eyes open. Further, we can usually "hear" the sound of their voice as they say our name. It is also possible to create such mental images regarding emotionally pleasant or unpleasant experiences. For instance, I can vividly envision my first bicycle, as well as the wild-eyed motorcyclist who separated my knee joint one day. Such mental images are etched in all our memories.

The term "perception" refers to the sensory information that registers in our brain, as well as the way we interpret this information. "Images" are what we retain and can readily recall of those perceptions, including all of their sensory elements. Some images (memories) can be repressed beyond conscious recall, such as often happens after traumatic experiences.

Such imagery is not limited to incoming sensory perceptions. It also includes emotions stimulated by the original perceptions. For example, we can recall and feel again the happiness of seeing a loved one after their absence, or the sadness of hearing about another's death. By the same token, I readily re-experience the anger, though at a reduced level, I felt if I recall a man I once saw whipping his dog.

Mental images associated with painful experiences may not be accompanied by actual pain, but they can produce negative emotional impressions. On the other hand, recalling a favorite comedian may not actually make us laugh, but we will usually feel emotionally positive. It is these positive and negative emotional aspects that have an important effect on dog behavior and behavioral problems, as we will see.

Learning and Memory

Konorski postulated that a dog's memories are comprised of mental images and are the result of what he termed "unitary perceptions" of experiences. That is, all of the sensory input and the emotional associations of experiences are stored in memory, with links to the various sensory, motor, visceral and emotional centers in the brain.

This sort of memory is believed to be stored so that information on objects, people, other animals, total contexts, odors and emotions can be used to guide the animal's behavior when these elements are encountered again. For instance, a juvenile wolf pup, once charged by a bear, would not live long if it had no memory of that harrowing experience to guide it in future encounters. With its memory of the previous experience, the mere scent of a bear would probably cause the pup to avoid contact with the bear.

Memory images in people tend to be more vivid when the experiences these images represent elicit a marked emotional reaction, especially fear, pain, anger, love or hate. If we consider hunger to be an emotion, as many behaviorists do, then it makes sense that images of food or of eating would be more vivid if we are hungry. Further, the emotional reaction to food would be much weaker if we are feeling "full." In fact, many fully sated people feel negative reactions, even nausea, when their favorite food is presented or even imagined.

Much of the foregoing discussion is based on studies of human subjects. However, some of these results can be extrapolated to dogs. For instance, any experienced professional dog trainer knows that a hungry dog will learn and perform already learned routines with more motivation than one that has just eaten its fill.

154

Sensory Priorities

It has been suggested that smell is the dominant canine sense. That is, smell is the dog's primary sense for identifying objects, people, animals, locations and even situations, as in the wolf pup and the charging bear mentioned earlier. So strong is this sense that many dogs appear not to hear their shouted name or feel a swat on the rump while sniffing a neighborhood canine scent post. In such situations, I have waved my hand across their eyes without eliciting a normal blink reflex. It appears that a strong olfactory stimulus can override any other competing sensory input unless it is exceptionally strong.

In contrast, I have found that a sudden auditory stimulus, such as a loud handclap next to the dog's ear, can produce a momentary motor response, ranging from an ear flick to a full-body jerk. This auditory reflex is an invaluable tool in correction programs. It appears to momentarily suppress or interrupt other mental activity. We can then use the time immediately following that sensory suppression to divert the dog's attention to more acceptable behavior. This is why we use a handclap or some other startling sound at the instant a dog perceives a stimulus that triggers unwanted behavior, to be followed by the Jolly Routine (see Chapter 7) or some other remedial action.

Practical Applications

Consider a dog that has become aggressive with arriving visitors. Such dogs usually are initially scolded, physically punished, and denied access to visitors, all of which formed negative memory images, including their emotional content. These negative images are activated at the first sound, sight or odor of subsequent visitors. The images associated with visitors are of the punishment the dog experienced. Though the dog, as an unruly youngster, may have once held positive images of visitors, the increasing strength of the owner's punishment eventually creates dominant negative images.

Before they become aggressive, most dogs with this behavior proceed through an intermediate stage, in which they exhibit anxiety as whining, pacing or barking when visitors arrive.

In correcting such behavior without further punishment or other negative treatment, the auditory reflex must be triggered the instant the dog senses visitors. Then a known positive stimulus must dominate the dog's senses. Eventually the dog associates visitors with positive images, without the need for handclapping or another auditory stimulus. This procedure may have to begin when a car door slams and then progress to the doorbell's ring, opening the door, and visitors entering, culminating with the visitors' petting the dog.

This procedure does not erase former negative images. Rather, new, positive experiences evolve to dominate recall processes.

Social/Sensory Aspects

Because the owner initially induced the negative associations with visitors, any negative images of the owners must be turned positive as well. It would be foolhardy, even dangerous, in such cases simply to suggest that the owners give the dog a tidbit or bounce a favorite ball so as to replace the negative images associated with visitors and the owner's punishment with positive images of food or a ball. This is particularly important in cases involving owners who are oversolicitous and inconsistent with their dogs and/or dogs that are bossy, leader types or that have assumed dominance over the owner through growling or biting. For this reason, as a foundation for virtually every correction program, we institute the "learn-to-earn" praise and petting ritual and other leader exercises (see Chapter 7). Also, scolding and all other forms of punishment are excluded so as to allow the dog to develop totally positive, nonconflicting perceptions of the owners. In this way, the dog's frustrations and anxieties about the owner are alleviated.

When we are frustrated or angry, we can talk about our feelings. For instance, we can tell a person who is aggravating us that they are doing or saying such-and-such and it is beginning to anger us, or that we will leave if they continue. If we find ourselves uneasy or anxious in another's presence, even if we do not understand why, we can either tell them and discuss it, or avoid their company. In dealing with our children, we explain that inappropriate behavior, if continued, will produce unpleasant consequences, such as a spanking or loss of privileges.

In contrast, dogs are limited to nonverbal communication and cannot be forewarned of the consequences of their behavior. Further, they cannot speak to tell us what is frustrating or angering them. Dogs *behave* in ways that reflect their feelings. This is not to say that a dog who chews up its owner's belongings is consciously trying to tell the owner it is angry about being left alone all day. Rather, the dog is communicating, probably without intent, that it is frustrated and misses the owner so much that it must taste objects that satisfy the gustatory/olfactory elements of its relationship to the owner. If the dog cannot see, touch and hear the owner, it can at least smell and taste the owner's belongings.

As with any theory, this concept of unitary perceptions is useful only so long as it: helps to explain to dog owners and behaviorists the processes of canine thought and, hence, behavior; and proves itself when the resulting methods are effectively *applied* to behavioral problem cases. At the time the first edition of this book was published, only my own clinical applications validated the concept. Since then, however, hundreds of behavioral consultants and countless dog owners have successfully applied its positive methods. Therefore, it seems appropriate to explain their theoretical and scientific basis in this second edition.

(This page intentionally left blank)

7

Puppy Behavior Problems

From the moment an individual or family decides to adopt a puppy, the quality of their mutual relationship depends on the way the owners choose to live with their new pet. The following information is designed to help owners select a puppy best suited to the personalities of its new owners, and to establish a rewarding relationship through enlightened care and handling practices.

All of the programs to train puppies and correct behavior problems described herein avoid scolding and physical punishment. Instead, the recommended correctional and training techniques use distraction followed by praise and redirection of the puppy's attention to desirable objects or activities. In this way, negative social associations are avoided and the relationship between owner and pup develops within a framework of positive interactions. This minimizes stress for all parties concerned.

One of the most frequently asked questions about these techniques is, "How can a puppy learn *not* to do something unless it learns that the behavior is *wrong*, or that I don't *want* it to behave that way?" The answer is that "right" and "wrong," as people understand them, are verbal-intellectual ideas that probably cannot be learned by dogs. However, puppies do learn quickly that behavior A will be interrupted by the owner, who guides it to behavior B, which is rewarded. While the pup may not learn that A begets the owner's disapproval through scolding or physical punishment, it readily learns that B is more attractive than A. Within a general environment in which the puppy learns to earn its social rewards, this sort of correction technique harmonizes well with its natural tendency to be and act like its leaders.

Since publication of the first edition of this book in 1975, I have heard from thousands of dog owners who have followed these principles faithfully and enjoyed what they described as the "best dog we ever had." During the same time, I have also spoken with many who have modified or combined the advice with various techniques, with less than satisfactory results. The obvious conclusion is that the program should not be tampered with. Only minor changes, mostly clarifications, have been made for this second edition.

A Behavior Test for Puppy Selection

Once a particular breed or mixed-breed litter has been selected from which to choose a puppy, the prospective owner is faced with a crucial decision: Which puppy should we choose? My interviews with clients indicate that most choices are based on the following considerations, in order of decreasing importance.

1. Physical appearance.

2. Behavior toward the prospective owner while with the litter.

3. Behavior toward littermates.

Unfortunately, a pup's behavior toward the prospective owner(s), without the social competition of its littermates, is seldom observed until after the adoption or purchase has been finalized. Too often this results in disappointment when the formerly friendly puppy avoids the owner in the new home. The former litter "wallflower" may then display excessive nipping, which had been suppressed within the litter.

I developed the following behavior test to minimize such misreadings and allow the prospective owner to experience at least the initial one-on-one behavioral tendencies of puppies while among the litter.

The prospective buyer should call to explain his or her intentions to the breeder, whose cooperation is vital, as the breeder must arrange the isolated area and the time required for the testing. It takes only about an hour to test a litter of 12 pups. Considering that a dog's lifetime companionship is at stake, it is time well spent. This test presumes that the puppy buyer has chosen the breed s/he desires and that all family members favor adopting a puppy. Family friction caused by a new puppy is the leading cause of puppy behavior problems. The best time to take pups home from the litter is at 7 weeks of age, and certainly no earlier than 6 weeks nor later than 8 weeks.

The examiner, alone, should take each pup singly to an isolated area new to the pup and as free of distractions as possible. The pups must be handled gently, with no spoken urging or praise during the test. If a pup urinates or defecates during the test, it should be ignored, as this is not uncommon. After all, housebreaking is yet to be learned by the puppy. Any mess should be cleaned up after the pup has been returned to the litter.

The test consists of 5 parts. Puppies are graded according to their responses, as shown in Figure 1.

1. *Social Attraction:* Immediately upon entering the test area, place the pup down gently in the center of the area, step away from the pup several feet in the direction opposite the door or gate by which you entered the area, kneel down and gently clap your hands to attract the pup to you (Fig 2). How readily the pup comes to you, tail up or down, or if it does not come at all, reveals the pup's degree of social attraction, confidence or social independence. When it gets there, or does not, take out your test sheet and score appropriately. Put the sheet away and immediately continue with the next part.

2. *Following:* Starting from a position next to the pup, walk away in a normal manner (Fig 3). How readily the pup follows you (watch closely as you walk) reveals its degree of following attraction. In each case, however, make sure the pup actually sees you walk away before scoring it as independent.

3. *Restraint:* Crouch down and gently roll the pup onto its back, holding one hand on its chest until it calms (Fig 4). How strenuously the pup objects to this or how readily it accepts this

Figure 1. Score sheet for puppy behavior test.

	Assign each pup a letter (A, B, C, etc). Circle the code letters scored under each pup's letter in each test section.											
	A	B	C	D	E	F	G	H	I	J	K	L
1. Social Attraction												
Came readily, tail up, jumped, bit at hands	(dd)	dd	dd	dd	dd	dd	dd	dd	dd	dd	dd	dd
Came readily, tail up, pawed at hands	d	d	d	d	d	d	d	d	d	d	d	d
Came readily, tail down	s	s	s	s	s	s	s	s	s	s	s	s
Came, hesitant, tail down	ss	ss	ss	ss	ss	ss	ss	ss	ss	ss	ss	ss
Did not come at all	i	i	i	i	i	i	i	i	i	i	i	i
2. Following												
Followed readily, tail up, got underfoot, bit at feet	(dd)	dd	dd	dd	dd	dd	dd	dd	dd	dd	dd	dd
Followed readily, tail up, got underfoot	d	d	d	d	d	d	d	d	d	d	d	d
Followed readily, tail down	s	s	s	s	s	s	s	s	s	s	s	s
Followed, hesitant, tail down	ss	ss	ss	ss	ss	ss	ss	ss	ss	ss	ss	ss
Did not follow or went away	i	i	i	i	i	i	i	i	i	i	i	i
3. Restraint Dominance (30 seconds)												
Struggled fiercely, flailed, bit	(dd)	dd	dd	dd	dd	dd	dd	dd	dd	dd	dd	dd
Struggled fiercely, flailed	d	d	d	d	d	d	d	d	d	d	d	d
Struggled, then settled	s	s	s	s	s	s	s	s	s	s	s	s
No struggling, licked at hands	ss	ss	ss	ss	ss	ss	ss	ss	ss	ss	ss	ss
4. Social Dominance (30 seconds)												
Jumped, pawed, bit, growled	dd	dd	dd	dd	dd	dd	dd	dd	dd	dd	dd	dd
Jumped, pawed	d	d	d	d	d	d	d	d	d	d	d	d
Squirmed, licked at hands	(s)	s	s	s	s	s	s	s	s	s	s	s
Rolled over, licked at hands	ss	ss	ss	ss	ss	ss	ss	ss	ss	ss	ss	ss
Went and stayed away	i	i	i	i	i	i	i	i	i	i	i	i
5. Elevation Dominance (30 seconds)												
Struggled fiercely, bit, growled	dd	dd	dd	dd	dd	dd	dd	dd	dd	dd	dd	dd
Struggled fiercely	(d)	d	d	d	d	d	d	d	d	d	d	d
Struggled, settled, licked	s	s	s	s	s	s	s	s	s	s	s	s
No struggling, licked at hands	ss	ss	ss	ss	ss	ss	ss	ss	ss	ss	ss	ss

Totals:	dd's =	3
	d's =	1
	s's =	1
	ss's =	0
	i's =	0

Figure 2. Social attraction is tested by crouching and clapping the hands. This puppy approached with its tail up, and then nipped at the examiner's hands. Score: dd.

position indicates the degree of dominance or submissiveness relative to social/physical domination.

4. *Social Dominance:* Crouch and gently stroke the pup, from the top of its head, backward along the neck and back (Fig 5). Whether or not the pup accepts this indicates its degree of acceptance of your social dominance or lack of it. Highly dominant pups will try to dominate the examiner by jumping up or

Figure 3. The following test stimulated this puppy to race ahead of the examiner and challenge her progress, biting at her ankles and feet. Score: dd.

Figure 4. Restraint dominance caused wild flailing of the legs and biting by this puppy. Score: dd.

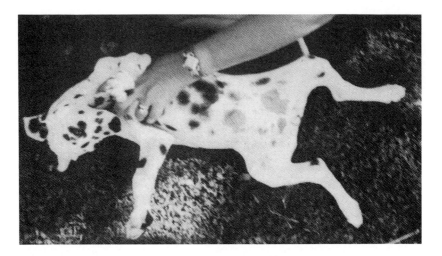

even biting and growling. The independent pup may simply walk away. In all cases, continue stroking the pup until a clearly recognizable behavior is established. Then score the pup.

5. *Elevation Dominance:* Bend over and cradle the pup under its belly, fingers interlaced and palms up, and elevate it just off

Figure 5. Social dominance of petting quieted this puppy, stimulating only a few licks at the examiner's hands and knees. Score: s.

164

the ground (Fig 6). Hold it there for 30 seconds. The pup has no control in this position, and the tester has total control. How readily it does or does not accept this situation indicates the degree to which it accepts your dominance. Gently put the pup down and score.

At this point, the pup, no matter how it responded, should be petted, praised and gently carried back to the litter. The next pup should then be tested. All pups must be tested in exactly the same manner for a true indication of behavior tendencies.

What the Score Totals Indicate

Two or more dd responses, with d's in other sections: These pups tend to react in dominant aggressive ways and may bite when handled. A poor environment for this type of pup is one in which small children or elderly people will contact the pup, as the nipping behavior may lead to problems. A fairly calm, adult household and nonphysical teaching methods best suit this type of pup, tending to mold a fine pet capable of aggressive protective actions in time of genuine danger.

Three or more d responses: These pups tend to be fairly outgoing and dominant. Consistent, gentle training methods yield quick learning. Small children in the home are not best for this type of pup.

Figure 6. Elevation dominance produced violent struggling but no vocal reaction in this pup. Score: d.

Three or more s responses: These pups probably fit most environments and are the best for children and elderly people.

Two or more ss responses, especially with one or more i responses: These are highly submissive pups that need plenty of praise and gentle handling to build confidence and bring them fully into the human environment. Normally safe with children, this type usually bites only when threatened severely, and even then only to protect itself.

Two or more i responses, especially if an i is scored in the Social Dominance section: These pups probably will not socialize quickly and may be difficult to train without special techniques. If they also have dd and d responses, they may even attack under such stress as traditional punishment. If they also have ss and/or s responses, they will tend to shy away under stress. These types usually do not interact well with small children.

A Mixed Bag: When a pup scores what appears to be contradictory results, such as dd's with ss's, it is best to repeat the test in another area new to the pup. Repeated mixed results indicate a pup who may behave unpredictably in the future, and may require special handling.

Final Considerations

A pup's score on the test may seem inconsistent with its behavior when in the litter. This is not unusual, as each litter has its own "pecking order." A pup that scored dominant in the handling test might not seem so with littermates because it ranks low or is even submissive when relating to littermates. If getting along with other dogs is important to the prospective owner, some time should be spent watching littermates interact.

It must be kept in mind that behavioral *tendencies* are being tested. The final and deciding factors in how the adult dog actually behaves tend to derive more from a pup's early experience in the human environment than from its litter. However, pups that are constantly vocal during the test may well respond vocally to later stressful situations. These pups may not be best for apartment dwellers but may be well suited to home owners.

Any test administered by a prospective owner is influenced by his or her emotional reactions to the pups. The results, therefore, lack the objectivity normally desirable in scientific testing. However, because our interest is in the pup's behavioral responses to typical people, this seems a necessary feature for optimum satisfaction. This fact also dictates that the test results are valid only for the particular examiner and may not be applicable to others. Each prospective owner must do the testing individually.

Final selection of one pup rests with the examiner, of course. This test is designed to assist the prospective owner to select a pup s/he feels most suited to the home environment and to avoid pups whose behavioral tendencies might be aggravated in this environment.

Introducing the New Puppy

When a pup is finally selected, it faces one of the most upsetting experiences of its young life: the transition from canine to human companionship. Whether or not this occurs during the 8- to 10-week fear imprint period, and the way it is handled by the new owners can shape a pup's initial and long-term behavior.

The Ride Home

If the pup is taken home in an automobile, it should ride beside the owner, or on his or her lap. Most pups whine during the ride, but the hum and sway of the ride usually put them to sleep within a few minutes. It is important to avoid any coddling in response to whining. This can teach the pup that whining is a way to gain sympathy, and the pup may use this throughout life as a way to attract attention when upset. It is better to keep close physical contact during the ride, making no special responses to whining. Above all, do not punish or scold it for whining or trying to investigate its surroundings during the ride. Merely holding the pet close in the lap and petting it when it settles are more appropriate. If the pup gets sick and vomits, make no special fuss. Just clean it up and remain neutral emotionally. Otherwise, a lifetime of carsickness may be imprinted.

The New Home

On arrival at its new home, the puppy should be first taken to the spot that will be its permanent toilet area. After the car ride, it will need to eliminate, and training to the toilet area should begin immediately. When the pup performs its duty, enthusiastic praise should be given at the site of urination or defecation. The owner should crouch right down, pointing at the spot and praising until the pup shows some sign of recognition of the waste matter.

The puppy should then be taken into the house and allowed to investigate freely. A regular dog bed or some type of bedding material should be placed where the puppy can find it when sleepy. A meat-scented nylon bone should be given to the pup for chewing. Avoid chewables that are easily destroyed or that resemble leather or fabric, as puppies tend to generalize chewing to other inappropriate articles of the same type of texture. If the pup shows no interest in the hard bone, it is advisable to play with the bone, teasing the pup to gain interest. If the pup shows chewing interest in electrical cords, shoes and socks, the bone should be introduced until it becomes recognized as *the* most desirable chewable item. Avoid punishment or tugging to remove inappropriate items from its mouth. Simply distract the pup's attention and then introduce the bone.

Housetraining

Have the water bowl and food dish placed adjacent to the door that leads out of the house to the established toilet area. If possible, design the situation so that the pup does not have to negotiate a maze to get from the feeding and watering spot to the toilet area. Providing as straight a course as possible simplifies housetraining.

During the remainder of the first day or evening, the puppy should be watched carefully and taken to the toilet area following eating or drinking, excitement, waking (even from a brief nap), chewing activity and vigorous sniffing. These are prime times for teaching the route to the toilet area and praising the animal for proper performance. Most mothers recognize this regimen as a standard potty-training procedure for children. Happily, pups learn much more quickly than children.

Social Aspects

During its first day in a new home, a puppy is naturally the object of attention and great excitement. First impressions are particularly lasting in pups, so it is important to make the first day as smooth as possible. Without creating a false and inhibited social atmosphere, it is best to be straightforward in the treatment of a new puppy. Overexciting it through excessive play or emotional displays may predispose the puppy to such behavior when the novelty has worn off. The result can be a pup that pesters its people for attention and then suffers the inconsistency of being scolded or punished for behaving in the very way it was taught to behave. Puppies normally let people know when they need physical comfort by approaching them and whining. At these times it is a good idea to pick up and comfort the pup, which demonstrates owner dominance. This should take no longer than a couple of minutes and is well worth the time spent.

Sleeping Arrangements

The first night in new surroundings is also a critical time for a puppy. If left alone in a strange area, most puppies whine, squeal and perhaps bark. This experience can lay the foundation for a lifelong fear of isolation, which, in turn, causes tension and the well-known cycle of tension-relieving behaviorisms, such as chewing, scratching, digging and barking.

The best solution is to place the pup's bed in someone's bedroom, preferably right next to the bed. If an overturned cardboard carton, with a little doorway cut out, is placed over the pup's bed, most pups sleep through the night (Fig 7). This arrangement has the added advantage of keeping the pup under surveillance for housetraining purposes. First thing in the morning, the pup can be shown out to its toilet spot and praised after elimination.

Most puppies enjoy the cozy atmosphere of their beds and actually begin to seek it during the daytime for naps. The bed can be placed in other areas of the house, such as the living room, family room, etc. This can become a further aid in housetraining, as most pups will not soil in the immediate area of their beds.

Feeding Times

The food fed by the breeder should be continued for at least 4 days after the puppy is brought home. Any change in diet should be done in gradual increments (see Chapter 5) to avoid digestive upset and related housetraining problems. Pups have poor con-

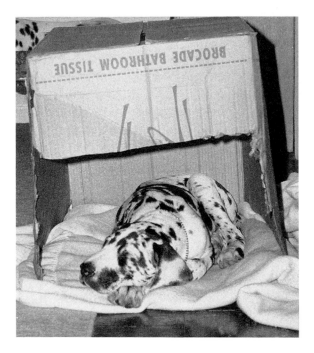

Figure 7. Most puppies enjoy the cozy atmosphere of an overturned cardboard box. Some even retreat to the box for daytime naps.

trol over loose stools, which often occur with radical dietary changes, and they cannot be blamed for resulting accidents.

A regular feeding schedule should be developed. If the owners work or are away on weekends, the pup should not be fed during those hours on the weekend. To do so would introduce a basic biological inconsistency into the animal's life that may cause anxiety when food is not forthcoming at the anticipated time.

Summary

Owners should show calm consistency during a pup's introduction to its new home. This avoids the risk of traumatic impressions associated with car rides, toilet duties, isolation from people, and feeding times, which may lead to problems later in life. If the transition from litter to human environment is accomplished smoothly, guided by confident and reassuring owners, the pup will tend to perceive the experience with emotional maturity. The procedures outlined above will not toally eliminate the pup's emotional stress, but they will minimize it and facilitate easier initial training within the new home.

Social Attraction

Despite the myth that a dog must be at least 6 months old to be trained, puppies as young as 5 weeks of age can be trained to some extent. Such early training takes advantage of a unique behavioral trait called *social attraction*.

Social attraction refers to the natural tendency of a pup to follow or attempt to be near its owners. Just as it is natural for a puppy to want to remain near its littermates, puppies also want to remain near their human companions when their littermates are no longer available. This natural tendency can be used to advantage during early training.

The threatening sounds and gestures of scolding or physical punishment, or the loud "whap" of rolled newspaper on the rump or a table top, can negate the positive effects of social attraction. While trying to teach "No, don't ever do that!", the owner actually stimulates the dog's reflex to fight, freeze or take flight. An 8- to 10-week-old puppy may develop a permanent fear imprint. The outcome may be a dog that is forever unsure of its relationship with the owner, and is panicked by fireworks, auto backfires and other loud noises. In the meantime, any attempt at correcting inappropriate behavior is rarely if ever permanently successful, and the owner's relationship with the pet deteriorates. Such treatment does not mean "No" in canine language.

Petting is another abused form of communication with dogs. When petted for no reason other than merely being there, a dog is soon spoiled. It becomes the canine counterpart of an over-indulged child, whose attitude is "The world owes me a living." In the world of dogs, it is the underlings that pet (groom) the "boss" dogs. So the coddled pup soon assumes a dominant leader role with its subordinate people. It begins leading the pack, even running away when called, given the chance. The more the owner chases, the more the puppy learns it can indeed lead.

The underlying problem may be the vocal/verbal abilities of people. Verbal language suppresses the need for more primitive, nonverbal forms of communication. Pet owners have lost their "animal sense," but somehow they expect their dog to learn words associated with physical punishment or manipulation, which is virtually impossible for dogs.

How can an owner effectively communicate with and "teach" a 6-week-old rough-and-tumble puppy? Every new puppy owner should take the pet out to strange, new (but not frightening) places and merely walk away from the pup, crouching down to praise it when it starts to follow. By following this procedure in several different areas and situations, the owner can develop a deep and lasting "leader imprint" in the puppy's mind (Fig 8).

The Role of Praise

In daily life with the puppy, praise and petting should be used as a reward when the pup actually does something the owner desires. Otherwise, praise should be withheld. When a new command is taught, the owner should accompany it with some physical sign to show the pup its meaning. As quickly as the puppy starts to make the proper movement, it should be praised. When the pup completes the desired action, it should be gently petted, preferably on the throat and chest.

An example of this highly effective form of instrumental conditioning involves teaching "Sit." If the puppy's name is followed by the word "Sit," and the hand is held about 3 feet above and slightly behind the pup's head, the pup will sit so as to keep its eye on the hand. After 3-20 such commands, the pup should sit without the hand signal. Each time the pup's haunches even begin to sink, the pup should be praised.

Figure 8. By merely walking away from this 11-week-old Springer Spaniel, this owner established an early leadership position with his puppy. Not wanting to be abandoned by his "leader," the pup follows.

Teaching sessions should be short, no longer than a few minutes, and should end with much praise and petting. A puppy so treated soon learns it must earn rewards of praise and petting from its "leader." In the family situation, all members should teach the puppy as a demonstration of consistency among the pup's people.

A puppy assuming a "follower" role with family members gains a behavioral foundation that makes all of life's later lessons more easily learned. Subordinate (follower) dogs do not violate (chew) their leader's belongings, steal their food, soil their property (house), etc. Therefore, a solid leader relationship with one's dog has the added advantage of avoiding most unwanted behavior associated with family dogs. This in itself seems a worthy goal for every dog owner to seek.

Most older dogs also respond well to this same regimen of teaching. However, because months or years usually precede such behavioral therapy, during which the dog has assumed dominance, the owner must be prepared to spend more time than is involved with a puppy. Two field trips on each weekend, coupled with short, happy daily teaching sessions, should span a 6-week period. Most dog owners begin to note that their dog is keeping track of them, rather than *vice versa*, on the second or third such field expedition.

A Natural Method of Housetraining

A factor common to all failed attempts by owners trying to train a dog or correct inappropriate behavior is that the dog appears to have no inkling that its owner is trying to *teach* something. This communication gap is never more painfully apparent than in housetraining procedures.

Puppies first become fastidious and avoid "messing" in their den area at about 5 weeks of age. If we can use this tendency in the pup's new home with people, the housetraining chore can be accomplished within days, rather than in weeks or months. The prerequisite is to *make the animal aware that we are actually going to teach it*. This is most easily done by first teaching a simple command, such as "Come." Most normal dogs or pups respond to the traditional method of teaching this command. It involves putting a long (15- to 30-foot) lead on the collar, then gently jerking the lead as the word "Come" is spoken, praising any movement toward the teacher. This method is time consuming but eventually effective.

Many pups that are either highly excitable, inhibitable or independent, however, may not respond to this type of training. At our faciltities, we prefer nonphysical techniques involving "body language," plus praise reinforcement. These take advantage of the dog's natural ability to communicate and avoid negative factors involved in physical methods.

Even the simplest command to "Sit," "Stay" and "Down" begins to establish a dominant leadership position for the owner. Regardless of which lesson is taught first, the first step toward housetraining is achieved; the owner is teacher, and the dog is the "student." The very first teaching session lays the groundwork for subsequent housetraining.

Most of us cannot recall how long (usually months) it took for our parents to potty train us. If we did, perhaps we would marvel at the fact that a pup can learn the procedure in a matter of days. Interestingly, the regimen is about the same for babies as for pups and older dogs.

Step 1

The first step is to feed a balanced, complete diet in accordance with veterinary guidance. Quantity and schedule must be adjusted so the pup produces firm, formed stools at every bowel movement. I generally recommend that the number of feedings equal the number of bowel movements. If the stools are loose, the feed quantity should be decreased 10%. This assumes that the stools are not loose because of internal parasites or another medical problem. The amount fed is continually reduced until a firm stool is produced. If the stools are chalky and very dry, the quantity fed should be increased until a firm but moist stool is achieved. A dog suffering from either constipation or overly loose stools cannot be expected to control its bowel movements on a schedule. I meet several owners a week who have been severely punishing diarrheic animals for something they themselves could not regulate.

When a dog feels the urge to urinate or defecate, it is not readily susceptible to conditioning (learning). Once the animal forms a habit of eliminating in one particular place, it usually seeks that spot when it feels the urge to eliminate. Therefore, it makes sense to teach the dog that the toilet area is a positively rewarding location. The location of the toilet area should be selected for easy accessibility, especially after mealtimes. For this reason, doggy doors are a boon to simplified housetraining.

The dog should be urged toward this location after meals, following every drink of water observed, upon awakening (even from a nap), after excitement and after any prolonged chewing on its toys. These are all times at which the animal may feel the urge to urinate or defecate. Once the pet begins to use that spot, whether it is on newspaper in an apartment or in the backyard of a house, we are ready to undertake Step 2 in housetraining. Most dogs learn their proper toilet area in 36-48 hours.

Step 2

Learning when and where *not* to urinate or defecate is the step that completes total housetraining of any dog, young or old. If the animal is alone from 8:00 AM to 5:30 PM, 5 days a week, it is folly to spend these hours playing doorman on the weekend days. Sphincter control can only be taught by keeping the dog inside the house and distracting it from urinating or defecating. During the hours when the pup is to be prevented from eliminating, it is helpful to take up its water bowl; in problem cases, give water only at mealtimes. This avoids triggering the reflex urge to eliminate during confinement.

Such punishment as putting the dog's nose into its urine or feces, or swatting it with newspapers is ineffective and negatively reinforcing. At best, it relieves some of the owner's tension. A more natural approach when finding an "accident" is to wait until the dog notices it too, then growl at the mess and shoo the dog out to its proper area, cleaning up the mess in the dog's absence.

Another device that has been helpful, especially with pups or older dogs that sneak away to do their "duty" indoors, is to hang 1 or 2 little brass bells on the collar. This helps the owner hear the dog's movements around the house, and especially during the night, to perceive when the animal wakens and moves around. We always recommend that the pup or older offender sleep in the bedroom with the owner during the housetraining period.

If this natural plan for housetraining is followed by all family members, most pups and older dogs become reliably fastidious in their homes within a week, though some animals take longer. The steps in this natural method of housetraining are summarized in Table 1.

Barking Puppies

Before undertaking any course of correction for excessive barking, we must determine why excessive barking occurs in the first place. The usual reasons are to protest social isolation, to gain a response from another animal, object or person, and to express alarm at unidentified sounds, movements, objects or odors. Most pups that bark excessively are vocally oriented. That is, in almost any stressful situation, they tend to vocalize by barking, whining or howling.

Table 1. Steps in the natural method of housetraining. This guide assumes the dog to be in good health, without internal parasites. Therefore, before starting the program, a veterinary examination is advised.

---

1. Teach "Come," "Sit," or some command at least 2 times daily.

2. Feed at the same time every day for a formed, firm stool. If the stool is loose, cut the feed amount 10%; if the stool is dry, increase 10%. No tidbits or between-meal snacks.

3. Establish only 1 toilet area. Take the dog there after eating, drinking water, awakening, excitement or chewing on its toys.

4. Once the dog begins to seek its toilet place, be sure to distract it from urination or defecation in the house during the hours it will be left alone.

5. When an accident is discovered, do not make a fuss over it, except if the dog notices. Just growl at it, then shoo the dog out to the proper toilet place. Avoid punishment or social isolation. Do not let the animal see you cleaning up the mess.

6. If the pup is sneaky about housesoiling, as is often the case with dogs that have been punished for their accidents, hang a small brass bell on its collar. Have the pup sleep in your bedroom at night.

7. Take up drinking water at night or when the dog is left alone. In problem cases, give water with meals only.

The most important method of controlling barking in any type of puppy is to make sure that corrective steps do not actually *teach* the pup to bark. This is a common error made by many owners. Inadvertently they reinforce the behavior by responding in ways that, either positively or negatively, stimulate feedback. The idea that punishment can perpetuate problem behavior is difficult for many owners to grasp. But when it is explained that more than a single stimulus (punishment) is acting on the puppy, a degree of understanding is usually achieved. For instance, when a pup isolated in the kitchen or service porch barks, the purpose of the bark is to attract attention so as to gain relief from the emotional discomfort caused by loneliness. After enough vexation, the irate owner appears and administers some punishment aimed at quieting the pet.

What has actually occurred, however, is that the pup has achieved its goal: the owner's presence. This is a source of positive reinforcement, even if accompanied by a slap on the rump or snout. From the pup's standpoint, discomfort of punishment is better than isolation. Because barking provides some relief from isolation, the excessive barking is continued.

Isolation Barking

A highly verbal 4-month-old female Keeshond had been shut in the kitchen at night due to the owners' fear that chewing or housesoiling might occur if the dog were left free in the house. This isolation had been practiced since the pup was 8 weeks of age, and resulted in incessant barking. Every night the husband got up 4 or 5 times, trundled downstairs, and punished the animal for causing a disturbance. The barking was becoming louder as time went by.

Barking was not the only behavior complaint. The clients also objected to the pup's destructive chewing and constant nipping at their young children. Further, the pup took every opportunity to run away from the house. Exhaustive chases were required to trap and return the Keeshond. Another problem was that the wife did not want a dog and placed full responsibility for its behavior on her husband's shoulders, even though she spent most of her time with the puppy during the day.

Correction involved building the woman's sense of responsibility for the pup's behavior, as well as working with the various problems themselves. The family undertook a 6-week puppy behavior program involving off-leash training of the pet to respond to commands to Come, Sit, Stay, Heel, Lie Down and Go to its own bed.

Night barking was extinguished by sound distraction. This required that the husband spend the first few minutes after bedtime outside the kitchen door and apply corrections when any activity could be heard in the kitchen. This kept the puppy away from the door and in its bed. Barking disappeared after 3 weeks.

Ordinarily, the barking problem would be solved simply by moving the pup's bed into one of the bedrooms. However, the wife was adamant that this not be done, even if it became necessary to get rid of the Keeshond. Her excuses were simple: the son had asthma and she *refused* to have a dog in her own bedroom. This was a highly emotional issue with her. Whether it might have been due to embarrassment about permitting the animal to witness marital intimacies is unknown. However, sexual inhibition is common in such cases and involves men as well as women.

The owners elected the most difficult method of correction. The barking problem was replaced by nightly urination, probably as a result of the pup's continued frustration. Fortunately, standard housetraining procedures, involving taking up the water early in the evening and at night, corrected this secondary problem in a couple of weeks.

Isolation barking can be corrected by not isolating the puppy. If this is not possible, the owner must gain a strong leadership position with the pup and stop reinforcing the barking. A distracting stimulus is used to quiet the pup *before* the bark actually occurs (as the pup is preparing to bark). This sound stimulus causes a reflexive response away from the object or situation stimulating the barking. I use an ultrasonic device for this purpose (see Chapter 15), but other common noisemakers include bean bags tossed at the door, a metal plate dropped outside the door or behind the pup, a heavy rap on a window away from the bark-stimulus locale, rustling of crisp paper between the hands and other novel sounds. The principle is essentially the same, regardless of the device used.

This type of correction for isolation barking succeeds where others may fail because it conforms to conditioning principles known to extinguish certain behavior. That is, if the barking behavior is not reinforced, the behavior will eventually disappear. Some pups bark more persistently than others and therefore require more patience, which is the most important characteristic of those interested in raising a well-adjusted puppy.

Alarm Barking

A pup that barks at unidentified sounds, movements or odors is often reacting normally. Owners who want a watchdog often make the error of encouraging this type of barking by reinforcing it with excited comments after the pup barks, such as "What's that, Tippy?" This sort of reinforcement can condition an otherwise normal puppy to become a problem barker.

Some highly excitable pups often overdo their bark responses with no encouragement whatsoever. Others are vocally oriented and may not have had sufficiently varied early experience, especially during the 5th through 14th weeks of life. These puppies often bark and circle unfamiliar objects. These include both the aggressive and shy (regressive, flight) types of pups.

Alarm-barking puppies tend to bark whether the owners are home or absent. The problem is more easily corrected at this time than later. Older barking dogs typically have been "shushed" so often when the owners are home that they only carry on their vocal antics when the controlling influence is absent.

The most effective correction involves training the puppy to bark only at the exceptional events, objects, odors, etc. Barking at everyday or nonthreatening stimuli should be extinguished (not reinforced). If the problem of barking is viewed in this way by puppy owners, the result is usually a well-adjusted and dependable watchdog. The following routine can be used to train normal pups and correct problem barkers.

Barking Correction for Pups

Step #1: The owner should ask someone to make sounds outside the house or apartment, walk a dog outside the door or fence (if the pup is in a yard), or otherwise visually stimulate the pup in a way that has caused the problem barking in the past or may do so in the future. As soon as the pup barks a few times, the owner quietly calls the animal to different parts of the house. In other words, the pup is taught to sound the "alarm" and then to seek the owner. It is a desirable trait for a dog that will function well as a watchdog to seek out its owner in the event of trouble. When the pup responds, the owner quietly praises it and remains silent thereafter. If the pup turns again toward the stimulus, it is quietly called back until it settles with the owner. Make sure that the outside assistant does not create unnatural situations to stimulate barking. Heavy footsteps, jimmying the door, trying to open a window, etc, are good agitations, but they must not be overdone either in volume or duration.

Repeat this procedure until the pup automatically seeks the owner after a couple of barks. Allow at least 2 1/2 hours between training sessions. Hold at least 2 sessions per day until the puppy seeks the owner and remains quiet after the alarm barking, without being commanded to do so.

In this procedure, the owners should *avoid*:

- Scolding or otherwise loudly or angrily reinforcing the behavior.
- Holding shut the pup's mouth (this only frustrates the pet and may cause problem barking in the owner's absence).
- Physically punishing the puppy, as this may negatively reinforce the barking.

The teacher should behave as the pup is expected to behave: mutely. This exemplary behavior requires patience but teaches the pup without harmful side effects to the relationship between the pup and owner.

Step #2: The puppy that continually barks when alone must be dealt with after the barking is brought under control in the presence of the owners. When this is achieved, a second person should create a situation that triggers barking. Immediately following the bark stimulus, the owner must introduce a distracting stimulus that the pup associates with a feeling of well-being. Some quieting distractions can be the rattle of a dinner dish or a door knob, a radio coming on, etc (anything associated with quiet behavior). A distraction that has stimulated barking in the past should not be used.

In any of these situations, the interrupting stimulus must be one that is practical to apply until the puppy quiets for longer and longer periods, up to several hours, even when additional bark-inducing stimuli are introduced.

This procedure may be time consuming and laborious only if the owner neglects that first step in the correction procedure: to control barking when at home with the puppy. Pups have been successfully silenced with this method in only 1 day; others have taken as long as 2-6 weeks. If the procedure is applied regularly, both night and day, an acceptably nonvocal pet will result.

Barking at Animals, People or Objects

When a pup barks at other dogs, cats, people or unfamiliar objects, it is usually the result of some frustration. I once had an ear-wracking lunch with a young couple who had taught their 10-week-old Labrador Retriever to "speak" for tidbits. The pup made conversation virtually impossible and, worse yet, the sheer volume of its barking seemed to inhibit the flow of gastric juices necessary to digest what otherwise might have been a delicious meal. This case is described in detail in the section on Begging. I mention it here because it is a classic example of inadvertent operant conditioning.

Most pups between about 12 and 26 weeks of age begin announcing their presence to strangers, attracting the attention of their owners, sounding territorial alarms at other animals or otherwise trying to stimulate some sort of response from unidentified objects, odors, sounds or movements. The secret of curtailing this natural tendency is to avoid reinforcing the barking, and it usually fades away. This requires ignoring the behavior. To a puppy, the act of vocalizing appears to be identified as just that – vocalizing. Therefore, shouting at a vocalizing, vocally oriented puppy to obtain silence merely reinforces the barking.

When the barking is aimed at someone or something the pup perceives as threatening (though this is not so), the animal's interpretation of the stimulus must be altered. This process takes from a day to a few weeks, and requires the same initial procedures used in alarm barking. That is, the pup is allowed a couple of normal "alarm barks" at the new stimulus, and then is taught to seek the owner and remain silent. When this has been accomplished, the act of barking takes on a functional significance for the pet.

Eliminating the pup's misinterpretation of threat by certain people, objects or sounds require that the owner introduce the pet to these stimuli while reassuring it with good-natured and jolly (but low-volume) words and phrases. If a visitor stimulates this type of barking, the owner should approach that person and behave in a friendly manner, crouching down while demonstrating friendly trust as an invitation for the puppy to approach. The puppy should in no way be pulled or ordered to the guest. Rather, it should be allowed to gain confidence at a natural pace. It often helps if the guest assumes the same crouched position as the owner, but remains immobile and passive while the pet begins to gain confidence. I have had successes with especially vocal and fearful pups by having the stranger or guest lie face down on the floor while the pup investigates the individual.

This same method can be used with a barrier between the pup and the inciting stimulus. The puppy can be taken to the other side of the barrier, whether a gate, fence, door or window, and introduced to the stimulus in a friendly manner. When this concerns other animals, more time and effort are required to obtain the involved animals and have their owners cooperate in correction. The same happy, jolly routine must be undertaken by the owners in these situations.

Where this procedure does not succeed, the pup should be stimulated between the time of the pup's initial orientation to the inciting stimulus and its overt barking, followed by jolly reinforcement. If the problem is caused by an odor, sound or movement, the pup should be escorted happily to the area from which these emanate and allowed to investigate, while the owner reassures it that no real threat exists.

In cases of previously reinforced barking, such as the dinner scene described earlier, an intervening stimulus is almost prerequisite to success. These types of barking pups resemble what I call "gimme kids." They yap to achieve some specifically learned reinforcement, even if only to gain the owner's attention. Correction entails withholding reinforcement, or using some neutral intervening stimulus to interrupt the inclination to bark, with a subsequent reward. The latter method generally takes less time.

Summary

All puppies normally bark or otherwise vocalize. If later problem barking is to be avoided, it is best not to reinforce this natural barking and also to avoid deliberately teaching the pup to bark for tidbits or otherwise encouraging barking.

A highly vocal pup may develop into a problem barker because of isolation, alarm barking or reinforcement. In any case, corrective procedures should rely on immediate orientation to the owner, nonreinforcement and/or application of a neutral stimulus, causing the pup to orient away from the inciting stimulus and, in nonisolation cases, toward a reassuring, happy reinforcement. The owner must remain calm and pleasant to achieve success. The time required depends on the pup's degree of previous learning, its tenacity, the owner's skill and patience, and the strength of the stimulus causing the problem. Correction can be achieved in a day or up to 6 weeks.

Begging and Stealing Food

Learning to beg or steal food is the easiest of all life's lessons for a puppy. The art is most often taught by the pup's owners. In some cases, it is learned when food is accidentally dropped on the floor, or left unattended where the puppy can get at it.

Human taste discrimination is so crude when compared to the dog's that many owners fail to appreciate the folly of giving their pups little treats of the family food fare. Many times it only takes one taste of highly spiced table food to ruin a puppy's appreciation for its less-seasoned commercial diet. The result can be a pup that turns up its nose at dog food and becomes a roaring menace around the dinner table.

In the previous section I mentioned a hectic lunch spent with a young couple and their Labrador puppy. The barker made social interaction impossible, and produced dyspepsia in the owners. The solution was time consuming and nerve wracking. The couple obtained earplugs and spent more than 3 weeks ignoring the vociferous pet at mealtimes before the puppy finally gave up and stopped barking.

Correction

The natural method of extinguishing begging takes time. The time it takes depends on the duration of the habit, the pup's tenacity, and the consistency of its owners in carrying out corrective procedures. It requires that absolutely no attention be given the begging pup, regardless of its antics in trying to gain tidbits.

In the case of food stealing, the natural method of extinguishing the behavior requires even more careful control of the environment, especially when young children are involved. They usually love to share their goodies with their pets, but it is impractical to explain the cause-effect relationship to such youngsters when they complain that "Tippy jumped up and stole my ice cream cone!" Children also tend to leave articles of food around on low tables and chairs, an irresistible temptation for most puppies.

To eliminate stealing, whether it is overt (taking food from children) or covert (pilfering the thawing dinner steak), it is necessary to initiate a program of at least 4 weeks, during which no food is ever placed within the pup's reach. It goes without saying that no tidbits should be given during this period.

Remedies that often fail include lacing some food with pepper or ammonia, saying "No-no" while tempting the pup, and physically punishing the animal when it approaches the family's food. These fail because they require the presence of some agent other than the food, either the aversive-tasting element or the owner. When these elements are not present, the pup is rarely discouraged from stealing the food. It learns to discriminate between treated and untreated morsels, and to avoid food in the owner's presence.

Use of an intervening stimulus to interrupt the pup's impulse to take the food seems to work well if applied several times a day for about 6 weeks. However, few dog owners are motivated strongly enough to work at it with the required dedication. Therefore, the best approach is the natural method. This involves totally ignoring the pup's begging behavior, avoiding dropping food, avoiding all tidbitting, and not leaving "people" food within the pup's reach for at least 4 weeks, or until the puppy no longer seems attracted by human food. As mentioned, this is difficult when young children are involved, but it can succeed eventually through the process of extinction.

Biting and Mouthing

The wife of a financial tycoon arrived at my office with an 8-week-old male German Shepherd puppy whose first response to my efforts to stroke it was to bite my wrist. "See what I mean?" the client said, displaying her own ravaged hands and forearms. I assured her that I empathized, and stood up to avoid further pain, but the pup then tried to place its dental tattoo on my right ankle.

The client explained that the pup was a gift from a well-meaning friend who bred especially large German Shepherds, and that its biting might possibly become rather dangerous one day. Possibly? That was the understatement of the year. A pup that emerges from the litter with such highly developed aggressive responses can definitely be described as a potential menace.

This case was extreme. Such unprovoked aggression seldom occurs in pups. Biting and mouthing the hands, pants, cuffs and ankles of people are usually an extension of play-fighting behavior in early litter life. This tendency is aggravated by owners who deduce that the way to solve the problem is to fulfill the apparent need of the pup for such activity. This leads the owner to engage in often violent tug-o'-war games with the naturally aggressive pup. This reinforces the behavior and also places the owner in a physically competitive situation with the pet. In highly excitable pups, tug-o'-war has produced viciousness as early as 13 weeks of age.

Correction

Whether the biting has been learned from the litter, from overstimulation by the owners, or a combination of both, attempts at correction are usually successful if the owner has the patience and fortitude to carry them out. Observations of bitches with mouthy and biting pups provide a clue to the best way of discouraging this. When the pup begins biting, the dam simply freezes so as not to provide any sort of feedback to reinforce the onslaught. If this is not successful (as is the case with many very aggressive pups), the dam makes a quick, snarling and menacing move toward the offending pup. This usually puts the "fear of Mom" into the puppy (the dam already has attained a dominant position with the litter) and stops the irritating behavior.

Particularly aggressive pups occasionally provoke their dams into actually nipping them. However, I have never seen a bitch exhibit vicious aggression toward a pup. Canine parents seem to instinctively avoid the type of corrective behavior that might quash a puppy's confidence. Unfortunately, this is not the case with many human parents when either children or puppies are concerned.

Using the dam's approach may take a few days, but the lesson tends to be well learned. The owner should first establish a strongly dominant leadership position with the pup. Teaching a few simple commands, such as come, sit and stay, is the initial step, as the act of teaching creates subordination in the puppy. Then comes the actual correction of overt biting or mouthing. The "freeze technique," as described above, should be tried, even to the point of exasperation.

If this fails (as it may with extremely aggressive pups), application of a distracting stimulus just as the pup *starts* the attacks is often successful. This stimulus may be a loud clap of the hands, tossing a favorite chewable toy quickly between the pup and its target, or even a startling countermove toward the puppy by the intended victim.

The standard techniques of holding the pup's snout shut and saying "No," cuffing under the chin sharply, slapping the snout, pushing a thumb down its throat, scolding or spanking with hands or newspapers, often work well with more passive or submissive pups. However, when these methods are used with aggressive, dominant types, the result is often heightened ferocity and subsequently serious problems involving aggression.

The German Shepherd pup mentioned earlier responded well after 3 weeks of command conditioning and correction with sound distractions. However, even when it had learned the "Sit-Stay" lesson, it would yap at the owner, complaining that it was required to respond obediently.

Another case involved an owner who had corrected the biting and mouthing problem by twisting his pup's tail whenever it tried to bite him. The problem presented was that now the adult male Labrador Retriever chased and bit its tail whenever it became frustrated. The client said he could live with the problem, except that the dog drew blood by biting itself and also became so frenzied that it knocked over furniture during these episodes. This case was solved when we discovered the dog was exceptionally leader-oriented (therefore easily stressed) and that it responded well to standard subordination command teaching procedures, combined with minimal corrections of the tail chasing and biting.

Summary

The standard methods of scolding and cuffing often succeed in correction of passive or submissive pups. However, the excitable, aggressive types that are presented as problem biters and mouthers usually respond to physical measures by becoming even more aggressive. Correction involves the owner's gaining a leadership position, combined with minimal corrections, such as freezing to avoid feedback reinforcement for the biting. If this is unsuccessful, a strong countermove toward the advancing puppy, or application of an intervening and strongly distracting stimulus usually stops the behavior. This procedure takes a few days to weeks, but nonphysical correction has the advantage of avoiding possible aggressive side effects that may be manifested later in the dog's life.

Finicky Eating

I have yet to see a pup emerge from a well-managed litter as a finicky eater. Usually the new owners create the problem by feeding the puppy "people food" as treats or changing its diet in the mistaken belief that variety is required for a happy pup. Feeding only kibble (dry food) as the morning meal and then providing meat (canned food) at the other meal(s) may cause trouble. It is always better to mix the meat and kibble. Let the kibble soak for 5-10 minutes to break down the binders used in the kibble and release its nutritional and flavor elements, then serve it to the puppy.

Another significant factor in finicky eating is the practice of overfeeding a puppy. Most pups eat until they appear on the brink of bursting at any given meal. Some owners are prone to give a puppy as much as it seems prepared to eat. The result is often loose stools (with poor housetraining potential) and a poor appetite at the next mealtime. When the pup turns up its nose at the following meal, the owner may resort to a diet change or a treat of "people food" to entice the pup to eat again.

Another element that should never be overlooked in the finicky eater is its health. If a properly fed puppy suddenly stops eating, it is time for a trip to the veterinarian. Poor appetite is one of the earliest signs of many common puppy ailments. The old saw, "Better safe than sorry," cannot be overused in this situation.

Correction

Given a healthy but finicky puppy, the solution is simple for the puppy but often difficult for its owners to carry out. A wholesome diet should be presented in the proper quantity (that which produces a firm and well-formed stool), with no variations. All food should be placed in the pup's regular food dish and no hand-feeding practiced.

> *I once had a client with an 8-year-old male Poodle that had always been handfed by its mistress. This was no problem until it became necessary to board the pampered pet. A change in diet from the usual "people food" tidbits, kibble and hamburger to a kibble-only diet, together with the altered feeding method (dish), caused a neurotic withdrawal from food. The client had to break off her trip to New York and return to Los Angeles to retrieve her starving Poodle, which had become emaciated after several foodless days of pacing, whining and barking in the kennel.*

In this case, as with all finicky dogs, the standard correction procedure produced results in 2-4 days. Given satisfaction of other needs, such as social contentment and minimal exercise, I have yet to see a finicky eater that has not responded positively to this program.

Sexual Mounting

Some puppies begin sexual mounting behavior at the tender age of 6 or 7 weeks, though it usually begins at about 12 weeks of age. It is self-rewarding behavior, in that it "feels good" to the pup. The problem rarely persists if the object of its attentions is made inaccessible. Unfortunately, many owners think that the behavior will disappear if they just let it run its course. They may allow the pup to mount until it reaches sexual climax. This, of course, makes the owner a subordinate sexual partner for the pet and can later develop into severe problems involving over-protection and biting.

Correction

Mounting should be discouraged by withdrawing the target (leg, arm, clothing) in as startling a manner as possible, as the pup *starts* the mounting rather than when it is under way.

Sexual experimentation seems to be a normal part of maturation in mammals, including people. Therefore, in cases involving permissive owners who allow the pup to persist in mounting, or where children actually stimulate the behavior (as one youngster told me, "just to see what happened"), all family members should be brought into consultation to explain the possible side effects of the problem.

The most dramatic case I have seen in this regard was a young, single girl who lived alone with her male German Shepherd. At about 3 months of age, the dog began to mount her leg or foot. She allowed this until it became a daily occurrence. However, as the dog matured it became more and more persistent, snarling if the girl tried to stop this behavior. By the time I was consulted, the dog (then 14 months old) had severely bitten 2 boyfriends and would mount the owner – freezing her in terror with its snarling – even when she entertained guests.

In such extreme cases, the owner must establish a leadership position with the pup or dog, preferably away from their home ground at first. This can be accomplished through standard obedience programs in some cases. However, a nonphysical approach to teaching is usually quicker, even if the dog is taught only to sit and stay on command. Along with this regimen, the aggressive Romeo must be distracted effectively *before* the overt mounting starts, with some strong intervening stimulus that takes its mind off the sex act. A food distraction is a poor substitute in most cases. Better is an invitation to play ball or otherwise engage in some strenuous physical activity that is enjoyed by the pet.

All unearned petting and praise must be stopped in cases of persistent mounting, even with very young offenders. If the pup pesters for attention, the owner should give it one of the simple commands until it obeys, then gently and briefly pet the animal and go on about some other business. After a few days to weeks of this type of correction, the puppy usually stops mounting and becomes oriented to the more typical play activity as a displacement mechanism.

This type of problem pup may persist in mounting inanimate objects, such as the owner's clothing, pillows or bedclothes, in the absence of its living sex object. However, this behavior usually fades away after a few weeks. One helpful corrective aid is to remove things that stimulate the behavior when the owner must be absent.

Chewing

The sense of taste is well developed even in newborn pups. However, applying a noxious substance, such as oil of citronella, to the bitch's mammary gland causes withdrawal of the nursing neonate's head. This has led to the marketing of several commercial substances designed to prevent destructive chewing by pups and mature dogs. If these are used regularly from the age at which conditioned responses are possible (3 weeks), investigative chewing may be minimized or prevented in later life, especially when teething becomes a stimulus for the problem. However, because the breeder would have to begin this type of regimen, and because most litters are raised under conditions that do not expose puppies to chewing taboos, correction is usually necessary.

Almost every owner recognizes that pups need to chew, if only to teethe properly. On the other hand, few appreciate that a dog's mouth is somewhat analogous to the human hand as an investigative tool, or that the healthy development of nervous and muscle tissue depends on hearty chewing exercise. The usual procedure is to give a pup numerous chewables, hoping these will be so attractive that electric cords, rugs, clothing and shoes will be saved from destruction – and the pet spared a possibly serious (or fatal) injury. However, furnishing many different kinds of things to chew may lead the pup to believe that *everything* is chewable.

Chewing appears to be an enjoyable experience for nearly all pups and many older dogs. So, the element of fun may also be part of chewing problems. The best approach to destructive chewing involves prevention and then guidance to chewable articles, such as a ball or bone. This helps the pup to discriminate between toys and inappropriate items. Practices that risk creating an orally oriented puppy include:

- Playing tug-o'-war.
- Allowing personal belongings (socks, shoes) to be chewed.
- Excessive attention to pup's mouth during teething.
- Punishment for chewing taboos.

Some pups are more oral than others. When this is coupled with an excitable or extremely inhibited nervous type, minor stress produces tension that tends to be released orally (rather than vocally or physically). Some of the causes for excessive tension in pups are:

- Very emotional departures and homecomings by the owner.
- Excessive attention to the pup.
- Social isolation.
- Barrier frustration.
- Delay of feeding.
- Inconsistent tidbitting by the owners.
- Monotony, boredom.

When 2 or more pups live together, chewing may result from competition for articles. Also, pups play games. When these involve articles of some value, the owner often attributes such chewing to spite or revenge. "Bozo's mad at me for leaving him alone, and he's getting even." This is seldom the case. Usually one or more of the aforementioned conditions are involved. As diligently as one might try to be a model puppy owner, it is obvious that few people can avoid all of the causes for chewing.

Among the best steps in prevention is to make sure that articles within reach of the puppy are expendable and nonlethal. Another practice that may help, if followed consistently, is to introduce some very attractive chewable, such as a meat-scented nylon bone or a fresh beef neck bone, immediately after each of the pup's postmeal toilet training sessions. This serves as an additional reward after praise for proper elimination behavior and also associates a specific chewable with chewing behavior.

When the pup begins to chew an inappropriate item, the best remedial action is to interrupt the chewing with some distracting stimulus, such as a clap of hands or shrill whistle. Scolding or otherwise vocally impressing one's presence on the pup tends to create a sneaky chewer that avoids chewing in the owner's presence but chews in the owner's absence.

Every new puppy owner should expect a certain amount of destruction from curiosity-based or tension-relieving oral tendencies of the pet. The preventive and corrective approaches mentioned above can help minimize problems while allowing the pup to develop a healthy relationship with its owners. Further causes and corrections relating mainly to mature dogs are presented in Chapter 10 and provide helpful reference.

Submissive Urination

The earlier an owner starts correcting the problem of submissive urination, the better. Most puppy owners are not aware of the underlying cause of this problem. Rather, they tend to feel their pup is displaying signs of cowardice and may not become a desirable adult dog. When the underlying reasons for the wetting are understood by the owner, correction may be accomplished in a few days to several weeks, depending on the degree of this tendency in the pup.

Causes

During the early neonatal period, a puppy's activities consist mainly of sleeping, blindly rooting around the litter group in search of the dam's teat, reflexive sucking for nourishment, and then being nuzzled onto its back and licked by the dam from stem to stern. The pup's unconditioned response to this licking is to urinate and defecate, allowing the dam to swallow the excreta and maintain litter sanitation.

The licking procedure occurs well before the puppy is capable of acquiring conditioned (learned) reflexes at a conscious level. However, at about the third and fourth week of life, there is an apparently conscious perception by the puppy that being turned over is a dominant behaviorism by the bitch, and that assuming a belly-up position is an appropriate response to this approach. Urination and/or defecation in these circumstances appears to be an acquired response on an emotional, rather than an intellectual, level of brain activity. When a solid food diet is introduced, the defecation response fades away, but submissive urination may persist longer.

Why submissive urination occurs more in females than in males is a matter for conjecture. One theory is that females have less of the hormones identified with dominant-aggressive behavior and are therefore more prone to submissive behavioral extremes than males. However, I have often seen the problem in mature males.

Because submissive urination occurs in response to dominant treatment, either by other animals or people, it tends to appear more often in submissive puppies than in dominant puppies. Originally the behavior filled a genuine physiologic need, that is, to evacuate so that proper internal and external health factors could be maintained. But if the behavior persists beyond this point, we can assume either that the pup is oversensitive to dominant stimulation, or that its submissive responses have been overstimulated and the behavior has become ingrained on an emotional level.

The term "emotional level" is appropriate here because a pup with this problem has no "conscious" awareness that it has urinated. It is doubtful that the puppy with this problem consciously concludes, "I'd better urinate because here comes my owner to reprimand me for chewing on that shoe."

Correction

The important point for owners to appreciate is that submissive urination is not deliberate. It just happens in response to dominant behavior. This being the case, punishment or other dominant behavior approaches are counterproductive. Scolding, picking up the pup, shaking, spanking or hitting it, pushing its nose into the urine or slapping newspapers at the bewildered and innocent animal are to be avoided.

These puppies lack confidence and therefore worry about their ability to cope with situations wherein they must be subordinate. To correct the problem, a pup's confidence levels must be raised and strengthened so that the conditioned urination is not triggered.

An environmental factor involved in most cases of submissive urination is that the pup is reprimanded far more often than it is praised for its achievements. In fact, most clients do not really consider their pup's need for praise. Most owners believe the pup should be punished for doing the wrong thing, especially if it is "caught in the act." This leads to that vicious circle mentioned earlier; urination is reinforced by the stimulus that causes it in the first place (punishment or dominant behavior).

A preferable corrective measure is to create situations wherein the pup can be praised both for doing the *right* things in response to its owners, and for not doing the *wrong* things. This approach is totally positive and avoids submissive urination in most cases. The puppy should be taught to respond to the simplest commands of "Come," "Sit" and "Stay," and be given immediate praise even for *starting* to make the appropriate responses. All teaching must be done without physical force, punishment or even gentle positioning of the puppy. These may be too closely associated with dominance behavior and could lead to urination.

Other recommendations include:

- Do not "hover over" the pup if this has caused urination in the past. When calling or petting the pup, the owner should crouch down. Petting is done palm up, under the chin and on the throat and chest, to avoid placing the hands upon the pet's head.

- If homecomings stimulate urination, ignore the pup for at least 5 minutes after arrival home. Then, when greeting the puppy, crouch as described above.
- Associate the phrase "Good dog" with petting and say it when putting down the pup's dish at feeding times. Then, whenever the puppy does something desirable, happily repeat "Good dog" a couple of times.
- Avoid all scolding vocal tones, especially if these have stimulated wetting in the past.

When these corrective steps, including the simple commands, have been practiced for at least 2 weeks, the pup should be gradually taken through situations (except those involving punishment) that have caused wetting in the past. Take only one situation per day. For instance, if merely leaning toward the pup and calling it has stimulated wetting in the past, try this a few times during a day. If the pup's haunches start to lower into the submissive urination stance, straighten up, walk away quickly and praise the pet to interrupt its behavior.

This type of program helps build the puppy's confidence in responding correctly to commands, as well as merely doing the "right things" without commands. A change in personality should be noticed within 4 days of starting the program, and the problem should clear up completely within 6 weeks.

Exceptions to the above regimen are pups that urinate only in excitement. This occurs at homecoming times or when some other of life's naturally stressful and/or exciting situations develop. To correct this problem, it is best to ignore the puppy at homecomings and at all other times urination tends to occur. If this is practiced for several weeks, the urination problem usually resolves permanently.

Sympathy Lameness

Sympathy lameness is a classic example of behavior resulting from psychic trauma. Almost every puppy owner has had the misfortune to step inadvertently on a puppy's paw. The result is predictable; the pup yelps, whines and carries the foot elevated until the pain is gone. Whether the experience produces lifelong sympathy lameness depends mainly on the degree of pain involved and the owner's reaction to the situation.

Many years ago our family dog, a feisty male that my parents chose to call a Toy Collie, developed the ridiculous habit of trying to exercise his herding skills on every passing motorcycle. One day the inevitable result found him writhing in the street with a broken pelvis. Our reactions were typical. We all gathered round, showed the greatest pity by applying liberal phrases of "puppy talk," and wrapped him in a blanket for the trip to the veterinarian. During the ride we cooed and petted him while he whined in a heartbreaking way.

After 6 weeks in a cast, our pet was able to use his repaired hip, which performed up to former standards when a few more weeks had passed, except when the dog was taken to the doctor, or when a motorcycle buzzed by. In either event, he would elevate his right rear leg or noticeably limp. If the motorcycle came close to the house, he would run after it in a most pathetic manner, the mended leg and hip almost dragging behind, a factor that probably saved his life in the long run. Never again was he able to catch one. However, if we threw a ball to chase, the little Collie ran as though he had never been injured. Routine trips to the veterinarian always produced whining in the car and a pathetic limping gait.

This example of sympathy lameness is well remembered because of the severe trauma involved. Most sympathy-induced behaviorisms are caused by trivial circumstances (such as accidentally treading on the pup's paw) that are soon forgotten by the owner and the dog.

The true cause of sympathy lameness in such situations is not the pain in the paw. Rather, it is the way in which the puppy, or older dog, *interprets* the incident. This interpretive factor usually involves not just self-pity, but *owner-induced* self-pity. This emotional conditioning is the basis of many canine behavior problems. The limping is an outward display of a conditioned connection from emotional centers in the dog's brain.

I recall a year-old German Shepherd bitch whose owners complained of chewing and general unruliness. The dog was adopted from the pound at about 7 months of age, and the owners were dismayed to find that their new pet seemed unable to tolerate confinement when left alone. In my office the Shepherd appeared to be genuinely claustrophobic. She paced, whined, tried to paw her way out the doors and even climbed on a couch in an attempt to crawl out a window. Unfortunately, my couch is on casters and it rolled out from under her, whereupon she crashed to the tile floor, striking an elbow.

When this happened, the owners cried, "Oh, my baby," and rushed over to the pet, which began to scream as only an injured dog can. I interpreted the dramatics as quickly as possible and suggested that we all go out onto our acreage and act happy. The couple looked at me as if I were out of my mind. However, I reassured them that the pet was not injured and away we went, with the now-limping dog tagging along and looking a bit confused.

When we reached the open spaces, we all ran and acted jolly about the situation. The owners were amazed to see their formerly hobbling dog now prancing about, jumping up at them and otherwise behaving as if nothing had happened. Even when we were back in the office, the now-rehabilitated bitch failed to revert to her limp. When I touched the injured elbow, she exhibited signs of pain by withdrawing, but the limp was gone.

The interpretive factor appears to be paramount in the cause of persistent sympathy lameness. In most cases, the dog interprets the painful incident in the way shown by people around it.

Correction

I have only known of 2 cases in which the owners found sympathy lameness to be a problem. One concerned a Golden Retriever that went lame in the field; the other involved an overly concerned owner with a Sheltie that went lame when a new pup was introduced into the family.

Remembering that the cause of the problem lies in the dog's emotional response to certain situations (usually involving stress), the solution lies in placing the dog in these situations and gradually inducing a different type of emotional response. It goes without saying that "sympathy" must be avoided during the procedure. Therefore, the owner's tone of voice is vitally important; any mewling at the dog is strictly forbidden. Only happy "Good dogs" and other phrases that are known to evoke tail wagging should be used.

This type of switch conditioning on an emotional level must start at the instant the dog exhibits anxiety about whatever stimulus triggers the lameness. This is often well before the lameness appears; therefore, this part of the correction is difficult for an owner to apply. Most people seem to want to see the lameness disappear, rather than prevent it. However, if applied properly, switch conditioning is successful.

In the case of the hunting dog that went lame in the field, the reconditioning procedure had to begin while the hunter and his dog were just getting into the truck at home, as it was at this time the Retriever began whining and otherwise showing anxiety. It took several field trips before she performed without showing her limp.

It is interesting that the initial cause of the Retriever's lameness was the owner's overconcern when the pup was first exposed to gunfire. We were unable to discover any association with pain involving the dog's legs.

The Sheltie that limped as a response to a new puppy in the household had been stepped on as a pup. The correction program involved the owners' "jollying" the pet whenever the new pup appeared. Complete correction required only a few days, where a 21-day course of tranquilizers had failed. While the dog was given medication, the lameness disappeared, but it reappeared on withdrawal.

Summary

Sympathy lameness is usually rooted in the owner's overly sympathetic reaction to some painful incident. This tends to fix an emotional response to stress in the pup, which may be generalized to other stressful situations. The motor response is the lameness.

Correction involves introducing the dog to situations that cause the feigned lameness and switching the response at the first signs of anxiety to an active, happy emotional mood. This should be done daily until the correction is complete.

Whining

Whining is one of the earliest vocal behaviorisms of puppies. Its first significance appears to be related to the stress of isolation, cold and hunger. When whining becomes a problem in a pet under 6 months of age, the cause is usually easily determined by defining when and where it occurs.

Causes

A pup whines to gain some objective. For example, the pup that is isolated in the kitchen on its first nights in a new home finds that sufficient whining gains the sympathy of the owners, who may then carry the pet into bed with them. This puppy often generalizes its whining to many other of life's frustrating stresses, and whines for relief. Another cause may be a genuine internal physical discomfort, such as gastritis or internal parasitism. If a problem whiner has not been thoroughly checked by its veterinarian for health problems, this should be done before any remedial behavioral steps are undertaken.

Certain Arctic breeds (Malamutes and Huskies) and some strains of German Shepherds are apt to emit an excruciatingly piercing whine whenever they are anxious. This type of anxiety whining is more complex and requires careful attention to the relationship between the owners and the pet involved than the simpler forms usually shown by young puppies.

Correction

In the simplest type of whining, that which is goal oriented, correction is straightforward: satisfy the need. However, if isolation is the cause, the problem must be solved with the same steps applied in barking. In the interest of brevity, these will be

199

mentioned here and the reader can refer to the Barking section for details.

The owner should stop isolating the pup, or, if this is impossible, gain a strong leadership position with the pup and use some distracting stimulus to interrupt the first *signs* of anxiety when the pet is isolated. This type of correction requires some play acting. The owner must pretend to be going off to work even on the weekends, and start the workday an hour earlier than usual to allow enough time for the correction procedure.

When whining results from generalized anxiety, the pup involved is typically a "bossy" type. These pups whine when the owner's attentions are withdrawn, even during initial consultations at our offices. They seem generally discontent in any situation they cannot control, such as car rides, when the owners have company and try to ignore the pup, or when the owner tries to make a telephone call. In other words, these pets become the canine counterparts of human children best described as spoiled brats. One way to test this causative factor is to keep the puppy away from its owners for a few hours. Interestingly, most of them cease whining within minutes of the owner's absence.

Correction in these pups involves the owner's gaining response to simple commands, such as "Come," "Sit" and "Stay." The puppy must be ignored at all other times insofar as praise, petting or other unearned social (or food) rewards are concerned. If the pup pesters for attention, it is immediately given one of the commands taught and then petted briefly. This teaches the puppy that the owners are in control of the relationship and avoids physical punishment, a step that is usually unsuccessful.

8

Aggressive Behavior

Aggression Toward Owners

A dog that growls at and/or bites its owner does so for some reason, even if the behavior appears "unreasonable" to the owner. If the case history reveals no environmental elements stimulating the aggression, then a *complete* medical examination, including tests for hormonal balance, neurophysiologic function and allergies, may reveal the underlying cause. This has been especially helpful in dogs that have swings in mood.

When growling or biting has erupted as a consequence of scolding or punishment for such behavior as chewing, jumping, general unruliness, or overprotection of food, these problems must be treated at the same time the program to correct aggression is initiated. Discussion on how to manage these problems are found in other sections of this text.

The Owner's Actions

Owners must understand that their dog growls or bites at them as a result of *defensive* feelings. Even the dog that growls when ordered off the couch is reacting defensively, as it feels its *dominance status* has been threatened. If scolding and punishment provoke aggression, the dog is reacting to a perceived threat to its physical safety. In either of these situations, the owner's threatening behavior is producing negative results. Increased punishment of these dogs is only counterproductive. When the dog is aggressive to everyone except the authoritarian member of the family (for example, an adult male), the "Beta-dog" syndrome is usually involved, as in the case of the shoe-guarding Shepherd mentioned on page 204.

Correcting Aggression Toward Owners

The solution, then, must be aimed at changing the way the owner and dog relate to each other. The owners must understand why the dog is behaving the way it is.

Once the reasons for the dog's aggressiveness are understood, as described in earlier chapters, the following program can be implemented. It has been highly successful in changing the dog's perception, hence *imagery*, of the owners, and has brought about dramatic improvements in behavior.

The "Cold Shoulder"

To convey to the dog that its relationship with its owner will be altered, this procedure is very effective. Most people have been the object of or have used this method in their relationship with other people, so it is easily appreciated. Even when we don't appreciate that we have done something to offend another, we are quickly aware of their change in attitude when we suddenly find ourselves ignored. So, the "cold shoulder" is particularly effective with bossy, dominant, leader-type dogs.

The "cold shoulder" procedure requires all members of the family to *ignore* the dog, except for feeding and other basic needs. Even saying the dog's name and making eye contact should be avoided. If the dog approaches for affection or attempts to otherwise gain attention by "herding," leaning or standing in the owner's way, they should merely move away and avoid contact. This must be done until it is apparent to the owners that the dog is concerned about what is going on. This will be shown by more persistent approaches for petting, etc. However, the dog must appear to be *asking* for the petting, rather than *bullying* the owner for it. When this stage is reached, usually within 4 days, the next step is instituted.

In the meantime, situations that have triggered the aggression must be strictly avoided. For instance, if growling while near the food bowl is a problem, the dog should be fed and then left alone. If the dog has growled while on the owner's bed, the dog should either be denied the on-bed privileges or kept out of the bedroom.

Learn-to-Earn: Each time the dog seeks affection, it must be pleasantly told to "Sit" or perform some other command, such as "Down." Subsequent petting and upbeat praise must be brief (under 5 seconds), after which the dog must be released with an "OK."

Leadership Exercises: Along with the learn-to-earn step, each time the dog precedes the owner when walking around the house or through doors, the owner must reverse direction. Though this may be inconvenient for a few hours, it will result in a dog that *follows*, rather than *leads* its owner around the house, through doors, etc.

When this program is combined with the correction programs for the problems that originally created the aggressive behavior, most dogs quickly become more manageable. However, the owners *must feel confident* that they are in control of the *emotional* reactions of the dog. Otherwise, the Jolly Routine may not be effective. Stated more simply, if the owner is "walking on eggs," the dog will sense it and may resume its aggressive behavior.

Jolly Routine: Whatever the situation(s) that produced aggressiveness, when the underlying problems have been dealt with, the owner should use the Jolly Routine at the instant the dog is beginning to become aggressive.

For instance, the dog growls or bites as the owner approaches the dog as it is lying in a doorway. When this situation occurs again, the *instant* the dog perceives the owner approaching, the single hand clap, followed immediately by ball bouncing, happy praise, etc, must be applied until the dog responds to the owner's approach happily *before* the hand clap. However, to reinforce this conditioned emotional response, the happy praise routine should be applied until the owner feels confident that the problem is solved.

This procedure for correcting aggressive behavior applies to more than aggression toward owners. It has been an effective foundation for correction of aggressive behavior in other circumstances. It avoids negative treatment of the dog and the possibly negative results. It will be referred to in the following discussion of other types of aggression.

Aggression Toward Outsiders

Dogs that bite or show aggressiveness toward people outside the family group usually feel insecure about their relationship with their owners and/or their property, or have been frustrated relative to people at barriers, on leashes, etc. Some of these dogs may have been mistreated by strangers or former family members, often unbeknownst to the owners.

Pack (family) and property protection tendencies naturally begin to appear at about 6 months of age. At this time the dog may show slight signs of hostility toward outsiders who threaten the integrity of its property or group. This behavior may become extreme in the following circumstances:

- The dog's owners do not have a uniform leader relationship with the pet (dog is submissive to some, dominant toward others).
- The family has very few visitors.
- Fear, hostility or aggression is commonly shown toward outsiders by family members (often by the children).
- At the dog's first signs of hostility toward outsiders, the owners have encouraged the behavior.
- The dog has been frightened or teased by outsiders.
- The dog has been shut away from the family when guests visit (often because of other types of misbehavior).

A family consisting of father, mother, 12-year-old son, 15-year-old daughter and a live-in housekeeper complained that their 2-year-old castrated male Shepherd-mix had bitten or threatened everyone but the father, and had also bitten visitors. These incidents always occurred in the father's absence. He had taken the dog through an obedience program a year earlier.

The main problem erupted when the dog began to "guard" the father's shoes or clothing in his absence.

One morning after the father left for work, the Shepherd would not allow the mother to get into the clothes closet to get dressed. The man had to return home from work to remove the diligent watchdog from the closet floor.

Scolding and physical punishment were unavailing. Correction involved weekly meetings of all household members to discuss nonphysical methods of correcting the dog's behavior. With show-and-tell teaching methods, the Shepherd was responding well to each person by the third week of the program. Incidents of hostility tapered off to zero by the sixth week, after which only one further episode occurred, this after the family boarded the pet for several weeks during an extended vacation. The Jolly Routine (described above) was applied and no further problems were reported.

An 18-month-old male Old English Sheepdog had viciously bitten its owners, a husband and wife. No children were involved. From 8 months of age, the dog had been shut away due to unruliness whenever guests called. The biting occurred when the owners were either pulling the dog from the house by its collar or, in the final instance, when the wife was trying to entice the dog out with a frankfurter as bait.

In addition to spontaneous viciousness, the Sheepdog displayed hyperkinetic signs. We were told of the case after the owners requested euthanasia. Before the quarantine period at the veterinary clinic expired, we suggested that the dog be given oral dextroamphetamine (1 mg/kg) in a meatball at 6-hour intervals for 2 days. Before treatment, the dog snarled whenever a hand was extended toward it, and any touching with hands elicited viciousness (Fig 1). Ninety minutes after it consumed the dextroamphetamine, the animal displayed lip smacking, but allowed us to lean against the meshed wire gate while it pressed its head against us. The dog still snarled when touched, but would allow us to gently pull the hair on its head.

Figure 1. This 18-month-old Old English Sheepdog was spontaneously vicious, and showed signs of hyperkinesia. Treatment with dextroamphetamine reduced signs of aggression.

Unfortunately, this case was closed before we had an opportunity to attempt rehabilitation. However, several other hyperkinetic dogs have been treated with some success.

We have obtained marked improvement in cases involving breeds whose hair covers their eyes. These cases involved dogs that appeared hyperreactive to hand movement in the visual field by displaying aggressive biting responses. When the hair was either cut off or tied back, the dogs appeared more relaxed and tolerated hand movements far better. Aggression toward hand movement reappeared when their hair was again untied.

I have observed only one apparently psychotic biting dog in action. This dog, a male German Shepherd of 6 years, ravaged my wrists to the extent that I was disabled for 2 weeks. The case deserves scrutiny because, after years of experience with hundreds of so-called vicious dogs, it was the only time I had ever been attacked.

> At 5 1/2 months of age, the German Shepherd had swallowed at least 50 mg of methedrine, inadvertently left within its reach. The convulsing pup was rushed to the hospital. Four days later, after appropriate treatment, the Shepherd was released.
>
> The dog had always been what the client described as "skittish," and had never been formally trained. The

first aggressive episode occurred when the dog was sleeping in the client's bedroom. The wife was in bed when the husband entered the room late at night from work. The awakened dog snarled and chased him from the room. The wife took the Shepherd by the collar and put it in the backyard.

After reflecting on the fact that his own dog had attacked him, the husband went to the backyard to "have it out" with his dog. He was bitten severely on the arms and legs.

No further incidents occurred for 6 months because the dog was banished to the backyard. Then a friend known to the dog was bitten on the knee while entering the yard. Also, another friend was bitten on the arm when meeting the Shepherd in the couple's house. The biting episodes were related to property protection and threats of a beating. The original bedroom episode was probably related to misperception in dim light. Behavior at the veterinary hospital was tolerable if mild tranquilization was administered, according to the wife. The veterinarian's staff reported no adverse behavior during treatment.

Despite the wife's reservations about it, I decided to see the Shepherd while it was off leash. The husband was not worried. "If you've got the guts for it, I don't think there'll be any trouble."

It was 90 degrees on a June afternoon when they arrived. From the air-conditioned car emerged "Thunder," followed by his owners, both of whom were perspiring. Thunder ignored me while we seated ourselves under a walnut tree's welcome shade.

After several stops to urinate, Thunder approached to within a foot, looked me in the eye and snarled viciously. In textbook style, I froze, wondering what might happen to my crossed knee. It was directly in the path of the dog's jaws. My blood rewarmed slightly as the snarl stopped and Thunder inquisitively sniffed the knee. I then said, "Good boy," and was allowed to chuck the dog under his chin. Thunder then trotted off toward our half-acre rear lot. We followed, chatting about the fact that the dog had asserted himself successfully and now probably would accept me as nonthreatening and subordinate.

Once in the open spaces, we stood talking while the dog investigated the terrain. I started to walk away toward a new area, saying "C'mon, Thunder." My act of group leadership triggered a full-blown, psychotic rage avalanche in the Shepherd. He brushed by my leg from behind, spun, then flew at my throat in less time than it takes to think, "Now I know why they were sweating inside that air-conditioned car!"

Thunder was subdued by the tail-lift method, only after I was severely bitten on the wrists and hands. When the dog was led away by its mistress, the avalanche had run its course. Put into the car, the dog appeared dazed and withdrawn, though it had suffered no blows, pain or injury.

During the ensuing 2 weeks, I gathered more facts about the animal from the owners and others who had encountered it. Initial fact-finding, it turned out, had been deficient. The husband mentioned that 4 men were required to restrain the dog on its last visit to the veterinarian, even though the dog was tranquilized. Previous biting had been more spontaneous than territorially related. Thunder had been constantly threatening toward the husband, to the point that the wife would not allow the 2 in the house together.

Thunder was fed a high-protein diet. The couple's veterinarian prescribed stilbestrol, which appeared to mellow Thunder, but not sufficiently to reassure the owners enough to attempt any behavioral modification.

Thirteen months later, after living in virtual isolation in the backyard, the dog growled viciously even when its mistress tried to open the door and bring food. Thunder developed a severe leg infection but could not be approached for treatment, and was consequently destroyed.

The indication of psychosis in this case comes from Thunder's obvious lack of contact with reality during the vicious episodes, at our facilities and at home. The owners' treatment (an autocratic master and permissive mistress), combined with probable early neural damage from methedrine overdosing, produced a type of paranoid mania often seen in violent human criminals.

Overprotectiveness

Clients who complain about overprotective behavior are usually concerned that their dog may bite someone. In most cases they state that the dog's on-guard behavior is acceptable and even desirable. However, the possibility of a lawsuit or the fear of being maimed usually motivates the owner to seek help. This type of ambivalence relative to the dog's behavior indicates some basic insecurity in the owner. When this can be brought into the open through consultation, the total problem can be placed in proper perspective and a corrective program becomes possible.

> *A woman who enrolled her 4-month-old Poodle/Terrier in a puppy behavior program complained of housesoiling, chewing, jumping up on furniture and people, and a lack of response to her. However, when I entered the office, the pup barked and even growled at me.*
>
> *"Wow! That's pretty aggressive behavior for a young-ster," I remarked above the racket.*
>
> *"Oh, I'm pleased about his wanting to protect me. It's one of the reasons I like him so much," she shouted back.*
>
> *"Who's running the show?" I asked.*
>
> *"What do you mean?" She leaned forward in her chair as if she hadn't quite understood.*

When I sat down, the pup immediately became quiet. While he sniffed my pantlegs, I explained what I call the "responsibility factor" in dog-owner relationships.

Who's In Charge?

In the daily interaction between a dog and its owner, most overprotective animals have devised various ways of telling the owner when to get up in the morning, when to open the doors out or into the house on cue, when to pet and stroke in response to nudging, etc.

On the other side of the ledger, these dogs only do something on command *when they want*. Commands to Come when called, Sit, Stay and various other commands are rarely if ever obeyed, except when the dog happens to be in the mood. In other words, the dog is in command and is naturally going to become upset when some outsider interferes with its concept of how life ought to proceed. The dog's response to such intrusions can range from submissive recumbency to a vicious attack on the interloping party.

An overprotective animal usually combines its jealousy of its owner's attentions with overdeveloped active defense reflexes. Overly developed defense reflexes usually result from the owner's deliberate encouragement of early signs of aggression toward strangers, lack of any attempt to control this tendency, or an excessively physical or emotional response when the aggression begins to emerge. In fact, most cases I encounter involve clients who have committed all of these errors.

In such cases, the dog behaves as if it feels responsible *for* rather than *to* its owner. Most clients can see the value of having a dog take its cues about protection from the owner, rather than allowing it to make the critical decision regarding toward whom it should be aggressive. The corrective procedure requires that both the owner and dog possess one vital personality factor: a sense of humor, an element missing in some older dogs. If this is absent, then devices must be improvised to develop it.

The Jolly Routine

I have yet to see the dog that does not wag its tail in response to some sort of pleasant stimulus, if only the suggestion that a ride in the car is in the offing. In rehabilitating an overprotective dog, these types of responses are used to gain a new kind of association for the dog with visitors, using the "Jolly Routine." This must be coupled with an overall environmental adjustment that requires the owner to teach the misbehaving pet to respond dependably to basic commands before receiving any praise or petting. Further, when the dog solicits petting or otherwise attempts to "direct" its owner's behavior, the owner must turn the tables and direct the dog in one of these simple command responses. This mechanism helps impress on the animal that the dog is now responsible to its owner, rather than *vice versa*.

Application of the Jolly Routine requires that we know what kinds of events stimulate the onset of the unwanted behavior. These can involve such things as a ringing doorbell, a knock on the door, a car door closing, footsteps on the walk, or the approach of another person. Whatever the key stimulus may be, it is at this *initial* signal stimulus that the Jolly Routine must begin. This is the time at which the dog's neurochemical responses begin, and therefore the time when switching to a "jolly circuit" is most effective. To wait until the dog is fully involved in aggressive threats requires stopping the avalanche of learned behavior in midcourse, which is ineffective. The following case illustrates this aspect of correction.

> *The owners of a 4-year-old male Spaniel-mix complained of aggressiveness toward any visitors to the house. They had tried every type of correction, from food treats by guests to muzzles and even a shock collar. The dog still snarled and menaced visitors with every type of aggressive canine display short of biting, which the owners prevented by physical restraint.*
>
> *In consultation, I discovered that the Spaniel had a sense of humor. It would wag its tail whenever the owners laughed. Further, the dog enjoyed playing fetch with a tennis ball.*

The doorbell initiated the onset of anxiety, before the actual appearance of visitors. The clients were advised to secure the cooperation of a few brave and understanding friends and neighbors in the following daily routine for at least 4 days.

1. Visitors ring the doorbell.

2. Family members all laugh and jolly the dog, avoiding any signs of "sympathy reassurance."

3. Steps 1 and 2 are continued until the dog appears happily (rather than aggressively) anxious.

4. The door is opened and visitors enter to a jolly greeting by the owners.

5. Visitors toss the tennis ball for the dog to fetch and return. Each visitor takes a turn until the dog relaxes, after which the guests and owners are seated for the remainder of the visit.

6. If the dog shows any renewed signs of aggression, everyone laughs and jollies the dog.

This procedure is not only effective if repeated daily for a few days, but it can also provide hilarious entertainment for everyone involved. In the above case, the client reported that after the first few rather strained and shallow chuckles by their edgy guests, the entire scene struck everyone simultaneously as being riotously ludicrous. The remainder of the evening was spent in spontaneous eruptions of raucous laughter, during which their formerly overprotective Spaniel interrupted its sleep in a corner to raise its head and feebly wag its tail.

The Insecure Owner

A 4-year-old male German Shepherd owned by a widow had become increasingly aggressive toward all callers during the 8 months since the husband's death, especially when out with the owner in the car. The dog was a severe leash strainer and constantly displayed anxiety behavior at the large front window of the family house.

Consultation revealed that the owner had become subject to increased feelings of insecurity since her husband's death. These feelings had manifested in plans to move from her home to another state. She admitted to particular fearfulness when out in her car, even though she had never been threatened in any way.

Whether a dog "senses" insecurity in its owner or actually observes certain subtle changes in the owner's actions and speech, we have noted definite evidence of mood transferrals from owners to dogs. In this case, the dog had a history of anxious behavior at the back fence and at the front window of the house in relation to other dogs and to people. The owner's heightened insecurity appeared to have been the deciding factor in the dog's final display of overt aggression.

As in all cases of overprotectiveness, the owner must institute the learn-to-earn praise and petting program and the Jolly Routine when situations that have stimulated problem behavior arise. When this has produced the desired emotional and behavioral changes, it is often advisable to have the owner enroll the dog in some sort of obedience work. In such an obedience program, an experienced professional instructor can assist the owner in gaining leash and command control.

Overprotectiveness Within the Family

An 11-month-old male German Shepherd had bitten the wife and growled at the husband when they had shown physical affection for their 10-year-old son. The husband was not as demonstrative as the boy's mother.

The dog had been obtained from friends, who had mistreated the dog with excessive physical punishment and isolated it in the backyard since about 11 weeks of age. The only person to have had a close relationship with the dog was the 10-year-old son. We learned that this boy objected to his parents' punishment of the dog, often crying hysterically when the animal was beaten.

The new family had immediately integrated the dog into their home, and the son quickly developed a strong rapport with the Shepherd. In our first discussion, it was obvious the boy did not approve of seeking help through me. He seemed to enjoy being the only one who could control the dog even in the face of physical danger to his mother. This was a fascinating consultation in that the boy was almost impudently disinterested in the proceedings. To gain a position of some authority in his eyes, I had to uncover the boy's lack of respect for his parents' authority, which, in turn, was the cause of the dog's overprotectiveness of the boy.

I said, "Tommy, I want you to understand that your mom and dad have brought you and Sparks to see me to avoid having to get rid of the dog. Did you know that if they hadn't heard about me, they would have taken him to the pound?"

Tommy ignored this question, responding to what was important to him: "Earl is not my dad. He's my stepdad." His eyes were on the floor and his voice had a slight tremor. His remark elicited a shrug and expressions of helplessness from his parents.

I could only answer in a way that would focus the boy's attention on the goal that was needed to salvage the situation. "OK, Tommy, I understand that. But, what we are really concerned with is that Earl and your mom have asked me to help them make a very serious decision about Sparks' future. And, from what I've seen and heard here today, I think that decision is going to depend mostly on you. What do you want to have happen with Sparks?

"I want to keep him."

"Even if he bites your mother?"

(Long pause.) "I never wanted him to bite her!" Tommy was on the verge of tears.

It was time to clearly define a goal that Tommy might value and work toward. I said, "OK, I'll tell you what I think it's going to take to get Sparks straightened out. Then you tell us if you can help us do it."

I outlined a procedure for Tommy and his parents that required them all to direct the dog before any praise or petting. This required 6 weeks of daily off-leash training by all of them, combined with weekly visits to our facilities for coaching and discussions.

During the first session in which the dog was taught to come on command, Tommy and Sparks displayed a remarkable degree of communication. When the father was teaching Sparks, Tommy would actually turn his back on the situation, whereupon the dog would run over to the boy and whine at him rather than go to Earl. It was also apparent that both parents were frightened of Sparks. They balked at crouching down to administer praise, a movement that is necessary to attract the animal in off-leash training. We were witnessing the boy's jealousy of the parents' relationship with "his" dog. Rather than abandon the session, I decided to shift the responsibility to Tommy, so I asked, "Tommy, how can we expect Sparks to be interested in learning if you're not interested?"

"I am interested."

"You'll have to show me by paying strict attention to what's going on."

He turned slowly and leaned on a post. I then got the family to call the dog alternately. This helps demonstrate to the dog consistency among family members. It is more time consuming than working with individuals, but it is highly effective when jealousy is a factor.

Once the dog was responding well to all, I had Tommy run to mother and hug her. This elicited only whining and some jumping up on them by Sparks, after which all 3 alternately, then together, petted the dog while acting jolly about it all. The dog responded with tail wags and the characteristic Shepherd whining sounds.

Back in the office, the dog settled by Tommy's chair while Tommy and his mother exchanged a familial kiss. Sparks did not seem unduly upset by this action. I suggested that this procedure be repeated back in the home at least 3 times daily; also that Tommy run to his stepfather happily and that Sparks be praised on these occasions. After the third week, the parent-oriented overprotectiveness was no longer a problem. The remainder of the program was spent dealing with the same behavior related to Tommy's many friends, a secondary complaint in the case. The same technique was successful.

Overprotectiveness Related to Socialization

A 4-year-old male Lhasa Apso was showing hostility toward visitors to the apartment of its owner, a recently divorced woman. Urination in the apartment was also a complaint.

The dog was extremely rigid in its movements when first investigating various urination posts in our consultation area. The dog continued to lift its leg numerous times, even though the dog was void of urine after the third time. When I tried to approach, the Lhasa growled menacingly and stiffened to a defensive posture. The owner complained of the same behavior whenever she tried to groom the animal.

This dog displayed no sense of humor. Its owner also showed a singular lack of this quality, so necessary for rehabilitation through the Jolly Routine. It turned out that Rex had been used for breeding in the apartment where the trouble first began. This can be a major contributory factor in urination problems, as it may heighten territorial protectiveness in certain dogs, especially those with strong leader inclinations.

It was interesting to note that when the former owner of this "little Caesar" attended a consultation, the dog's entire demeanor changed to one of almost puppyish joy. It wagged its tail and jumped up on the former owner, interrupting this happiness only to become stiff and hostile when the current owner or I tried to influence it in some way. The former owner, a breeder, had kept the dog for a year before selling it to the current owner. It was obvious the breeder alone enjoyed the needed benefit of an early relationship involving the period of critical socialization.

Despite the owner's wistfully sad outlook on life in general and her problem in particular, I still recommended that the Jolly Routine be attempted, not only in specific stressful situations, but also in the overall daily interaction with the morose animal. I also suggested that the owner gain off-leash control of the recalcitrant dog, and undertake a basic housesoiling correction program.

Though the hostility was brought under control to the point that Rex was no longer a potential menace to the owner and outsiders, the inappropriate urination did not cease entirely. This may have been due to the fact that the dog continued to be used for breeding on its home territory.

Narcissistic Overprotectiveness

This type of protection-of-self and/or of the dog's "belongings" deserves special discussion because such dogs may progress to biting their owners. Narcissism, or self-love, usually has its roots in puppyhood and often centers around owners who dote on their pets. If the dog tends to dominate and has matured in an environment in which its wishes have been fulfilled, at 6-12 months of age we often see aggressive tendencies when the owners attempt to physically manipulate, scold or otherwise impose their wishes on the pet. This tendency has been noted in pups the first day after leaving the litter, but such cases are rare and generally involve the litter "bully." If taught by nonphysical methods, these pups usually respond well and eventually develop into worthwhile pets. Given excessive physical punishment, however, they can become dangerous adults.

> *A 2-year-old male Doberman Pinscher growled menacingly at its owners when scolded. From puppyhood, the Doberman showed self-protective tendencies, even under veterinary examination. At 3 months it had persistent diarrhea, but no physiologic cause was found. The owners were required to obtain rectal temperature readings twice daily for a period of several months. During this time the Doberman received constant sympathy and doting attention from the couple.*
>
> *The case was referred to me after the dog had viciously menaced the wife when she tried to approach and take away a stick it had brought into the house. The first meeting at our facilities indicated an extremely self-oriented, leader-type animal tending toward overprotection of the wife. When released, the dog urinated excessively on scent posts, circled my chair and raised its hackles in response to my speaking its name. Though the dog had been thoroughly obedience trained, commands (especially Come) were only grudgingly obeyed.*

A 6-week behavior program, involving nonphysical methods, was used to gain instant responses to commands. The Jolly Routine was recommended for situations involving strangers (to whom the Doberman showed consistent hostility), as well as when the dog tended to become menacing with the owners.

One milestone in this case was that the attitude of the owners changed from autocratic to leadership by example. It is interesting that many of these types of dogs have owners who believe the dog ought to "accept" punishment in order to be a good pet. When owners understand that they have the type of pet that will respond aggressively to threats (probably due both to innate and acquired tendencies), they must decide on a different (nonphysical) method of teaching. When this method produces a behavioral change in the dog, owner attitude normally changes from autocratic to that of an enlightened leader. At this time the Jolly Routine takes on sincerity that has tremendous impact on the dog. The switch from hostility to lightheartedness usually brings quick results.

A serious detriment to this procedure is the owner's understandably cautious approach to the dog. One aspect of the Doberman case illustrates the problem: the dog was particularly sensitive about its rear quarters. If the owners attempted to touch or manipulate the dog's rear quarters, it immediately froze, turned its eyes rearward and growled dangerously, apparently on the verge of biting. The first signal to the Doberman that it should feel concerned about the procedure was the owner's hesitancy about handling it. "Once bitten, twice shy" translates to "once growled at, twice shy" in these cases.

In an effort to demonstrate the method that generally works well with this type of case, I jollied the dog, and it responded with tail wagging and generally giddy behavior. While the upbeat vocalizations continued, I rubbed its ear and moved my other hand along its back to the rump. The dog appeared to be unaware of this invasion into formerly forbidden territory. The final test was to cease rubbing the ear, continue the vocal jollies and see what happened when the dog became aware of the hand manipulating the rear quarters, legs, gonads and anal area. The Doberman remained cheerful.

When this was demonstrated, the client was invited to join in the merriment, to the delight of the pet. The dog continued its good natured acceptance after the behavioral "ice" was broken, and the problem resolved itself with only daily sessions.

A word of warning: this approach should not be undertaken suddenly with self-oriented aggressive dogs, or in a way that tends to surprise the animal. In the Doberman case, I told the veterinarian that the dog would accept physical manipulation as long as the manipulator laughed a lot while so doing. Because the dog was hypersexual and intermittently displayed signs of possible prostatitis, it was examined by the veterinarian the following week. The doctor initially approached the Doberman suddenly from behind a counter, "ho-ho-ing" like a Santa Claus. The surprised dog lunged toward an equally surprised doctor, who has since been less than enthusiastic regarding the Jolly

Routine. However, once the element of surprise was overcome the Doberman allowed prostate examination peacefully while the owner and the doctor chuckled more appropriately.

There is nothing funny about being viciously threatened by one's own dog. When the owner understands the problem's cause, environmental changes are made, and specific corrective techniques are mastered, such behavior can be corrected.

Other Methods of Correcting Aggression

Dental Treatment: Biting has reportedly been corrected by grinding the canine (eye) teeth to a level just below that of the adjacent incisors. As reported in the feline literature, transection of the infraalveolar and infraorbital branches of the trigeminal nerves in mouse-killing cats caused the cats to normally stalk and pounce on the mice, but not bite them. Dr. Joseph Stuart reported success in correcting biting in a St. Bernard and a Cocker Spaniel, as well as fighting between Foxhounds in a kennel, after grinding down the canine teeth as described.

These findings suggest that impairing proprioception of the canine teeth may inhibit biting, though more clinical evidence is needed. In dogs and cats treated in this manner, the procedure did not affect the eating habits or dental health.

Castration: Castration has sometimes been effective in curtailing fighting between male dogs. However, castration has been unrewarding in correcting aggression toward people.

Drug Therapy: Numerous reports in the veterinary literature indicate that progestin therapy has also been unrewarding. Tranquilizers and antidepressants, such as amitriptyline (Elavil: Merck Sharp & Dohme), have been reported in a limited number of cases. However, I have not asked referring veterinarians to prescribe them due to the possibility of the problem behavior recurring after withdrawal of the drugs.

Summary

Dogs who bite outsiders require the same general remedial programs as those who bite their owners. This is because similar canine and owner *attitudes* are at work. The dog perceives its "targets," often including the owners, *negatively.* Therefore, the relationship between the dog and its owners must be converted to a *positive* one, after which the owners can use the Jolly Routine, combined with continued learn-to-earn and leadership exercises, to change the dog's perceptions, imagery and behavior toward outsiders.

Aggression Toward Other Dogs

Dogs that fight tend to have any or a number of the following characteristics:

- Are dominant in their relationship with their owners.
- Lacked exposure to other dogs during critical socialization periods.
- Have been attacked by other aggressive dogs.
- Fight only when a neighborhood bitch is in heat.
- May have been the litter bully as a pup.
- Usually become excited when stressed.
- Are jealous because of owner favoritism.

Most fights between unacquainted dogs are related to the territorial boundaries or property (human owners in some cases) of one or both combatants. This type of aggression is easily understood but difficult to correct. Another type of aggression that is difficult for owners to understand and correct involves dogs that live in the same household. Though both dogs receive what appears to be the same treatment from their owners, they engage in savage fights. Though the causes vary, corrective methods involve the same principle. Correction centers around converting the feelings of hostility to "happy" emotional responses. This requires extreme self-control on the part of the owner, but it has proved effective when performed properly.

Territory and Property Fights

Among wild dogs and wolves, the integrity of the home territory is normally well respected by roaming loners or intruders. An especially bold or aggressive stranger may test the degree of protectiveness of a home-pack leader or other pack member, but this is rare. The usual sequence of events consists of: approach, confrontation, threat display by the established animal, and retreat by the intruder (Fig 2). In situations involving people, this type of behavior becomes seriously distorted, not by the dogs but by people.

Neighborhood Urine Marking

A commonly accepted myth among dog owners is that dogs, especially males, have a fundamental need to spread their urine widely in order to be emotionally well adjusted. As a result, the dog is often taken off its own property, to dutifully sprinkle up, down and across the street. In addition to methodically despoiling the area's greenery, the owner is allowing the dog to extend its protective feelings beyond its natural home and yard. An aggressive dog consequently begins to defend what the ignorant owner has "taught" it to consider its territory. This is especially true when the 2 dogs involved both suffer the misfortune of having equally ignorant owners. Each dog tries to protect its own extended boundaries. This type of defensive behavior predominates among males, but also has been noted in females.

When the foregoing facts are appreciated, one portion of a remedial program becomes rather obvious: the owner must not allow the dog to "brand" the neighborhood territory. Further, in dogs that are fighters, whenever and wherever they go off

Figure 2. Two dogs "square off" when first meeting. The German Shepherd, with tail and ears erect, is the aggressor in this situation. A fight could ensue if the Dalmatian does not show signs of submission.

their property, it is best *not* to allow any urinating at all unless 5 or 6 hours have passed and the dog genuinely must urinate. This avoids one of the most common canine rituals preceding aggression: urine marking.

An example of this took place when I was taking photographs of biting dogs. A local guard dog company graciously brought out an old German Shepherd to accommodate my need for an aggressive display. When it first came into the area and faced me (on leash), it was commanded to "Watch it!" Even though I crouched and made threatening gestures, the old warrior did not seem perturbed.

However, during a pause in the proceedings as the handler and I pondered our problem, the Shepherd went to a nearby bush, hiked its leg and branded the area, after which it turned and gave me a most convincing, throaty growl (Fig 3). Thereafter I was intruding on the dog's marked territory.

Freedom Frustration

Another cause of dog fights lies in constant frustration by barriers between excitable, aggressive animals and other dogs that they find threatening (Fig 4). When this situation occurs as part of the fighting dog's environment, it is best to remove the animal from the area, even if it means making major structural

Figure 3. Guard dog showing signs of aggression upon command by its handler.

Figure 4. Dogs that are constantly restrained, such as this male Pit Bull Terrier, tend to become very aggressive because of frustration with captivity.

changes. I have seen good responses with the addition of an inner fence-within-a-fence, whereby the dog is unable to approach nearer than 6-8 feet to intruders and *vice versa*.

Fighting With Other Resident Dogs

Fighting between canine members of a household usually involves dogs of the same sex, often littermates. Trigger people in the family often stimulate such fights, though sometimes food or another dog may also stimulate fighting. To avoid such fights, it is best not to obtain littermates of the same sex, particularly those that appear competitive within the litter. Also, when a new dog is adopted into the family, it is a good idea to pay more "jolly-type" attention to the resident dog(s) than was shown before the newcomer's arrival. Make the additional pet *fun* for the resident pet. Allow the new animal to fit in and adjust with less attention than is shown the older members. This will cause resident dogs to have pleasant associations with the new animal.

If a fight should erupt, never induce more hostility into the situation by shouting, screaming, scolding, hitting, kicking the heads or bodies of the fighters or pulling them apart by the heads or necks. Most serious canine quibbling I see involves owners who induce hysteria into the original battle, which, if allowed to reach its conclusion naturally (if the owners had left the scene or remained passive), more than likely would have concluded bloodlessly and with one permanently dominant and one submissive dog.

The most effective method I know for stopping a fight requires that someone pick up the more aggressive of the warring pair by the tail, just high enough so its hind feet cannot touch the ground. If both dogs are aggressors, then both must be elevated. Lack of hindquarter traction often quickly short circuits hostility. If either dog has a docked tail, the hind legs may be picked up to equal advantage. There are exceptions, of course. I know of one Pit Bull whose owner had to carry an axe handle to pry the determined gladiator off other dogs or people's legs or arms. One must, of course, use extreme caution when intervening in any dog fight so as to avoid being bitten.

A common underlying cause of persistent fighting is owner hysteria when such fights break out. Most owners of multiple dogs who do not have such problems did not become hysterical when fights or hostilities initially erupted.

In more than 95% of sibling-type fighting, the dogs never fought unless the owners were present. A good percentage of them were boarded together in the same run without hostile signs. This brings us to one type of remedial program that is often successful: boarding the dogs together on neutral territory, there to be visited by the family under controlled conditions after a week or so. If no fight ensues, a daily series of visits, followed by rides in the family car to other neutral areas, will often help if the plan spans 3-6 weeks. After this, a daily trip home can be included.

Dogs fighting for any reason must be taught to respond to simple commands to Come, Sit and Stay when the owner directs. All fondling, coddling or solicitous behavior toward the pet must be avoided. This helps the owner assume dominance over the dogs involved and is prerequisite to all procedures recommended.

Correction of Fighting

The Jolly Routine: This method of rehabilitating fighting dogs in all categories requires owners who possess a sense of humor and some theatrical ability, plus a dog that tends to wag its tail or otherwise show the signs of canine joy when hearing its owners laugh. Fortunately, this is the case in most of the situations I encounter. When I meet a Grim Jim or Gripey Jane owner with an equally sullen fighting dog, I flatly tell them that to succeed they will have to figure out some way of laughing a lot during their time with their scrapper. Then, when the pet begins showing signs of a more pleasant disposition, we can offer assistance.

The Jolly Routine requires precise timing to achieve an emotional change from defensive feelings to predominantly pleasant ones. Whatever the trigger mechanism (stimulus) that normally creates the very first outward sign of fighting, it must be accompanied by the owners' laughter and movements or activities that have happy meaning to the offender.

For example, if the mere sight of another dog creates aggression, then other dogs must be brought into view. As soon as the fighter perceives them, the Jolly Routine must be initiated and continued until the upset animal is imbued with happiness. If the simple odor of a sibling through a door creates hostile reactions, the aggressive dog must be exposed to the odor and the Jolly Routine undertaken by the owners.

Depending on the dogs involved and the degree of success with early attempts using the Jolly Routine, the potential antagonists should be brought closer more often. In some cases this occurs on the very first day, often within an hour. In seriously ingrained cases, it may take up to 6 weeks of conditioning to achieve success.

I have seen good results when the dogs involved have been handled on leashes in conjunction with this routine. We find that a sharp sound distraction used at the instant the trigger stimulus appears, followed by the Jolly Routine, makes the task considerably quicker and easier than with any other training aid.

Other elements necessary to rehabilitate these dogs include:

- Instant command response at least to Come, Sit and Stay.
- Total avoidance of solicitousness toward the dog(s) by family members.
- The owner's ability to act jolly when stimuli triggering hostility appear, plus the dog's tendency to respond with tail wagging or other pleasant behavioral reactions.

- Discontinuance of all territorial urine marking.
- Where freedom frustration is a factor, the physical environment must be modified so as to alleviate the animal's proximity to frustrating stimuli.
- Avoidance of emotional displays or threatening handling by the owner in the event fighting occurs.
- Removing the involved dogs from the home territory (in the case of sibling fighting), combined with increasingly frequent visits by the owner before field trips, concluding with a return to the original situation.

As mentioned previously in the section on Biting, fighting between kenneled Foxhounds ceased after the dogs' canine teeth were ground down to a level just below that of the incisors.

Killing Other Animals (Predatory Behavior)

Dogs have not travelled far along the evolutionary road since the time they hunted and killed for food. In fact, some breeds are still selectively bred for their tendency to chase or stalk prey and at least capture, if not kill and/or eat them. Notable among these are the Terriers, Dachshunds, sighthounds and various hunting breeds. It is no wonder then, that pet dogs occasionally succumb to their ancestral tendency, even without special training.

Dogs are often inadvertently trained to kill. For example, many dog owners have urged their pets (sometimes playfully) to chase cats, squirrels and stray dogs, and are often horrified when their dogs bring home the neighbor's Teacup Poodle as a trophy of the chase. Sometimes other animals, usually cats, have "trained" dogs to become killers. These animals do this unknowingly by sitting on fences, rooftops, in trees or beyond fences, tantalizing the dog from a safe vantage point. After enough of this teasing, the dog becomes sufficiently frustrated to attack an animal when the opportunity presents itself.

Dogs that kill other animals are usually, but not necessarily, of the excitable type and react aggressively or dominantly to other species or smaller dogs. The killing of smaller dogs or cats by larger dogs is usually the case in urban areas. However, when dog packs operate as hunting groups, much larger animals become the prey, sometimes even people.

Most dogs that have killed people, either by themselves or in packs, select children as their prey. Child killings (especially those committed by lone dogs) have usually occurred at or within the dog's "territory," or have involved a child who screamed shrilly when first approached or knocked down. A small percentage of dogs appears to be stimulated in the most primitive way by the screaming of any animal: their reaction is to kill that animal. Wild canids have killed members of their own pack that cry out after they have become trapped or are injured.

Dogs that kill other animals should be differentiated from those with a fighting problem. Most dog fights end before either of the combatants is seriously injured. These episodes rarely result in the death of either dog. Predatory attacks aimed at killing the prey animal are deliberate, with the fangs aimed at the base of the prey's neck just above the shoulders. If the prey is on its back, the soft flesh of the throat or belly is attacked. A predatory attack also usually includes violent shaking of the victim. Rarely does a domestic dog actually eat its kill, though some that prey on chickens and other fowl tend to do so more often that cat or dog killers.

Correcting Predatory Attacks

The method I advise has worked well, even with older dogs. In principle, it involves desensitizing the offender through intense exposure to the chosen prey. This avoids force or punishment such as that involved in the often-recommended methods whereby the prey is forced into the dog's mouth and the mouth taped shut, or where the prey is hung around the dog's neck until it virtually rots off the collar. Both of these rather harsh methods have worked with many dogs. However, it is rare that an owner will carry them out. Especially with very excitable or aggressive dogs, the situation can become much worse and produce other behavioral problems.

Whatever the prey involved, a sufficient number of prey animals must be obtained for retraining sessions at least 3 times weekly, or twice daily with several hours between sessions. In a controlled situation (dog on leash if necessary), the dog must be exposed to the potential prey and its response converted from an aggressive response to a happy, playful response, first toward the owner and then toward the prey animals. This Jolly Routine is essentially the same as that used for fighting, general aggression, biting or shy and fearful pets.

The routine works most effectively if some novel, intervening stimulus can be applied to distract the offender at the *instant* the dog notices the prey. Each retraining session should end when the dog shows signs of genuine relaxation in the presence of the prey and seems content to undertake some other activity. This may include playing fetch, performing basic obedience routines (the most helpful pastime of all) or simply ignoring the prey animals. The routine should take place on a regular schedule spanning 6 weeks for permanent correction. If at the end of this time the dog has still not learned to adjust to the prey animals, the program should be extended.

If the dog attacks its prey only in the presence of one or more owners, it is necessary that all the owners gain a strong leader position through off-leash command responses to Come, Sit and Stay. Without this degree of control and orientation, the program will probably be unsuccessful. All fondling should be stopped, and brief petting should be given only as a reward for response to commands. For example, if the dog approaches and nuzzles for attention, it is immediately told to Sit, after which the owner may say "Good dog," and pat the dog a couple of times for its performance. In some cases involving bossy leader dogs, this command response training should be continued for several weeks before actual exposure to prey so the owner can gain the proper position of leadership. The value of this part of the program is seen in the owner's increased confidence when directing the jolly sessions.

Grinding the canine teeth down to a level just below that of the incisors has reportedly curtailed fighting and biting in a limited number of cases. No cases involving killing animals have been reported. However, the technique may be useful.

Chasing Vehicles and Other Moving Objects

For no apparent reason, the instinct to chase seems to be stronger in some dogs than in others. In sighthounds (Greyhounds, Basenjis, Afghans, etc), this tendency is understandable from a genetic standpoint, in that their early selection favored strong sight and low thresholds for chase reflex excitation. In other breeds not of the sighthound class, the tendency is probably genetic in its initial stages (the dog as a pup probably displayed strong chase tendencies) but develops into problem behavior through frustration or reinforcement. The dog may be behind a barrier or on a tether relative to fast-moving objects, or may even have been encouraged to chase vehicles through naive behavior by the owner. An example of this inadvertent stimulation of chasing is the owner who chases bike-mounted neighborhood children off the sidewalk. A dog witnessing this a few times thereafter assumes the guard-duty function.

Another element often present in dogs that chase moving objects is an overdeveloped sense of territorial defense that has been allowed to extend well beyond the dog's own yard. Aggressive dogs with overprotective tendencies often attempt to keep their territories clear of invading vehicles. This tendency is frequently noted in dogs that are either allowed to wander around their neighborhood or that are taken on regular walks during which they urine mark beyond their own territorial limits. Females as well as males may claim "street right" and chase cars.

Correcting Chasing Behavior

In young pups or dogs that have only chased a few times, correction is far simpler than if the dog has been chasing for more than a few weeks. Early correction can usually be made by transforming the stimulus, whether it is a car, bicycle, motorcycle, children on skates, etc, from an attractive to an aversive stimulus. One of the most effective methods involves the "monkey-see, monkey-do" principle. This requires the cooperation of one or several car owners who are prepared for the dog and stop their vehicle before any injury can be sustained. If bicycles, motorcycles or other stimuli cause the chase, these of course should be employed.

The owner should walk with the dog toward the street from various starting points the dog has used in the past or would be likely to use in the future for its attacks. Just as the dog starts to break into its run, the owner should suddenly reverse direction away from the vehicle, shouting as if fearful. The vehicle's operator must slam on the brakes, screeching the tires to a halt, after which the vehicle and operator must remain still until owner and dog have retreated to their own property and have gone from sight. Then, the vehicle should be driven or pedaled onward and a repeat performance set up.

The process must be repeated until the owner no longer needs to reverse his direction to stimulate the dog to retreat back to its own property. This may take as many as 20 repetitions, with the cooperating operators and vehicles rotating their appearances. When this is accomplished, the same method is used, with the owner absent from the scene, to test the degree of conditioning obtained. If the dog resumes chasing the vehicles, the procedure should be started anew until success is achieved.

The value of this method is best demonstrated in young dogs or those that have recently acquired the behavior. In older and more experienced dogs, more preparation and work are required. The tenacious chaser is usually one that has been at it for more than a few weeks. Underlying causes frequently involve more than simple satisfaction of a chase reflex. Many affected dogs have suffered severe injuries from their "conquests" after catching up with the mechanical prey, and yet have persisted in their folly to chase cars and other fast-moving vehicles.

In these cases, the total environmental and behavioral background must be examined to determine the causative factors; these must then be removed. Possible inciting causes include:

- Barrier or tether frustration.
- Wandering free around the neighborhood.
- Regular walks and urine marking.
- Tendencies acquired through the owner's previous anxiety or overt chase behavior of vehicles or children on skates, skateboards, bikes, etc.

In any of the above situations, the dog is usually aggressive and excitable, and often in a leadership role in its relationships with its owners and with other people. For such dominant dogs, correction proceeds as follows:

- The owner must gain a strong off-leash and nonphysical leader relationship with the dog through command teaching and general environmental adjustments. If the dog pesters for an owner response, the dog must respond to a command before any petting or other action.
- Neighborhood roving, walks, barrier frustration, and any owner hostility toward vehicles must be stopped.
- The method described above for young or novice chasers may then be applied after a minimum of one and a maximum of about a dozen sessions involving up to 6 vehicle setups per session over a period of 3 weeks.

This correction method takes time and patience. However, the habit in these cases is ingrained and the owner must be prepared to accept that "unlearning" usually takes longer than the initial learning of such a serious problem.

Other devices that have been successful are described in much of the popular literature and involve applying some sort of unpleasant stimulus to the chasing dog. These include the dangerous actions of squirting the dog from the vehicle with lemon juice, diluted ammonia or some other noxious fluid, throwing chains (up to even more than 1/2 lb) at the animal from a hidden vantage point, shock collars, tying a long lead (up to 60 feet) on the dog's collar and yanking it as it approaches the vehicle and, incredibly, accompanying the dog on the chase and then suspending it by a choke collar until the animal becomes unconscious. These methods may work with some animals, but the risk of heightening anxiety and aggression toward the chase target, coupled with the reluctance of most owners to apply such measures, dictates that a better way is usually desirable in everyday practice.

One boasted to me that he had "cured" his dog of car chasing by shooting it with rocksalt from a 20-gauge shotgun. His only complaint about his now-adult pet was that every New Year and July 4th, the dog tried to eat its way through the back door. The obvious side effect had cost the owner more than $150 in screen and backdoor replacements. The fellow was genuinely convinced that his dog was neurotic. I could only comment at this point that *something* was surely neurotic about the situation!

Another client spread thumb tacks in the street and then allowed the dog to chase the cars. In doing so, he had not solved the problem, but had succeeded in training the dog, a 2-year-old Doberman Pinscher, to long-jump almost 15 feet over the tacks to carry on its merry chase. In this case, the standard method outlined above succeeded in a matter of 2 weekends involving about 4 sessions and 5 vehicles.

Sexual Mounting and Jumping Up

Problems concerning sexual mounting and jumping up are combined in this section because they tend to be caused by similar owner actions; corrective measures are closely related. In basic canine behavior, the act of placing the forefeet upon another animal indicates dominance as is the act of mounting.

Causes

In puppies, mounting seems to have some roots in physiologic development or conditions. However, when mounting or jumping up persists in a dog older than 6 months, the cause is usually found within the external environment. Often the owners have either tolerated or encouraged this behavior. Among the physiologic causes of sexual mounting are: proestrus or estrus (in bitches); male response to estrus in a neighborhood bitch; and hypersexuality in males, evidenced by frequent erections when petted, general excitability and aggressiveness.

Most cases of jumping up involve dogs that have been rough-housed extensively, inconsistently allowed to jump up onto the owner's lap or, in large breeds, allowed to place the feet upon the owner's chest or shoulders. In other words, the problem behavior has been taught and the owners naively think their dogs can discriminate between guests who permit such behavior and those who do not, the types of clothing worn by people (it's OK if I'm wearing my old clothes, but not if I'm wearing my good ones), inside jumping vs outside jumping (you can jump up in the yard, but not in the house), etc. In these cases of inconsistent treatment, the owners are unaware of the potent training methods they are using. That is, intermittent and random reinforcement teaches more effectively in many situations than methods involving regularly applied reinforcement.

Correcting Sexual Mounting

Sexual mounting has been successfully treated in many cases by neutering the offender. However, when the behavior is psychologically ingrained, this may be ineffective. If the dog (male or female) is neutered in an attempt at correction, environmental/behavioral alterations are also advisable. It should go without saying that the owners must not allow or encourage further sexual mounting.

> *An example of inconsistency involved a couple with 2 teenage boys and a year-old mixed Shepherd. The parents went on a 2-week vacation and left the boys to fend for themselves. On their return, they were horrified to see the dog mounting their younger boy (14 years old) with the tenacity of what the mother described as a "sex maniac." The dog literally had to be pried off the boy's leg by 2 people.*
>
> *In consultation, the boy indicated that the objectionable behavior began shortly after the parents left for vacation, which was also the time that the dog was allowed to sleep on the boy's bed at night. The boy was an exceptionally sound sleeper, but he had been awakened several times by his pet's amorous clutching at an elevated knee. This was discouraged by lowering the knee and scolding the dog, but subsequently the behavior became worse and the dog would often be put outside to sleep. This produced a secondary behavioral probelm: the dog barked when left alone in the yard at night.*

This case did not seem to include the usual permissiveness or even encouragement of mounting by the owners, an element that is prevalent in most sexual mounting problems. It was probably true that the boy slept so soundly that the dog actually experienced satisfaction without the sleeping partner's knowledge. Though most of my cases do not include extensive discussion about permitting or encouraging the act, I have had clients who mentioned rather elaborate sexual rituals with their pets. In these instances I have found it helpful to maintain a neutral profile while listening to the descriptions, and then explain the relationship of the activity to the problem. Clients have always made the behavioral adjustments necessary to eliminate the causes of the problem.

Doting or fondling of the dog must be stopped. If the dog pesters for attention, it should be given a command before any reward of spoken praise or petting. Rewards should be friendly and brief, no longer than a few seconds. I say "a few seconds" because in some cases the owner may use the dog's response as an excuse to pet and fondle it for as long as 10 minutes. This, of course, encourages the practice that contributed to the problem in the first place.

When correcting sexual mounting, it is best to distract the dog to some other activity before it becomes firmly attached to a leg or other part of the owner's anatomy. The early signs of mounting are usually easy to spot. A rather vacant stare as the animal approaches, pawing at the owner's legs, a "humping" motion, or penile erection signal the onset of some sexual action, and mark the ideal time for distraction.

Distracting agents I have used include throwing a ball or some other plaything, followed by several minutes of intensive play-exercise; issuance of a command to Sit and Stay, to be maintained until the dog appears settled; and application of a sharp sound as an intervening stimulus, followed by quiet praise when the dog stops the mounting attempts.

Traditional corrections that usually fail include stepping on the hind toes to discourage mounting; sharply raising the knee into the dog's chest area to knock it away from the leg; and picking up the offender and shaking it while saying "No." Less traditional, and equally ineffective, approaches include hitting the dog on the muzzle, holding a lighted cigarette in the target area of the romantic pet, and shouting, screaming and other hysterical behavior.

Severe physical punishment may lead to other behavior problems. Also, with aggressive dogs, the act of sexual mounting is sometimes closely related to general aggressive tendencies, and a strong physical rebuff can produce biting, even in puppies under 6 months old.

If mounting is accompanied by penile erection in male dogs, castration combined with correction of the causative factors has been successful. The effects of neutering may not become evident for up to 90 days, though in most cases some lessening of sexual aggression is noted within a day or so. In spayed bitches with masculine tendencies, progestin hormone therapy has been helpful when carefully supervised by a veterinarian.

Correcting Jumping Up

Jumping up on people is a highly social and usually dominant way for dogs to say "Hello." Play-fighting by dominant types involves similar behavior. The socially bold dog that is isolated often jumps excitedly when a person enters its area. Removal of the causative factors, such as excessive isolation, horseplay between owners and their dogs (or neighbors, friends, etc), or what appears to be genuine hyperexcitability, must be accompanied by some recognition by the dog of the leadership position of its owners.

The jumper that does not respond to traditional knee, stomp or push methods of correction is usually the excitable and socially bold type. Such a dog's response may be even more tenacious (albeit usually good-natured) malbehavior. If simple command responses are taught on a nonphysical basis, the corrections are generally easily accomplished. Dogs that respond readily to Come, Sit and Stay commands are quick to recognize behavior that displeases their leaders.

One method of stopping the jumping is to crouch down so the object of attention, the owner's face, is where the pet need not jump to achieve its greeting (Fig 5). This requires physical stamina and patience in the case of extremely exuberant pets, but it yields excellent results quickly in mild cases.

A method that often works with highly reactive dogs is a quick, toward-the-dog movement, almost like a cha-cha dance step, followed by absolute stillness of the owner. The sudden movement toward the pet often stops its approach; the following stillness secures calmness. If a jump is still in the offing, a quick side step, followed by absolute stillness, is called for. This method takes more time than some others, but the cure is lasting once achieved.

Use of a distracting stimulus has proved effective when applied as the dog approaches with the intent of jumping. This may involve throwing a ball or some other unique stimulus. After a few such distractions, the dog will be conditioned not to jump up. If a ball has been thrown, a frantic search for the play object is a substitute behaviorism often welcomed by harassed owners or guests.

In all cases of correction, the dog must be praised with a soft-spoken "Good dog" and petted, if at all, in a slow and calming manner. This helps reinforce following behavior and instills calmness to replace the previous excitement.

Another effective deterrent is to allow the dog to jump, then grab the forepaws and hold them until the dog *starts* to pull them away. Then the paws are instantly released, the hands are put behind the owner's back, and praise is spoken. This reinforces the reflex to withdraw the feet from entrapment. Putting the hands behind the back avoids calling the dog's attention to them, as some dogs have substituting hand-biting for jumping when this has not been done. A few corrections usually solve the problem.

Figure 5. A simple way to prevent jumping up when a dog greets you is to crouch down.

When small children or other animals are involved, correction takes longer, as the adult owner must supervise the correction sessions. Dogs that jump up on children are usually stimulated to do so by the child's behavior. Therefore, the child must run or play with the dog while the parent applies correction before outright jumping takes place. In these cases, distraction with a sharp sound is especially valuable because it represents a neutral stimulus (one not requiring the owner's voice or movement). Therefore, the dog's conditioned behavioral inhibition will more easily relate to the child than to the owner's presence or voice.

Some clients have told me of success in correcting jumping related to children through use of pebbles tossed at the dog, BB guns shot at the dog's rump (a dangerous practice for canine and child eyes), and water thrown on the dog or squirted through a hose. All of these were effective in some instances, but aggravated the problem in others. The methods I recommend avoid the aggravation of physical punishment or injury while allowing the owner's position of leadership to control the pet's general behavior beyond the immediate problem.

(This page intentionally left blank)

Unruly Behavior

With all types of unruly behavior, the fundamental relationship between the owners and the dog must be modified at the time corrective programs are applied. Such modifications include:

- *Instituting the learn-to-earn praise and petting regimen.* The dog must be pleasantly told Sit or Down when it seeks attention or when the owners feel like petting. After compliance, the dog is petted and praised briefly (3-5 seconds), and released.
- *Applying the leadership by movement exercise.* In daily activity with the dog, any time it begins to move ahead of the owners, they must immediately clap hands *once* and reverse directions until the dog follows them dependably.
- *Avoiding emotional homecomings and departures.*
- *Avoiding physical punishment and/or scolding.*

Dashing In or Out of Doors

About half of dogs that dash out of doors do so because they are frustrated by captivity. The others are either trying to get into the house to socialize with their owners or to continue their social contact by attempting to leave with the owner.

Whatever the basic motivation, the act can be both financially and emotionally costly. Such door-dashing has seriously injured children and elderly people, caused premature birth in pregnant women, resulted in injury and death of the dog and, in one case, caused an automobile accident when a motorist swerved to miss the dog.

Causes

When the problem involves a dog that dashes merely to get *out there* to run about the neighborhood, avoiding its owners' pleas to return, the pet is usually unruly in other circumstances as well. These cases often involve an independent, self-oriented (spoiled) dog. Other factors may involve an early history of unrestricted outdoor activity, followed by restriction because of some problem that has arisen outside (fighting, car chasing, etc).

Some cases involve continuous frustration relative to neighborhood activities, such as the dog's "fretting" behind a gate or at a window. Depending on the excitability of the animal, it may develop the same type of stereotyped behavior seen in fence-running dogs. Simple freedom-dashing may be tension relieving in itself, or the escaped dog may have a frustration target, such as passing cars, playing children, mail carrier or other animals.

Correcting the Freedom Dasher

By the time I see a freedom-dashing dog, the pet has already failed to respond to traditional methods of scolding and/or punishment. Some punishments are inordinately harsh. One client had repeatedly shot his dog in the rump with a pellet gun whenever it tried to escape. I strongly disapprove of such dangerous methods. Another rather harsh method that has succeeded (usually inadvertently) entails shutting the door on the dog as it proceeds through. This risks physical injury and is not recommended. Depending on the degree of tenacity shown by the dog, either of 2 methods can be used. A prerequisite to both is that the owner gain off-leash command responses, at least to Come, Sit and Stay.

Given a moderately severe problem and a dog that is easily stimulated by quick movement, the first method requires that the owner, other family members, and friends perform the following steps.

1. Approach the door or gate. (Of course, the door-dasher will be close by.)

2. Given an inward-opening door, abruptly open it no more than 2 inches and slam it loudly. An outward-opening door should be opened no more than an inch and then closed very quickly, or the dog may push through.

3. As the door is slammed, the owner must abruptly move away from it at least 8 feet and praise the dog for following, after which the owner should be encouraged to remain still for at least a minute (Fig 1). If the dog remains at the door, steps 1, 2 and 3 must be repeated until the dog retreats along with the owner.

4. Step 3 must be repeated until the dog *stays* away from the door when the owner approaches it and when the door is opened. When this occurs, the door should be opened a full foot. If the pet dashes, the door should again be slammed shut and Step 3 applied with this larger opening.

5. Step 4 is repeated until the door can be opened to its normal exit width, with the dog staying at least 8 feet away from it. When

Figure 1. As the dog dashes toward the opening, the gate or door is slammed shut, causing the dog to withdraw. Repetition teaches the dog to accept open gates or doors without dashing through.

this is accomplished the owner must stay inside, close the door, return to the dog and praise it quietly. Then the owner should remain in the house, going about some other activity for at least half an hour before repeating the procedure.

6. When the dog stays away from the door on the initial approach, the owner should then proceed outside, close the door and stay away for at least 15 minutes, after which s/he should return as nonchalantly as possible (Figs 2, 3).

If this method is applied daily for a few days, most dogs begin to ignore the comings and goings of their owners. Dogs that are extremely tenacious in their efforts to dash through a door ahead of people often have a long history of frustration about barriers, or are highly motivated by a strong stimulus on the other side of the door.

A word of caution about using the command "Stay" to solve a serious dashing problem: It might seem practical to simply tell the dog to Stay, and then proceed through a door. The trouble with this method is that people often forget to give the command or are not aware that the dog is lurking nearby, ready to make its frantic dash. If a command is needed to stop the dog, all is lost. On the other hand, the leadership by movement exercise conditions the dog to respond in a certain manner to a particular situation without a command. This conditioning is permanent and eliminates the difficulties of inconsistent verbal commands.

Figure 2. These dogs have been taught to refrain from passing through an open gate or door, even if their owner appears to be leaving.

Figure 3. The dogs bolt through the gate only after being released with "Okay!"

Jumping Fences

Of all behavior problems, fence jumping generally requires the most careful consideration. When, where and why the problem occurs must be determined before corrective measures can be taken. When this is understood, the solutions become apparent.

Causes

Most dogs jump fences when their owners are absent. This leads us to ask just why the pet is shut out of the house when the owners go away. Destructive behavior in the house is often the underlying complaint. A solution to the destructiveness is more pertinent than an effort to correct fence jumping.

If the dog is jumping out at a location where the fence or gate is only 3 feet high, a simple physical adjustment may entail raising the level of the barrier (Fig 4).

Fence jumping usually involves social factors. The dog is often seeking the company of other dogs or people. The social aspect is most evident in dogs that are shut out of their homes and jump even when the family is present. These dogs generally wind up scratching at the front door to get back into the family group. Installation of a dog door may clear this up rather quickly.

The cause of goal-oriented fence jumping usually relates to the animal's ultimate activity when it is free of the yard. For

243

example, one dog jumped the fence only on Thursday mornings. Many dogs were allowed to roam free in the neighborhood, and tended to congregate on Thursday morning, which happened to be garbage collection time. The normally content pet needed only the extra stimulus of the weekly dog pack to sufficiently motivate it to jump a 6-foot block wall. The solution to this problem involved keeping the dog in the house on Thursday mornings for a few weeks to break the pattern. After 6 months, the clients were still keeping the pet inside and seemed content with the arrangement, and the dog displayed no anxiety.

The sexually motivated jumper is more difficult to correct, especially if its behavior has been rewarded. The simplest correction is to keep the dog or bitch indoors until the season is over. When this is impossible and no physical adjustments can be made, some sort of conditioning to reshape the jumping is required. This will be discussed later.

Dogs that are permitted to roam or are regularly walked in the neighborhood and allowed to urinate freely may jump fences for the purpose of re-marking their territory and/or fighting with other neighborhood dogs. When these elements are present, the walks must be stopped as part of the correction. Urine marking can develop into a habitual pattern. Urban pet owners

Figure 4. If the dog jumps the fence at a specific location, the height of the fence in that area can be raised.

believe this activity is necessary for the happiness of their dogs, especally male animals. It may appear to be rewarding, but it is actually an idiosyncrasy of city dogs rarely noted in their rural cousins. The primary reason for this behavior is that owners allow it to occur. If all owners prevented their pets from urinating around the neighborhood, a major cause of fence jumping would be eliminated.

Several cases have involved dogs that apparently perceived the yard itself as an aversive stimulus at certain times. For example, one dog with a history of digging tended to jump the fence just before its owners arrived home. The animal had been severely punished when the owners arrived home and found fresh holes in the yard. Therefore, the dog began to relate the existence of holes and the presence of its owners with punishment. When the dog's biological clock told it that the owners were due to arrive, the animal left the yard.

Frustration with confinement is also responsible for a good deal of jumping. A dog that is isolated and does not receive enough social interaction will often try to escape. Freedom then becomes a goal in itself, no matter the consequences in terms of later punishment or further confinement.

Correcting Fence Jumping

In addition to such obvious corrective measures as getting the dog into the house, installing a pet door, raising the wall, and curtailing neighborhood walks and urination, the following steps have proved helpful.

Sometimes it is effective to erect an inner fence to interfere with the animal's approach to the barrier. In some cases, an inner fence of only 30 inches has proved effective. If the pet climbs the main barrier, an inward-slanting overhang can be installed along the top of the wall. One bright client saved the expense of raising his wall by digging sunken gardens around the inside perimeter. The dry moats interrupted the dog's approach and raised the effective height of the wall.

Corrective measures should never include use of shock collars, tethers, hobbles, physical punishment, electrified fences and noxious chemicals applied to the wall. Though I have heard of instances in which these have succeeded, the risk of injury and adverse behavioral side effects is great. Complications from use of such measures have included viciousness, death from hanging by a collar, physical burns from caustics on the wall, self-mutilation with hobbles, and poor owner/dog relationships resulting from punishment.

"Invisible" Fences: With "invisible" electric shock fencing, an electric shock is emitted from a collar on the dog's neck if the dog crosses a wire around the perimeter of the yard. To delineate for the dog the area beyond which the dog should not pass, the perimeter should be marked with obvious cues. The procedure requires a great deal of time and effort, and the devices are expensive.

While manufacturers and adherents of the "invisible" fencing devices claim many successes, the system has more drawbacks than traditional fencing relative to safety of the dog and possible trespassers. These warrant serious consideration. First, aggressive stray dogs or malicious people are not affected and are free to attack or harass the electrically confined pet. Second, the pain associated with the perimeter may also be associated with passersby, including children. If the "fenced" dog feels aggressive toward outsiders and they cross the property line, the result could be unfortunate for all parties concerned.

In the urban setting, the most obvious correction is to move the dog into the house during the times it tends to escape. If underlying problems, such as housesoiling, destructive chewing, or jumping out windows, are involved, these problems must be resolved initially.

Straining on the Leash

"Who is walking whom?" This question pops into my mind whenever I see owners being dragged down the street by their dogs. Leash pulling usually becomes a complaint only after a large dog has finally succeeding in pulling its owners off their feet, with resultant injury or embarrassment.

Most cases of leash pulling involve dogs that have accommodated to the discomfort of a choke chain or leather collar. Some of them cease pulling only long enough to regurgitate or take a few deep breaths, then continue struggling forward. Reasons for leash restraint in such dogs include biting at whatever is beyond reach, jumping up on people who approach, and running away from the restricting influence of the owner whenever the opportunity presents itself.

Correcting Straining on the Leash

Most leash pullers are leader types, so more than one problem must be solved. One simple correction might be to teach the dog to heel on command. Then, walks would be spent with the animal dutifully positioned alongside the owner. However, this method avoids solving the primary problem. If the dog is not told to Heel, it generally reverts to straining on the leash. Other steps are needed to solve the basic problem.

Leash pullers often respond well to a technique that incorporates the dog's natural tendency to follow. If the dog moves ahead, the owner simply turns around and walks the other direction. This puts the dog behind the owner. A 6-foot leash is needed for this method. Only about 4 feet of it are used; the remainder is reserved for slippage, as the leash is never allowed to pull on the dog.

The leash is tightened only at the moment of correction, when the leash is jerked with a quick wrist action (Figs 5, 6). The procedures should be practiced with another person holding the dog's end of the leash. When the assistant feels no continual tug, but only a sharp jerk, it can be tried with the dog.

The direction of the leash jerk is also important. It is almost impossible to hold a large dog back from directly behind it without actually stimulating the animal to pull away. Holding the dog from behind is one of the elements in training sled dogs to pull, and guard dogs to attack. If, on the other hand, the jerk on the leash is toward one side of the dog, it affects the dog's balance and usually triggers an orienting reflex. Spoken praise gains the animal's attention as the trainer walks away in another direction. The new path is then followed as long as the dog remains slightly behind the trainer. If the dog starts to overtake the trainer, a quick 180-degree left turn in front of the dog places it again behind or at the side of the trainer.

This process results in a rather chaotic walk with one's dog, but it teaches the animal to be oriented to the owner's movements rather than to its own. The first sessions should be held

Figure 5. When the dog begins to move ahead of the owner, a sharp 180-degree left turn again places the dog behind the owner. If the dog has already moved ahead of the owner, one can make a sharp 90- or 180-degree right turn while suddenly jerking on the leash.

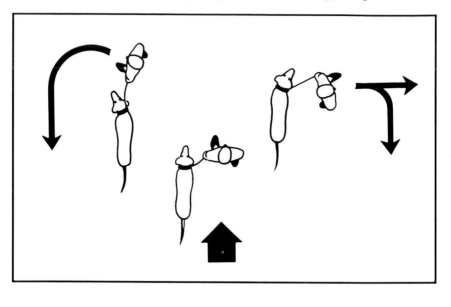

Figure 6. The leash can be held behind the back during training to give a quick tug if the dog moves ahead or strays off course. The leash is kept slack and only jerked as needed.

in an area with minimal distractions and at least 30 feet of walking distance in all directions. As the pet becomes more responsive, it should be taken to larger and more distracting locales, as well as smaller areas, such as in the house. Daily practice for 2-6 weeks normally gains harmony of movement between owner and dog.

Jerk and Praise: When a pet resists moving on a leash, which is not uncommon in puppies, a different technique can be used. Pulling the animal usually only succeeds in frightening it and creating more resistance. Success has been achieved with the jerk and praise method. This requires that the leash be placed on the dog, after which the trainer walks ahead a few feet, crouches, claps and praises the recalcitrant dog, applying the quick jerk only if the pet refuses to move.

If the praise does not bring the dog, even after a couple of quick jerks, the trainer must then move behind the dog. A good deal of happy praise must accompany this procedure so as to keep the pet oriented to the trainer. Once behind the animal, the trainer crouches again, praising, clapping and otherwise behaving pleasantly. If this directional switching is continued long enough, even the most obstinate dog responds by approaching.

Overcoming fearfulness takes time. An older dog that resists moving on a leash has had some frightening experience relative to the leash and/or the individual handling it. Care should be taken to avoid rushing the pet. The first session may only produce a single approach by the frightened animal. One should then try the next day and aim for gradual rehabilitation, rather than creating more problems by expecting too much too soon.

If the above procedure does not produce results within 4 days, the owner should try putting the leash on the dog before feeding. For a few days the owner walks with the pet to the food bowl, letting the leash drag behind. When fear of the leash has disappeared, the leash may be picked up and the "jerk and praise" technique tried again. This sequence is usually successful.

The weight of chain leashes stresses the dog's neck. Also, because this system of correcting leash pulling requires the trainer to hold a 6-foot leash at 4 feet, a chain can present difficulties. A leather leash is more desirable because of its light weight and soft texture.

Running Away

A dog that runs away from home has somewhere to go. It astounds me that in most cases the owners cannot tell me where their dog goes. The usual answer is, "Just out in the neighborhood to see the other dogs or something."

These dogs have a definite objective in mind and habitually cover the same route during each journey. Why is that route or objectives more appealing than its home environment? It must be that its own environment is lacking in some respect. The root of the problem usually is the owner. The dog is often either overdependent or is not in a subordinate position in relation to the owner. All corrective procedures must start with the relationship between dog and owner, except when minor external environmental adjustments are needed, such as gaining a misguided neighbor's cooperation to stop feeding the dog when it comes around.

Correcting Running Away

The relationship between dog and owner must always be considered first when solving a runaway problem. When the dog is overdependent or too independent, it must be taught, without tethers or physical manipulation, to Come, Sit and Stay on command. The owner must make a general environmental adjustment and avoid all fondling or other stimulus-response situations that subordinate the owner to the dog's whims. For instance, a dog that nudges for petting, food tidbits, or to be let outside must be given some simple command, and then told "Good dog" and petted briefly when it obeys. The pet should then be ignored while the owner continues whatever activity was interrupted by the dog's solicitation. This helps reorient the dog to its owner's control and reverses the leadership position. Combined with daily training sessions and other corrective measures, this procedure produces results in 1-3 weeks.

Owners who allow their dogs to roam free in the neighborhood are contributing to the runaway problem, and should be made aware of the dangers related to this practice. The pet's safety and health are at risk because of poisoning, road accidents, fighting, and diseases contracted from other animals. The animal may become lost, picked up by animal control officers or stolen. What is seldom considered also is that the owner may be subjected to civil suit or criminal charges if the wandering pet causes destruction of property, including fights with other dogs, or human injury.

If an owner cannot appreciate the folly of allowing a pet to roam, any attempt at teaching the animal to behave at home is wasted. When the dog has been taught to accept the confines of its own property, the problem of running away is solved, and such associated problems as dashing in or out of doors, jumping fences, and other escape behavior can be dealt with effectively.

Licking and Sniffing at People

The first licking experienced by a puppy comes from its dam even before the pup's eyes are open. Licking is used to groom the pup and, after feeding, to cause urination and defecation. It is doubtful that a young pup consciously considers licking a dominant behavior. However, the act of licking can acquire various other meanings to puppies as they mature and gain feedback from other animals (including people) they lick. Licking by neonatal pups is usually aimed at the dam's mouth and, at least in wild canines, elicits a gratifying regurgitation of food by the dam for its offspring. This behavior is also seen in domestic litters, even though it seldom results in a meal from the bitch.

This section discusses dogs that lick objectionably (to the owners) as a device to attract some response from its owners or another animal. Licking involved in self-grooming is discussed in the section on self-mutilation.

Problem Licking

Licking another animal can broadly be classified as care-seeking behavior. However, in some bitches and apparently "feminized" males, licking may occur as a genuine mutual grooming gesture, which could be considered dominant behavior in such situations. When one dog tries to lick the genitals of another, the behavior is considered submissive. This is usually practiced by submissive pack members toward their dominant counterparts.

Licking seems to acquire different meanings when the puppy is brought into the human group. The significance of licking then depends on the type of feedback provided by the pup or its owners. The old idea that dogs lick our hands to benefit from the salt on our skin rarely applies to licking problems. Rather, the problem generally involves a submissive dog and a permissive owner. In these cases, early episodes of licking are permitted (some people feel genuinely flattered when their dog licks them) and the dog appears to enjoy the owner's response.

Only once has a client complained to me of a licking problem. In this case the objection was not about the licking *per se*, but that the dog practiced the habit in the middle of the night and ruined a good night's sleep. Otherwise the owner tolerated and even enjoyed the ritual.

In many cases, licking is a factor in another type of problem behavior. These usually involve the dog's use of licking to dominate the owner's attentions or to demonstrate its dominant feelings relative to the owner.

Correcting Problem Licking

Licking is a problem only when the owner is present. Therefore, licking is usually easily stopped merely by telling the dog not to do it or by moving away and avoiding it. After a few days or weeks of this rejection, the problem disappears. However, this procedure does not correct the basis of the problem, that is, attempts to dominate the owner through such behavior.

In addition to discouraging licking, the dog must be taught to respond to commands, and owner adjustments made if the dog is "coddled" or otherwise doted on. When it seeks petting or tries to dominate the owner, it should be given a simple command, such as Sit, and then petted briefly as a reward for obedience.

I also usually recommend use of some intervening stimulus when the dog begins to pester the owner. Whether this involves introduction of a chewable toy that the pet is urged to fetch, or a sharp sound, the goal is to divert the animal's mind off licking and onto something else. During the initial stages of correction, there may be seen many types of substitutional behavior, such as whining, pacing or self-licking. If ignored, this behavior usually disappears in a few days.

Pestering Problems

Many dogs are described as "perfect pets," except that they become constant, good-natured pests when guests visit or the owners' attentions are diverted, such as during telephone calls, reading or watching television. If scolded or punished, these dogs react by coming back for more. Though their dog does not develop problems of aggression, submissive wetting or self-mutilation, the owners would like to curtail the pestering while preserving the pet's generally pleasant personality and behavior. The following program usually meets these objectives. It does not use punishment or scolding, yet curtails the pestering behavior.

1. Put the dog on the learn-to-earn praise and petting program. It must be told pleasantly to Sit or Down to earn its rewards.

2. Command the dog to Sit (praise), Down (praise), Sit (praise) and Down (praise), then release it after 4 commands. Do this until all 4 responses are performed quickly (within 5 seconds for small and medium-sized breeds, 7-8 seconds for large breeds).

3. Whenever the dog begins pestering, the target person initiates the sequence of 4 commands, as outlined in Step 2. If a set of 4 commands does not calm the pet, the commands should be continued until the dog noticeably slows down in executing them. Then it may be released.

This routine has proven extremely effective with good-natured pestering dogs. It is interesting to note that the dogs usually wag their tails excitedly as they perform the exercise! Therefore, it is not rational to consider the procedure as punishment. The most plausible explanation seems to be that the sheer *intensity* of the exercise, though apparently enjoyable to the dog, fills its need to *interact* with the person commanding the exercise.

Most pestering dogs are good natured but "bossy." Many of these become vocal during the exercise, with yapping or mild howling, even though the tail is wagging. This can be considered good-natured objection, but the vocalizing does not diminish the effectiveness of the procedure.

Stealing Food and Other Articles

Dogs steal food for obvious reasons. The problem is easily managed by keeping food items out of reach. Stealing other articles, however, is a more complex problem and requires more extensive investigation before correction is attempted.

Food

Stealing food is simply eating that which is appealing. My Dalmatian, for instance, had to be taught not to drink my martini when the opportunity presented itself. Because she was encroaching upon her leader's beverage, correction involved only a gruff "get away from that," followed by my own ingestion of the martini. Correction was simple because the Dalmatian recognized that the martini was mine; the drink was never present except in the context of the person drinking it. In most problem cases, the pet has been given food items in certain situations, and expected to ignore the same food at other times, or a naive dog has the opportunity to take food when the owner is not present

The simplest approach to correcting a food stealing problem is the realistic approach. This requires that the owner take special and basically sensible measures to deprive the pet of the opportunity to steal food. It also avoids the need for punishment or the more sophisticated and time-consuming methods used with puppies. The puppy-training methods may be tried if the owner wants to make the sacrifice, but only in conjunction with the standard rule, "Never leave food within the dog's reach."

Other Articles

When various articles, such as shoes, clothing and hair brushes, are stolen, the dog is usually displaying a lack of respect for the owner's leadership (particularly when stealing occurs in the owner's presence), or the dog has learned that its actions instigate an enjoyable ritual, such as a tug-o'-war. These motivations differ somewhat from those of a dog that takes the owner's articles and chews them when alone or when it feels excluded from social activities.

When a lack of leadership and/or tug-o'-war are central to the problem, the pet must be taught simple command responses without punishment so as to reestablish the owner's authority. All fondling of the pet must cease, as well as tug-o'-war and other orally stimulating interaction between owner and dog. As in the case of food stealing, any articles likely to be stolen should be kept out of reach.

If the dog is caught trying to steal an article, the dog should be given commands to Come, Sit and Stay, and praised lavishly for its responses. The gruff "get away from that" warning also helps if followed by praise for positive response away from the article.

Dogs also can be distracted from articles with a sharp sound, but this is usually unnecessary. If this method is to be employed successfully, the sound must be made at the instant the pet appears to be contemplating the theft. Any distracting noise stimulus can be used in the same manner. This could be a slap on a tabletop or stomping on the floor. I never recommend slamming a rolled newspaper, as the paper becomes closely associated with the owner's presence and therefore tends not to inhibit the behavior except when the owner is on the scene. Whatever type of distracting stimulus is used, the owner must maintain a neutral posture so as to avoid owner-dependent inhibition.

(This page intentionally left blank)

10

Destructive Behavior

Destructive Chewing

Irksome and sometimes expensive, destructive chewing usually takes place when the owners are not with the dog. Therefore, correction when the dog begins to chew or is in the act of chewing is impossible. The client who returns home to find the sofa arm hanging in tatters usually becomes upset and punishes the dog, to no avail (Fig 1). A quick look at a dog's eyes during punishment (they are either shut or watching the owner) indicates that the dog's attention is not on the damaged furniture but on the source of punishment. Harmful side effects can ensue, including even heightened chewing activities due to owner-induced tensions when the dog's biological clock tells it the owner will soon arrive.

Causes

There are many causes of destructive chewing. They lie not so much in the dog as within its environment. Some dogs chew to relieve tension. Other dogs bark, howl, pace or dig. The solution to chewing problems involves removing the environmental causes of tension, and diverting the dog to chew on appropriate articles instead of forbidden objects.

Figure 1. This dog has destroyed a chair by chewing. Note that the arms of the chair, on which the owner's scent is strongest, have received the most attention.

Puppies are the most common problem chewers, for obvious reasons. Teething irritates the gums, and chewing seems to ease this irritation. With such teething puppies, we recommend diverting the chewing to appropriate articles, as described below. Time and maturation eventually resolve such problems.

Table 1 lists environmental factors that tend to evoke destructive chewing in older dogs.

A Boxer literally ripped apart a living room couch. The dog often sat on the couch, watching street activities through a window. A neighborhood cat made a practice of sitting on the outside ledge, throwing the dog into a frenzy that was "taken out" on the couch. The solution involved putting an outside shade on the window where the dog could not tear it down. Also, the nightly street walks were stopped, as the dog was overprotective about its neighborhood, having been allowed to urinate along the street for several years.

Correction of Destructive Chewing

Once the factors that create tensions in the dog are recognized, a program of correction must be started. The key factor in all corrective programs involves the owner's gaining a powerful leadership role. The most difficult cases are those involving

Table 1. Factors that tend to evoke destructive chewing in older dogs.

Owner-Related Factors

- Tug-o'-war games.
- Providing personal belongings to chew on.
- Pulling things out of the dog's mouth.
- Providing leather chew toys and/or fabric toys.
- Excessive attention to the dog's mouth during teething.
- Excessive punishment of the pup's mouthing tendencies.

Stress-Related Factors

- Emotional homecomings and departures of the owner.
- Lack of owner leadership.
- Excessive attention to the dog when the owner is home.
- Isolation during critical socializing period (5-12 weeks of age).
- Isolating the dog as a punishment.
- Barrier frustration at doors, windows, gates.
- Psychologic trauma associated with locale or situation.
- Physical punishment administered too long after chewing.
- Marked emotional upset of owners, though not directly involving the dog.
- Delay of feeding or other habitual routines.
- Inconsistent tidbitting practices by the owner.
- Boredom.

---

overdependent owners. Dogs that are especially overprotective tend to have owners who feel flattered by the dog's aggressive tendencies. However, once the owner understands that his dog does not feel responsible *to* but *for* the owner (the dog is taking the dominant position), adjustments can be made.

Leadership of dogs mainly involves movement. Though command responses on a leash are of some value, they unfortunately do not relate to the dog's off-leash behavioral problem. Most owners have some degree of verbal control over their dogs. Whatever the command is, such as Sit or Stay, the owner must run through a short twice-daily exercise of these commands to assert control of the dog. The exercise must be performed in many areas, not just within the home. The owner should take the dog to areas remote and new to the dog, and literally walk away, praising the pet when it follows. This should be done once a week for at least 6 weeks.

We have had excellent results in reorienting a dog's chewing objectives by taking all inappropriate chewables and introducing a meat-scented nylon bone, available at most pet stores. This bone is made the focus of fetch-and-play sessions at least twice a day. The owner's scent and the meat scent make it an appealing object for chewing (Fig 2). Any attention toward forbidden objects should be immediately distracted as the bone is introduced to the dog. When the dog is to be left alone, the bone is handled by the owner before leaving. Because the bone, rather than such other articles as socks, shoes, leather or fabric toys, now has become the focus of interaction between dog and owner, most dogs divert their attentions to the bone.

Of prime importance in most cases is to minimize emotional displays at homecomings or departures by the owners. On these occasions, the owners must ignore the dog *totally* for at least 5 minutes preceding departure or after arrival. Eye contact with the pet should be avoided. When a greeting is given at least 5 minutes after homecoming, it must be calm and *away* from the usual portals of entry or departure, as these are generally where the dog manifests frustration and anxiety behavior in the owners' absence. This is not a simple procedure for many owners because they enjoy being greeted. When the problem has been resolved, the owners may resume *quiet* greetings on arrivals home and subdued goodbyes when departing.

If the dog has destroyed an item, such behavior should not be reinforced by calling attention to it or scolding or punishing the dog. Upon discovering a chewed item, the owner must ignore the mess and, after 5 minutes and a quiet greeting away from the

Figure 2. A meat-scented nylon bone can be used to redirect a dog's chewing attentions. This dog's inappropriate chewing was corrected with fetch-and-play sessions using the bone.

chewing area, get the dog out of the area of the chewed article, cleaning it up without emotion.

The dog is likely to revert to former chewing habits if the daily leadership or bone-play sessions are applied inconsistently. However, if the program is carried out daily for 6 weeks, the problem usually can be permanently resolved. The positive nature of the program appeals to most owners who have tried the traditional punishment and scolding methods, as these are forbidden in this corrective procedure.

Another purely mechanical approach to destructive chewing has been successful in over 65% of cases tested by my clients. The basis for correction lies in the fact that most dogs exhibit withdrawal defensive behavior when surprised by a hissing sound. If this is associated with a mild but novel odor, a dog may withdraw from the odor alone. The procedure is as follows:

Obtain a can of aerosol, dry, unscented (to people) underarm deodorant (one that does not contain hexachlorophene). In the area where the chewing takes place, kneel in the dog's presence, holding the spray can so it will squirt at a 90-degree angle to the dog's nose (Fig 3). When the pet is about to sniff the can, depress

Figure 3. An aerosol spray can be used to distract dogs from destructive chewing. Note that the spray is oriented at a 90-degree angle to the dog's muzzle.

the button briefly as you move the can smartly toward the dog's snout (do not hit the dog's muzzle). If the pet's response is to withdraw quickly, simply put the can away. Without the dog in the area, take the can and lightly spray the articles the dog has chewed or might be likely to chew. Continue this process daily until the problem clears up. If no success is achieved, follow previous advice regarding chewing problems.

Digging

If an owner complains about a digging dog, it must be determined where and when the digging occurs. When those questions are answered, the cause for the digging usually becomes clear, and corrective action may be planned.

> *The owners of "Misty," a 2-year-old male Irish Setter, complained that it had ruined their entire back lawn by destructive digging. The traditional corrections they had tried unsuccessfully reflected the degree of their own growing frustration. First, they simply showed Misty the hole and spanked the dog's rump and snout. They then tried burying chicken wire under the earth. This resulted in torn paw pads and medical expense. Next, the holes were filled with rocks. Then the dog's own feces were buried in the holes. Finally, they filled a freshly dug hole with water and forced the hysterical dog's head into it, holding it under until the animal was nearly unconscious. All of these actions merely caused Misty to change the site of digging activities. Further, the clients' relationship with their pet suffered severely. Whenever the dog saw either of its owners approaching, it now urinated submissively. In desperation, the clients sought my advice.*

Misty appeared normal and healthy, a happy-go-lucky type. "Where does he dig?", I asked. "All over the place," was the disconsolate reply. "All over" tells us nothing, so I asked where the very first digging occurred. The digging began next to the back door. However, punishment relative to that site motivated Misty to dig farther out toward the lawn's center. Thereafter, the rocks, feces and water-in-the-hole treatments spread the digging even farther.

"When does Misty dig?", I asked. "Whenever our backs are turned," anguished Mrs. Client. "He knows it's wrong, but he does it anyway." She was on the verge of crying. "When we leave him alone now, we put him in the garage. And, do you know what he's doing? He's actually eating the door!" In an effort to calm her, I explained that their problem was not unusual and that Misty could be a well-behaved pet, but that we would need a little more information as to what happened when excavating activities first began.

"What does Misty do in the house that made you put him out in the yard?", I asked. It seemed that Misty was unruly when guests arrived, sniffed in embarrassing places, and licked and jumped up on people. As a result, the hapless Setter was hauled by the collar to the backyard and banished from the social activities of the family. Frustration built tension, which must be normally released through some activity. Misty began to dig. In the first instances, the dog's digging was aimed at the object of frustration: the door leading back into the house. After sufficient punishment, merely being placed in the backyard produced tension, and digging became a tension-relieving mechanism. Another dog that was vocally rather than physically oriented would bark in the same situation. An orally oriented dog would chew when isolated.

Once these aspects of behavior were clear, the clients agreed to a controlled program of rehabilitation for Misty. Because the underlying cause for digging was isolation following household unruliness, the dog was kept inside the house as much as possible. Guests were forewarned of the problem and Misty was taught to lie, on command, on the throw rug that served as a bed. After a dozen guest arrivals over a 5-week period, Misty was behaving well. Because both husband and wife had jobs, the dog was left indoors on weekdays. Some investigative chewing occurred during the first 2 days, but stopped thereafter. A daily regimen of command response sessions gave Misty a more functional relationship with people, thereby calming his general demeanor considerably.

The factors in Misty's case are evident in nearly 90% of all digging problems I see. Underlying household misbehavior may range from housesoiling to viciousness with guests, but the causes rather than the symptomatic digging must be dealt with.

Causes

Some dogs dig by example. "Monkey see-monkey do" is normal canine as well as primate behavior. Clients who spend the weekend gardening often complain that their handiwork is destroyed by their pet the minute their backs are turned. Though deliberate, the pet's digging was probably not done in malice. In such situations, the best remedy is prevention. The dog should be kept out of sight during the gardening.

Digging to escape from a yard is usually caused by some stimulus outside the yard. If the stimulus cannot be removed, the dog should be kept in another area, preferably inside the house. Many dogs dig in an effort to catch gophers. The correction, of course, is to eliminate the gophers.

Simple boredom is another common cause of digging. A program of intensive interaction between the dog and owner, such as playing fetch with a ball in the area of the digging for no longer than 15 minutes daily, often results in correction. Teaching the dog to Come, Sit, Stay or Lie Down on command in the area also helps alleviate tension.

Dogs of the northern breeds, such as Huskies, Malamutes and even German Shepherds, may dig cooling holes and lie in them (Fig 4). Dogs that dig cooling holes should be guided to a spot in the yard that is naturally cool, preferably close to the house, and encouraged to excavate there. This has worked well if the owners are willing to make the area available.

Most digging reflects the target of the dog's frustration. Once the causes are clearly defined, corrective action can be started. Though traditional punishment sometimes is successful, more often its deleterious effects on the pet-owner relationship make such steps inadvisable.

Digging on Furniture

Many dogs seem to want to rough up the material on which they lie. When this occurs on chairs, couches or beds, it becomes expensive. With this type of problem, it is best to find out which family member tends to occupy the damaged areas on the furniture. Bitches often dig spots occupied by male family members, and male dogs may seek out furniture used by female family members. When a bed is involved, the digging usually occurs in

Figure 4. Dogs of northern breeds often dig holes in the dirt so they can lie in them and cool off.

the area of the bed from which scents emanate. Correction of this problem centers on the owner's establishing a strong leader relationship with the dog. There is usually a strong element of sexual misorientation that leads to the problem. Once this has been resolved, the behavior usually ceases.

> *One case that did not fall into the preceding categories involved a 4-year-old male Terrier-mix that dug only after guests were entertained, and only on the furniture occupied by guests. The dog, affectionately nicknamed "Gopher," also barked incessantly at guests and usually was put into a bedroom as a result. Jealousy was an element in other areas of its relationships with the family. Gopher even barked if the owners attempted to talk on the telephone. The little Terrier did not accept being ignored.*

In this case, the usual correction by establishing leadership was accompanied by distraction with a sharp sound during barking episodes. Both destructive digging and barking disappeared after several weeks.

Jumping Out of Windows

Jumping through screens, glass windows, or an open window is about the most dangerous escape behavior a dog can display.

This also applies to jumping through various openings into a house. In either case, the causes are similar.

Causes

The most common cause for jumping through windows is social isolation. Most cases generally involve dogs that do not accept being left alone in the house and escape to seek some social contact in the neighborhood. Some escape and remain on the front porch to await the return of their owners. Most of these dogs have experienced some sort of highly gratifying social interaction when outside. Males or bitches in heat may escape to obtain sexual satisfaction. Others have been fed by neighbors or otherwise welcomed into their homes. Some have been generally allowed to run loose when their owners are at home, but are confined when the owner is away.

A less common cause is genuine fear of confinement inside the house or in the yard, causing the animal to jump out of the yard and/or into the house. In these cases, there has usually been some sort of experience involving the area in which the dog is confined. Such traumatic events may include severe physical punishment, extreme hunger (one dog was left without food or water for 2 days), pain from BB shots or rocks thrown at the dog, and firecrackers or other explosions nearby or in the yard. Such distress has caused some dogs to jump out of windows as well.

Correcting Window Jumping

When the dog escapes to achieve social interaction in the neighborhood, the owner must establish a very strong leadership role with the dog. This tends to fulfill its need for socializing within the confines of its own home, a step necessary for complete correction. This can be accomplished through basic obedience command responses, practiced daily over a 6-week period.

Some problems of this type have been solved by installing frosted glass in the dog's favorite escape window, eliminating its view of the outside. However, several dogs have switched to other windows when this has been done, so the owner must be prepared to face this possibility. The more important adjustment is to eliminate the social gratification formerly sought, such as "bumming around." If neighbors are feeding or otherwise accommodating the dog, their help must be sought to stop this.

It is always necessary to determine *when* the dog jumps out of a window. If it occurs shortly after the dog is left alone, the owner must leave the house, sneak back to the premises and apply some strongly distracting stimulus as the dog begins to prepare for the freedom leap. In every case, a period of initial anxiety behavior, such as whining, pacing or barking, precedes the actual leap.

If the jumping occurs just before the owner arrives home, the owner should arrange to come home earlier than usual to apply the corrections. Just as in barking cases, the distracting stimuli should not be painful, but should take the dog's mind off its anxiety. This may involve a rap on a door some distance from the escape scene, and (as in one case mentioned by a client) even stomping on the roof while monitoring the dog's behavior by listening through an air vent.

If jumping is associated with fear of surroundings, it is necessary to change the area in which the dog is confined (the simplest method) or to switch the dog's emotional association with the area from fear to contentment. This may be difficult because the fearful response usually occurs when the pet is alone; conditioning requires the presence of the owner or some other intervening factor. However, if the dog has been severely punished in the area, especially at homecoming times, it is often practical for the owner to stop the punishment and virtually ignore the dog when arriving home. Any interaction between the owner and dog at other times should consist of play, training work for command responses and quiet activities, such as just sitting around. This sort of correction takes several days to weeks.

If jumping *into* the house is the problem, the simplest correction is installation of a pet door. This removes the barrier between the pet and its goal: the inside of the house. In most cases, however, the dog has been relegated to the yard because it is destructive or not housetrained. Therefore, another problem must be solved before approaching the jumping problem, However, it is worthwhile to work on the problem that caused the jumping rather than to try to force the pet to accept confinement in the yard. It is easier to correct housesoiling or chewing than to curtail isolation-induced misbehavior.

Many of my clients state that the dog is left outside because it needs the fresh air and exercise. I answer this by asking the owner to take 2 pieces of plain white paper in the morning and place 1 outside in the open air and the other inside the house. A comparison of the 2 in the evening should convince any city dweller that the air outside is less clean. As for exercise, 10 minutes of tossing a ball in the yard will fulfill most dogs' requirement, and is more wholesome than the perilous activity of jumping in windows and tearing down screens.

If a pet door is installed, the dog can make its own choice of air and exercise area. In cases involving fear of the yard, where no problem exists, the pet door alone is a splendid solution.

Scratching At Objects

Destructive scratching is related to escape chewing, digging and jumping out of windows. That is, the dog normally undertakes the behavior when it has been confined and wants to escape.

Causes

To discover the causes of this troublesome and sometimes expensive behavior, one must determine when and where the scratching takes place. Aside from obvious causes as the bitch next door being in heat, or confinement because the dog is a social pest or is being punished, the usual causes relate to confinement alone.

One exception is the dog that scratches on the seats or cushions of furniture or through bedding or mattresses. These excavators are usually digging a hole for themselves to curl up in or are scratching in frustration at their owner's anal and/or genital scents (see Digging). When pillows and clothing are the target, the dog may be attempting to masturbate with them (see Chapter 12).

Correcting Destructive Scratching

Scratching for escape can occur in dominant or overdependent dogs. In either case, correction involves the same methods as for destructive chewing. The owner must teach at least the Come, Sit and Stay commands without use of force. These commands should be used whenever the dog nudges for attention. The dog should be praised for desirable responses. If punishment has been used, this must be stopped, as this is usually counterproductive.

To minimize the contrast between the owner's presence and absence, all unsolicited attention, such as talking to the dog, petting it or playing with it in response to the dog's attention seeking, should be stopped. Examples of these taboo activities include tug-o'-war, wrestling, chasing the dog, and playing fetch when the owner must force the dog to give up the ball or stick. In other words, interactions must involve the dog's responding to the owner, rather than *vice versa*. Homecoming receptions and/or guilt-ridden departure rituals also must be avoided. It is also helpful to leave a radio turned on at normal volume at all times to stabilize the acoustic environment.

Most dogs begin destructive scratching soon after the owner leaves or just before homecoming times. When this can be ascertained, the "sneak 'n peek" method of correcting the overt behavior is sometimes practical (see Jumping Out of Windows). This procedure must be carried on until the dog literally forgets about the scratching. However, if the dog is also vocally oriented, care must be taken not to induce barking as a substitute behavior. If barking does occur, the sound level of the stimulus should be lowered so as not to be upsetting.

If the cause of destructive scratching is known, that cause should be eliminated, if possible. If a confined male dog is scratching because a neighborhood bitch is in heat, use of some medication for the bitch in heat has proved successful, providing the bitch's owners are willing. If not, and if the problem is recurrent with a male that is not to be bred, castration has proven helpful if combined with the other steps outlined here. If the dog is unruly or shut away as punishment for some other behavior, the basic behavior problem should be corrected.

(This page intentionally left blank)

11

Vocal Behavior

Note: The term "barking" is used throughout this chapter. However, the discussion also pertains to such other forms of vocalization as howling, whining and yowling.

Causes

Barking is one of the most *reasonable* behavior problems in dogs. They bark at or about something for several reasons:

- To announce their presence.
- To answer another dog's barking or to stimulate another dog's bark response.
- To alert the pack (or human family) to some perceived threat.
- To warn outsiders that they are encroaching on the dog's territory.
- To indicate impending defensive behavior, such as biting.
- To seek relief from some disturbing condition, usually social isolation.
- To relieve tension created by frustration, generally related to socal isolation.

Correction of Problem Barking

When barking becomes a problem, the cause must be determined so the appropriate remedial program can be used. The following programs have produced excellent results.

More than 75% of the barkers that are kept in the backyard or on the porch are isolated because of other problems, such as chewing or housesoiling. In these cases, the underlying problem should be identified and corrected, at which time the dog can be readmitted to the house and the barking usually ceases.

Dogs that bark to relieve tension caused by frustration need a simple, but consistent program to remove the source of their frustration. Even if the barking has been inadvertently reinforced by owners who have *returned to the dog* to punish it, the following program has been highly successful.

Learn-To-Earn and Pushups: The learn-to-earn praise and pet program can be used in correcting barking. Each time the dog seeks affection or attention, it must be pleasantly told to Sit, then praised and petted briefly (3-5 seconds), then released from the Sit.

The dog should also be taught to go Down on command after being told to Sit, then Up to Sit from Down, then back Down from Sit, then released and petted briefly. This exercise, called Pushups, can be used as described later.

Limited Barking Permitted: If the dog barks when the owners are at home, it should be immediately called to the owner on the *first* bark and *very quietly* told to Sit. If the stimulus that caused the first bark is known *not* to warrant barking (the barking was unnecessary in that situation), the sitting dog should be quietly released and immediately recalled, and the routine repeated until the dog settles down.

If the owner believes the stimulus should be investigated, the dog should be called, told to Sit, then released, at which time the owner should go quietly to investigate the stimulus that caused the barking. If the cause for the bark is not worrisome, the owner should quietly tell the dog again to Sit, release it and return to former activities. This teaches the dog that its bark is important, but that *the owner is in control of the situation, not the dog.* If the dog starts again to bark during this procedure, it must again be called and the routine repeated. When this is done consistently, the dog will soon begin to give a single alarm bark, then seek the owner for further guidance.

This exercise is very important in that it teaches the dog it has a *function* in the family group. At the same time, it learns *not* to sound the alarm at stimuli that are not important, such as neighbors returning home, visitors arriving, or sirens sounding.

Defusing Homecomings and Departures: At homecomings or departures, the owners must avoid all emotional interplay with the dog. This requires behaving matter of factly. In many cases, even eye contact with the dog should be avoided if it causes excitement. Homecoming greetings should be delayed at least 5 minutes and then should be low key, with minimal petting and a few quiet words. If the dog barks for attention, the greeting must be ignored until the dog becomes quiet.

Leadership Exercises: Many barking dogs are leader types. That is, if the owner walks from one room to another, the dog rushes ahead of them. The owner must understand that this is the dog's way of *leading* in their relationship. To reverse this situation, the dog should be taught, by movement (the dog's language), that the *owner* is in charge of movements around the house. This is not difficult, but it must be applied consistently.

Each time the owner starts to go somewhere and the dog begins to move ahead, the owner should produce a single hand clap and *reverse direction*, which puts the *owner* in the lead. If the dog catches up and again starts to move ahead, the hand clap and direction reversal are repeated. This should be done if the dog rushes ahead of the owner when the doorbell or phone rings, or at meal times, until the dog begins following its new leader. If the dog is a backyard barker, this exercise should be applied there as well as in the house.

Staging for Correction of Isolation Barking: Staging "setups" must coincide with the times of day or night at which troublesome barking occurs. For instance, if the dog barks when the owners leave for work Monday through Friday, setups should be staged during weekend days at those times.

The owner should quietly leave the dog, but be prepared to monitor it for *any signs of restlessness or anxiety*. This may mean sneaking to a window, listening at a door, or peeking over or through a fence (downwind of the dog). If the dog shows anxiety or starts to bark, a single, loud sound should be made to startle the dog and reorient its attention. This can be a hand slapped on a wall, or a sharp knock on a window. Then the owner must remain silent. If needed, this should be repeated each time anxiety behavior or barking occurs until the dog settles down.

At least 5 minutes after the dog has settled quietly, the owner should return, again with *no emotional interplay*, waiting at least 3 1/2 hours before repeating the procedure. This period between setups allows the conditioned learning to "incubate" better than if the sessions were conducted over a shorter time.

The time the owner remains away can usually be doubled between sessions. That is, the owner initially stays away for 5 minutes, then 10, 20, 40, 80, etc, until the dog has quieted dependably.

More Pushups: If, after 4 days, all of the foregoing steps have been strictly applied with little or no progress, the setup should be repeated by leaving the dog and applying the single, sharp sound stimulus one time. Then the owner must literally *rush* into the area where the dog is and pleasantly, but with *urgency*, apply the pushup routine of "Tippy, sit. Good. Sit. Tippy, down. Good. Down. Tippy, sit. Good. Sit," etc, *until the dog shows signs of tiring*. At this time, and again with no emotion or eye contact, quietly leave the dog, again to monitor and repeat the routine until the dog is quiet for the required minimum of 5 minutes. The time the owner spends away can be increased by doubling, as previously described.

Correction of Anticipation Barking: Many dogs bark in antic- ipation of the owners' homecoming. This usually can be resolved using the steps outlined above. When barking persists, the owner must arrive home early, applying the setups at the first signs of anxiety or barking.

Remove the Cause: Some vocal dogs bark in response to stimuli that can be removed. These dogs may bark at neighborhood cats or other dogs. If the neighbor's cat or other dogs can be kept away, the barking may stop. Some dogs gazing out their favorite window may bark at people or other animals. Keeping the drapes drawn often resolves these problems. Many dogs that bark in the backyard for entry to the house benefit from a pet door.

Debarking: Surgical removal of the vocal cords, while often successful in removing the noise associated with barking, does not address the *cause* of the barking. Debarking, however, may not be totally effective, as many debarked dogs can still make objectionable noises or the vocal cords may regrow. If surgery is elected, the preceding program should still be used.

(This page intentionally left blank)

12

Introverted Behavior

The term *introversion* generally refers to people whose attention and interest are inwardly oriented, while *extroversion* refers to people who direct their interests outwardly.

For our purposes, we will use *introversion* to refer to such behavior problems as pica (eating nonfood items), coprophagy (eating stools), carsickness, inappropriate urination or defecation, and self-mutilation.

The basis for correcting all of the following problems is a regimen of earned praise and petting, leadership exercises by the owner, and discontinuation of scolding or punishment.

Phobias

Unreasonable fear of any situation or thing, such as thunder, social isolation, certain people or objects, is termed a *phobia*. Phobias often develop in dogs when the owner first notices anxiety in response to a specific stimulus, such as a thunderstorm. A high degree of concern and sympathy by the owner toward the dog usually reinforces the dog's fears. This worsens the problem instead of eliminating it.

Phobias are combatted by directing the dog's attention to happy activities. To accomplish this, the owners must be viewed by the dog as its leaders, or they will not succeed in diverting the dog's emotional responses from thunder, gunshots, veterinary offices, certain people, etc. Before treatment for phobias is initiated, the following steps must be accomplished:

- The earned praise and petting regimen (Chapter 8) is practiced, wherein the dog is told pleasantly to Sit whenever it seeks attention or the owners wish to pet it.
- The dog dependably *follows* rather than leads the owner in daily movements around the home (Chapter 1). This requires a single handclap and reversing directions any time the dog begins to move ahead of the owner.

After these conditions are met, attempts are made to recreate the situation that stimulates the phobic response. At the *instant* that stimulus occurs, the Jolly Routine (Chapter 8) must be applied and the situation repeated until the dog responds *on its own* with happy behavior before the owners can even apply the single handclap. One of the most difficult phobic situations to recreate is that related to thunderstorms.

Storm Phobias

Many dogs that fear storm activity also fear other sharp percussive noises, such as gunfire, exploding balloons, or low-frequency sounds from a sound system capable of rattling the windows. Because storm noises originate outdoors, any attempts to simulate storm noises or other loud sounds should originate there. These can be tested and used with the Jolly Routine, which involves a single handclap, followed immediately by praise and introduction of some toy or other stimulus the dog associated with happiness. These staged performances should be repeated until the dog acts happy in response to loud noises, without use of the Jolly Routine. After this stage, it is still advisable to follow the same steps required for dogs that do not respond to staged percussion (see below).

If gunfire is to be used in these sessions, the shells used must be handloaded, low-powder blanks. The gun should be fired *outdoors* into thick, soft material, such as an old pillow. Only adults experienced with firearms should be involved. Also, neighbors should be forewarned of training sessions.

If the dog does not respond to attempts at recreating storm sounds, the solution becomes more difficult, as one cannot conjure up storms at will. However, one can watch the weather forecasts carefully and make preparations at least 3-4 hours before a storm is due. This long lead time is necessary because many phobic dogs begin to show anxiety as falling barometric pressure indicates impending storms. In these situations, the Jolly Routine must be applied at the first sign of anxiety in the dog, and then reapplied until the dog shows upbeat behavior instead of the former anxiety, without any need for the routine.

Sedation: If the owner cannot be present to apply these procedures before and during storms, sedatives and tranquilizers may be used to reduce the dog's anxiety. However, without behavioral therapy, such drugs have not been effective over the long term.

Desensitizing With Sound and Light: Though several authorities have recommended playing low-level thunder recordings and gradually increasing the volume as the dog accommodates to it, I and several others in this field have not been successful with this technique. In the 1970s I used recordings of thunder, coupled with flashing strobe lights, without success. This is probably because of 2 factors unique to storms. First is the lack of barometric pressure changes. Second is lack of the intense (to the dog) percussive effects of low-volume thunder recordings.

Situation Phobias

In dogs with phobias to such loud noises as gunfire, firecrackers, auto backfires and slamming doors, the above program, as described for storms, works especially well. When the phobic situation involves visual, nonpercussive auditory, olfactory or tactile senses, alone or in combination, the leadership program and Jolly Routine must be used in conjunction with staging of the *total* situation. Distinct from storm and other percussive sound phobias, these situations can be approached by starting at low levels of stimulation and then increasing the intensity.

For instance, if a dog is phobic about a certain person or place, the Jolly Routine is applied as that person or place is first perceived at a distance. When the happy response is achieved, the person or place is brought or approached closer. This is repeated until the dog dependably "jollies" with no sign of anxiety.

Carsickness

A dog that gets carsick is a genuine victim of motion sickness (rare in dogs), a leader-type animal that becomes ill as a psychosomatic response to its inability to control its circumstances, or one that has experienced traumatic reinforcement in a car or at the journey's end.

A prime example of a trauma victim is a dog that always gets ill on the way to the veterinarian, but seldom on the way home, In several cases, this predictable reaction was used in correction. The dogs were driven *away* from home, in the opposite direction from the clinic, then back toward home and thence on to the doctor. No illness occurred. Different routes were used on later trips.

Correction

Most carsickness cases are not so easily corrected. Where no emotional basis is found for the problem, administration of motion sickness medication has proved helpful. If excessive salivation accompanies vomiting, atropine sulfate (by veterinary prescription) may alleviate the problem. In cases involving behavioral relationships, a combination of general environmental and leadership adjustments succeeds.

Most of the carsickness cases I encounter involve a leader-type dog. Therefore, the first step toward correction is for the owner to gain a dominant leader position. Together with teaching a few simple commands, all general petting of the dog must cease. Any solicitation for attention by the dog must be countered by a command, with a few seconds of petting and praise if the dog responds appropriately. This regimen impresses on the dog that the *owner* is in control of the general tenor of life.

In addition to command training, the dog should be taken for an upbeat car ride around the block at least twice daily. The owner should act jolly toward the dog throughout the ride, reinforcing happy behavior. These trips may then be extended in time and distance over a 6-week period, after which permanent correction is usually achieved.

Fear and Shyness

Fear and shyness are combined in this section because in many dogs, fear is an outgrowth of shyness. That is, a shy dog is more likely to become fearful than a bold, gregarious animal. Extremely strong or prolonged fear-producing stimuli are required to induce generalized fearfulness in a dog with a well-balanced nervous system and a sanguine personality. On the other hand, extremely excitable or inhibited pets are often quick to develop fearfulness.

Fear of falling is thought to be the only inborn emotional fear response. All other fears are presumed to be learned associations. However, because fear is a subjective emotion, it might be wise to define behaviorisms associated with problems in fearful dogs. The first startle responses in puppies are to sudden movement and loud noises. Distress vocalization appears when pups are isolated from their litters. These responses will not be dealt with here because they do not usually trigger the types of overt problem behavior under consideration.

For our purposes, fear and shyness may describe a submissive response to relatively normal stimuli. For example, extreme panic accompanied by defecation, urination and expression of anal sacs is not a normal reaction to a sudden loud noise, a car ride, or handling by the veterinarian. Nor is a submissive posture (ears back, tail between legs, slinking, urinating) a normal response to the mere presence of people or other animals.

Submissive responses of course would be more prevalent in submissive dogs with passive defense reflexes. A fearful or shy dog with active defense reflexes would be more likely to growl, bark or bare its fangs in response to a fear-producing stimulus. Fear biting may occur in either type.

Understanding the Shy Dog

Two important questions should be answered before any attempt to modify shy behavior:

- *What does the dog actually do?* (for example, tail tucked under, head down, freezes, retreats, rolls over).
- *What stimulates the shy behavior, and when was it first noticed?*

281

If a dog displays shyness only before its owners, one must consider its behavior with other people. If shyness is absent with other people, most likely the dog has been overpunished. If it has not extended its shy behavior to people, it may be basically aggressive.

Most dog owners confuse genuine shyness with submissive behavior. Wolves are shy; when approached by people they retreat if possible, responding to the instinct for self-preservation. A pet dog faced with its owner's threats often finds retreat impossible. Therefore, the pet behaves submissively (tail down, whining, rolling on its side, urinating, etc) to tell the aggressor (owner) that the point is well made (Fig 1).

Because owners who overpunish their dog are not attuned to canine behavior, the pet's submissive gestures fail to ward off the threats and/or punishment. If the dog continues to be overpunished, it will act submissively when approached by anyone. This learned behavior is then misinterpreted as shyness.

Most of the "shy dogs" I see fall into the above category (overpunished). Due to excessive scolding, threats or physical

Figure 1. This Italian Greyhound displayed submissive behavior in response to people. The animal lacked broad socialization, and chewed destructively when left alone.

abuse, they display submissive behavior to their owners or to all people. In either case, the corrective procedure is the same.

Correction

A dog that has been overpunished lacks self-confidence. Therefore, such dogs should be allowed to succeed. This is fortunately a simple process with dogs. They are dramatically quick to learn from people when taught by nonphysical methods. Even a simple 3-part exercise, performed daily, can bring about a behavior change in a few days.

All that is needed is to crouch down, say "Rover, come," and heartily praise when it responds, even if it only looks at the owner. If the pet urinates on the way, the praise must be continued. The wetting usually disappears as confidence improves. When the dog comes all the way, it should be petted, preferably on the throat and chest to eliminate fear responses that may be caused by hands over or on top of its head. Most shy dogs usually come readily to a crouching figure.

The "Sit" command is simple, once the pet comes dependably. A hand is held up over the dog's rump as the words "Rover, sit" are spoken. The dog usually looks upward, and should be praised by happily saying "Good, sit," but without bending down or petting. If this is patiently repeated a few times, most dogs will sit down. The spoken praise should be followed by petting.

It is important not to bend over from the waist to pet shy dogs, as this movement often signals possible punishment. Crouching avoids bending over, and is friendly and reassuring. Pushing down on its rump, holding, or otherwise manipulating the pet must be avoided. Physical force is at the root of most submissive behavior and interferes with effective learning.

The second part of therapy requires that owners avoid punishing the pet. If other behavior problems exist, these must be resolved using the methods mentioned elsewhere in this book. Self-control is a major challenge to most dog owners; however, after they see the progress usually achieved in a few days, their feelings that the pet "needs to be told it has done wrong" usually abate. Any backsliding on the owner's part is quickly reflected by regression in the dog. This feedback provides an effective control mechanism to which most owners are highly sensitive.

A third step in correction is used for dogs that respond submissively to persons outside the family. If a few friends are gathered to reinforce the owner's teachings, the dog usually responds satisfactorily. Correction in most cases requires only a few minutes on 2 or 3 occasions. Older dogs with a persistent problem may require longer training periods.

This approach to correct overly submissive behavior in shy dogs assumes the pet is healthy, so that no possible organic influence interferes with the learning capabilities of the animal. Total rehabilitation can be expected in 6 weeks when the process is carried out daily.

'Kennelosis'

The behaviorisms mentioned above may be displayed by either extremely excitable or inhibited dogs. Extreme submissiveness is typical of a syndrome called "kennelosis." Such cases usually involve prolonged isolation and lack of broad geographic-social experience, excessive punishment, improper management by the owner, or extreme psychic trauma associated with other animals, certain areas, odors, sights or sounds. Leader-type dogs are seldom affected.

A 4-year-old spayed German Shepherd, which was fearful of loud sounds, strangers, clinical care, fast movements and unexpected touches, had been raised in a large family from 6 weeks of age. The dog snapped at visiting children and made violent escape efforts when left home alone, either in the yard or house. These resulted in split toenails and severely torn pads. From puppyhood, the dog had been fearful of sudden noises. To correct the behavior, the family had coddled the pet. The only effort at training was made by the father, who taught the dog to come and sit.

When the family arrived at our facility, the dog, hackles abristle, barked at me and then proceeded to investigate the perimeters of the property, apparently in search of an escape opening. The dog's behavioral history indicated an extremely excitable nervous makeup, which we discussed. It took about 45 minutes before the dog lay down near the owners. At this point a cabinet door was slammed somewhere. The dog's reaction was to leap up and run to the family sedan, onto the roof and into the car through the sunroof.

The corrective program required all family members to "jolly" the pet after loud noises or when any fearful or shy reactions started. Everyone took part in daily off-leash teaching sessions, during which the dog displayed independence and at times stood and barked at the owners in response to their teaching efforts. The owners were often exasperated, but no physical punishment was used and persistence finally prevailed over the dog's excitable resistance.

Accentuated startle responses were alleviated about 3 weeks after a stress diet was initiated (see Chapter 5). Within 7 weeks all exaggerated responses were absent. Though the dog was not gregarious with strangers, fear and shyness were replaced by tailwagging and friendly approach behavior when strangers knelt or sat down.

> *Gemini, a female Doberman Pinscher, was adopted at 6 1/2 months of age from a kennel environment. The new owner, an intelligent teenage girl, had visited Gemini twice in the kennel and had once taken the dog to her home. On these occasions Gemini crept along fearfully, rolled over submissively, and urinated when approached. Because the dog was bought as a deterrent to burglary, this behavior was unacceptable.*

This case was typical of moderate kennelosis. On referral from the family's veterinarian, I was asked to assist Gemini's socialization, and to teach the dog to bark when strangers approached the yard and display mild aggressiveness on command. Considering the dog's background, this seemed an impossible task. The extreme shyness of kennel dogs often precludes rehabilitation. However, due to the dedication of the owner and the age of the dog, significant progress was made.

Correction involved 2 stages: socialization with family members and others, including strangers; and instilling territorial possessiveness. Stage 1 included daily off-leash command training sessions, plus maximum contact with people through field trips. The game of "fetch" also increased the dog's confidence. Stage 2 involved nightly "patrols" of the property by dog and owner, with the owner acting worried about sounds outside the yard.

Within 12 weeks the Doberman was extremely responsive to family members, and was sufficiently confident to meet strangers without displaying submissiveness. Soon the dog began barking at unfamiliar sounds, and was "on guard" at appropriate times with strangers.

Summary

Fear may be an integral part of a dog's general reflex mechanisms. Dogs that exhibit fearful or shy behavior usually have passive or flight tendencies that tend to dominate in stress situations. However, more than the dog's response is involved in problem cases of this type. The manner in which owners react to the dog's behavior can reinforce shyness or fear, or reduce such emotional reactions.

The term "shy dog" should be qualified by examination of the dog's actual behavior and the things that stimulate the shyness. Dogs may display submissive behavior because of overly harsh treatment. Others may suffer from kennelosis or other improper socialization during early critical periods. In all cases, the dog's level of confidence in its interactions with people must be increased.

Rehabilitation requires gradual socialization, demonstrative teaching for command responses, and avoidance of physical manipulation. While this is being accomplished through training exercises and general environmental adjustments, the "Jolly Routine" of acting happy and gaining tail-wagging responses in place of fearful or shy behavior usually solves the problem after a few weeks.

Housesoiling

Though most dogs, male and female, choose to "brand" their territories with urine, many also defecate to mark their turf. Housesoiling with defecation most often involves females. Though the following corrective programs refer to micturition and urination, they apply equally to marking by defecation.

Housesoiling is the complaint most often mentioned by dog owners. It can be divided into several categories: the naive unhousetrained dog; the diet-change victim; and the insecure dog. The first 2 types are not associated with introverted behavior and are discussed elsewhere. The insecure dog requires detailed attention because the problem usually has its roots in emotional influences in the dog's environment. Fact finding, therefore, becomes a more delicate matter, as human factors as well as canine and human interactions are involved. Fortunately, explaining the principles of behavior to the owner is usually productive.

Causes

To "brand" it as theirs, dogs urinate around a territory, on an object and, infrequently, upon another animal or even a person. Leg lifting is more pronounced in males, but females also do it. Wild dogs mark whelping and hunting area perimeters for obvious reasons. Emotional conflict within the pack sometimes leads to dominant dogs urinating on subordinate animals. Pack leadership contests often start with the contestants comparing urine scents, and sometimes end up in a pitched battle.

Other notable causes for this problem include: the dog's being shut away because of some other undesirable behavior when guests visit; a neighborhood bitch in heat; pubescent girl experiencing her first menstrual cycle; and moving, either out of or into a home. In all cases, a strong leader relationship must be established by key family members to relieve the anxieties of the "insecure" dog.

Owners of dogs that urine mark indoors must consider where and when the urination occurs, and when the problem began. This information may reveal the source of the problem. Two cases from my files typify the problem, and subsequent corrective actions.

A 2-year-old male Sydney Silky had been urinating on furniture and draperies for 11 months. The owner, a pregnant mother of 2, had been told by her husband to solve the problem or get rid of the dog.

She explained that the urination always occurred near the front windows of the living room. I asked,

*"When does he do it?" She answered, "Any time he gets
the chance!" Further discussion indicated that the dog
had been physically punished at the urination sites and
now urinated only when nobody was looking. Lately the
dog had responded to the client's attempts to punish or
even groom him by snarling and biting her. The Silky
moved very stiffly in my office and, within a few moments, urinated on a recent dog scent on my sofa.*

No specific time of onset was apparent, so I questioned the
owner regarding general practices with the dog. He was taken
for morning and evening walks up and down the front sidewalks,
and allowed to "sprinkle" indiscriminately as he walked. Further, when not kept away from the large front window, the dog
spent daytime hours monitoring "his" territory, fiercely barking
at both canine and human passersby. The frustration of this
daily experience caused the Silky to relieve tension by urinating
on drapes and furniture in the front room. The owners also
fondled the dog and on many occasions he had growled at them
when not "in the mood" for petting.

Such reactions indicate a dominant personality, the result of
pampering and lack of owner direction. Correction was achieved
through withholding all praise and petting, except during daily
teaching lessons for command responses. The daily walks were
stopped and a single toilet area in the backyard was established,
using praise for performance as reinforcement. In 5 days the
client was able to groom the dog with no sign of hostility, and
household urination ceased by the end of the third week.

In some cases, household urination might be aptly labeled the
"new baby syndrome." Older children sometimes begin wetting
the bed on arrival of a new baby bother or sister and the resulting
loss of parental attention. With dogs, the reaction is often more
immediate, and the cause more obvious.

*Two 9-year-old Dachshunds, male and female, had
been relegated to the backyard because they began to
urinate in the house after the owner adopted a Minia-
ture Poodle puppy. A compounding factor was that the
dogs also defecated in the house. This is not uncom-*

mon, as new puppies also often defecate indoors. All family members expressed disgust for the offending Dachshunds and freely admitted they believed the age of the dogs precluded correction. Euthanasia was thought to be the only alternative.

After I explained the probable causes, the dogs were granted a 1-week trial period. During this time, the owners were to have the older dogs inside the house, praising them whenever the pup appeared. Everyone was instructed to pay more attention to the Dachshunds than to the puppy. Four days after starting the trial, the problem had cleared up. This was unusual. We typically experience poor success when such trials are attempted, primarily because the owners have already prejudged the pet as "hopeless." This negative attitude diminishes their effectiveness as teachers. The best situation for correction is the owners' total commitment to the dogs.

Correction

In all cases of housesoiling, I advise against any form of punishment, either physical or social, such as scolding or isolating the dog. Usually these methods have already been tried unsuccessfully and often are implemented hours after the act, contributing to the dog's neurotic behavior.

Following are suggestions on correction of housesoiling.

- *Avoid all fondling of the dog.* Praise and pet it only after it has responded to some command.
- *Feed a steady diet only, on schedule.* Never tidbit.
- *Take the dog to the same restricted area for elimination* only at times the owner is normally home during the work week, even on weekends.
- On weekends, *correct all sniffing* of furniture, etc. Praise enthusiastically after each correction.
- *If urine or feces are found in the house, do not make a "big deal" of it.* Avoid scolding in any way. Apply correction when the dog looks at the soiled spot, then immediately take the dog to the proper toilet area and await some sort of sniffing, praising it with "good dog," and wait for urination

or defecation. Then, praise and pet the dog, pointing to the spot.

- *All household members must treat the dog in the same manner,* using the same method.
- *Run the dog through command exercises* twice daily and whenever it seems to be getting "bossy."
- *Avoid bringing other dogs into the house* until the problem is cleared up.
- *Remove sources of water when the dog is to be left alone and at night.* In severe cases, give water only at feeding times.
- *Clean any soiled spots* with a 25% solution of white vinegar. Soak any residue of this solution out of materials by pressing with paper towels. Do not let the dog watch the cleanup!
- *Have the dog examined by a veterinarian* if disease is suspected or the dog does not respond to correction attempts. The corrective program assumes the dog to be in excellent health. Disease may be responsible for the problem.

Masturbation

Masturbation is apparently normal among bitches and dogs. It becomes a "problem" for owners when it is a source of personal embarrassment, is esthetically distasteful to witness, or damages property (upholstery, pillows, clothing, etc). Incessant masturbation is rare, but it does occur.

Cause

Some offenders are hypersexual and have histories of precocious sexual behavior. Many cases also involve owner permissiveness.

When the behavior is destructive to furniture and bedding, investigation usually reveals that the target articles bear the owner's scent. One possible explanation is that the dog is venting its frustration on the owner's property to relieve tension. Often the dog receives an inordinate amount of attention from its owner and, as with chewing problems, tends to be overly anxious when the owner is absent.

Excessive masturbation is generally associated with owners who tend to fondle their pets or, on the other extreme, give them little if any petting. Regardless of the cause, methods of correcting the problem are similar.

Correction

In all cases, the owner must gain some degree of response to simple commands (Come, Sit, Stay) without handling or touching the dog. All fondling must be stopped. The dog should be praised and petted only after it responds to some command. These social rewards should be brief, especially in dogs that constantly pester the owner for attention.

If the dog masturbates when the owners are present, the dog must be distracted and then praised in a jolly manner for stopping the behavior. The nature of the distraction is not important, except that it must divert the pet's attention *toward some external activity*. One client distracted her 2-year-old Boxer by dropping a tin can, then got a dog toy and tossed it as further reinforcement. Masturbation ceased within a week.

In puppies, masturbation is never a problem if the owners have begun obedience training before puberty (about 12-14 weeks). After dealing with hundreds of cases involving puppies, I have concluded that early establishment of strong leadership by the owner helps avoid the problem.

Pica

Causes

When a dog starts to swallow nonfood articles, owners often wonder if perhaps they have a neurotic pet. After all, why should a dog swallow rocks, pins, wrist watches, panty hose or toilet paper? The logical answer is that such behavior must make the pet feel better. That is, it probably relieves tension.

In all cases, the dog's diet and feeding regimen must be considered. Underfeeding or overfeeding may be an underlying cause of pica. Older dogs should be fed 2 times a day. The quantity should produce a formed, firm stool, with no looseness. Puppies should be fed as many times as they have bowel movements per day, in amounts that produce formed, firm stools. If a particular food does not produce firm stools, the diet should be changed to one that does.

Most pica cases hinge on an unsatisfactory relationship between dog and owner. There is usually an element of over- or underattentiveness on the part of the owner. Most cases involve nervous, inhibited dogs. It is also interesting that most cases involve puppies that were either orally oriented to begin with, or were made so through excessive oral stimulation (tug-o'-war, etc) during early life with the owners.

> *An overindulged, orally oriented male Dachshund was shut out of the house because of unruliness with the owners. Soon thereafter the dog was taken to the veterinarian because of extreme pain and failure to eat or defecate. X-rays revealed blockage in the intestines, but no object was apparent. A pair of panty hose was surgically removed from the intestine. The dog, having been severely weakened by starvation, failed to survive the operation.*

Correction

Corrective measures are straightforward in most pica cases. All fondling of the pet is stopped and some degree of command response is established, using nonphysical methods. If the dog pesters for affection, it is directed to perform some previously learned command response before it is rewarded with petting.

As in chewing cases, I recommend that a scented nylon bone be employed to fix the animal's oral orientation on an acceptable object. Even if the owner teases the dog with the bone, this substitute object has proved helpful in correction. If the animal is kept outdoors because of a chewing problem, the underlying problem must be corrected and the dog reunited with the family before dealing with the pica problem. Correction usually takes 1-6 weeks.

Self-Mutilation

A dog that licks or chews on itself is manifesting stress or frustration about something. The problem may start because of some frustration relating to environment, but soon develops into a self-reinforcing habit, as the licking or chewing causes inflammation. Further licking or chewing can provide at least temporary relief, but this ultimately perpetuates the problem.

A complete veterinary evaluation should precede the behavior program for rehabilitation. Flea or tick infestation must be ruled out as a cause. Possible allergies also should be considered, as the problem in many self-mutilators stems from food or other environmental allergies. Many practitioners recommend hypoallergenic diets, even in the absence of clinical symptoms, as a matter of "insurance."

Correction

Corrective measures must consider the environmental factors that bear on the problem. However, a general plan involving nonphysical, off-leash training and stabilization of the owner-pet relationship provides satisfactory results. Owner leadership is established by withholding petting and praise, except when the pet responds to some directive from the owner.

If licking or chewing occurs in the owner's presence, some strong and neutral distraction must be applied. I use an ultrasonic device for this purpose, but other distracting stimuli have been equally successful. These have included a loud rap on the wall, a ball tossed, or a tin can dropped.

If a specific stimulus is associated with mutilation, such as sirens or footsteps, this must be "staged" and correction applied until the dog's reaction stops. If self-mutilation occurs only in the owner's absence, the owner should hide and distract the animal with a neutral stimulus (ultrasonic device or tin can dropped); otherwise, final correction hinges on the owner's presence.

Coprophagy

Eating stools is not always abnormal behavior, disgusting though it appears to the owner. For example, the dam eats her pups' stools as a hygienic measure.

Causes

Stool-eating in older pups and adult dogs may indicate disease that impairs normal digestion of food. Examples include pancreatitis, parasitic infection, malabsorption, and other intestinal problems. For this reason, it is best to have the stool-eating dog examined by a veterinarian for possible physical abnormalities.

Overfeeding is a common cause of coprophagy. This includes overloading the digestive system by feeding a full day's ration in a single meal. Because the digestive system of some dogs cannot fully digest the nutrients in a single large meal, many nutrients are passed in the stool. The dog, later feeling undernourished, then feeds on the stool.

Some dogs learn to eat stools after watching their owners pick up stools. Some housesoiling dogs have learned to eat their stools to avoid punishment, hiding the evidence, so to speak.

Correction

Adult dogs that eat their stools must be fed, twice daily, an amount that they totally consume at every meal and that produces a formed, firm stool. Puppies should be fed as many meals as they have bowel movements, with the same standard for stool firmness.

Assuming health and feeding problems are uninvolved, correction is fairly straightforward. Most dogs defecate soon after eating. Knowing this, the owner must monitor the dog after meals. As soon as the dog finishes its bowel movement, a single, sharp, distracting sound should be made. Immediately thereafter, the owner should praise the dog and distract it to some happy activity, while moving away from the stool, preferably back to the house. Toilet area stools must be removed after each deposit, but when the dog cannot see the owner.

This routine must be repeated after each feeding until the dog moves away from the stool *before* the sound stimulus and jolly routine can be instituted. Praise should be given to reinforce this conditioned reaction. After 6 weeks, the correction is generally permanent, even in longstanding stool eaters.

13

Problems of Old Age

Problems that most often lead to euthanasia of elderly dogs are deafness, loss of sight, incontinence, physical soreness and irritability. The fact that old age in dogs is accompanied by inconvenience to the owner is often overlooked when a puppy is bought. Many people tend to compare the experience of dog ownership with that of having a new baby in the house. But there is a major difference: few dogs outlive their owners.

The owner of a puppy should be aware of the entire spectrum of life so that geriatric problems will not adversely influence the owner-pet relationship. The owner should also know that these problems can be minimized by veterinary care, training, and certain environmental adjustments.

Some problems cited here, particularly loss of sight and deafness, may occur in younger dogs. I have not discussed these in the Puppy Problems chapter because few puppies are spared when the breeder recognizes a handicap. However, methods of dealing with geriatric problems have been equally successful with younger dogs.

Deafness

Loss of hearing or congenital deafness is often a greater handicap to the deaf dog's owner than to the affected dog.

Usually the dog's other senses compensate for lack of hearing. Problems associated with this condition involve a lack of response to the owner's spoken commands, and the pet's tendency to wander into the road or otherwise endanger itself. The solutions to these problems are not too difficult.

The deaf dog must be taught to come by a *sign*, rather than by a spoken word. Once this is accomplished, hand signs can also be used to teach Sit and Stay. Teaching the dog to walk with the owner requires both hand signs and signalling the pet to come back when it starts to wander away from the owner's side.

Because voice communication is useless, direct physical contact is the only truly reliable training tool for deaf dogs. The method I recommend requires an innovative owner willing to devote the time necessary to teach the dog. The only supplies required are beanbags (these may be made from dried beans and old nylon socks) and pea-sized pebbles. Throw-chains and other heavy objects used by some trainers are entirely unnecessary and inhumane.

The deaf pet must learn to keep its visual attention on the owner at all times. Therefore, teaching sessions are held in safe but distracting areas. Each time the pet's attention is distracted from the teacher, a beanbag is tossed at its legs and the teacher turns and walks away from the animal. It must be remembered that dogs have greater peripheral vision than people and are therefore better able to track objects in their peripheral field of view. Several times during the conditioning process, the teacher should try walking away before tossing the beanbag to test the dog's visual tracking and response. If the dog turns to follow, the teacher should crouch down and make beckoning movements to attract it. When the dog approaches, it should be petted for a few seconds before the process is repeated. When the dog follows reliably, 5 or 6 times in a row, without the need for tossing a beanbag, the session is ended.

Sessions should be no longer than 15 minutes and about 3 hours apart. The process should be repeated at least twice daily over a 6-week period in increasingly distracting circumstances. For instance, the first few sessions might be held in the backyard, in the house, or in the front yard. Then the dog is taken to neighbors' homes and yards, neighborhood tennis courts, fields, on quiet streets, then busy streets. An assistant should come along to stop traffic if necessary.

Once the dog is well oriented to the owner (when no beanbag tosses are required for a few days), field trips can be conducted, using only a few pebbles as substitutes for the beanbags. If the pet starts to stray or becomes distracted, a pebble is tossed as a reminder to pay visual attention to the owner.

The daily teaching process should involve every family member who may need this type of control, even children, as the pet may respond only to those who teach it. Once the dog keeps its eye on its human companion and stays close, hand signals may be employed to teach Sit, Stay and Heel (walk with me).

Deaf dogs that wander into dangerous areas or that tend to chase (cars, motorcycles, other dogs, etc) should be taken through the above owner-orientation process. This often eliminates the wandering or chasing problem. However, some dogs chase when their owners are absent. These animals must be taught, through the behavioral response communicated by the owner, that such activities are to be avoided. For this reason, the owner orientation of deaf dogs must be reliable.

The deaf dog should be exposed to dangerous situations in controlled circumstances. That is, the vehicle or other dog must be under the control of a person who is cooperating with the owner and will react quickly to ensure that the dog is not injured. The dog is walked toward the dangerous area (for example, a quiet street). As soon as it exhibits the *first* sign of recognition of an approaching car (driven by a cooperating companion), the owner must toss a beanbag at the dog's legs (to gain attention) and then *withdraw* from the area, displaying the most horrified expression that dramatic abilities allow. This procedure must be repeated until the deaf animal exhibits retreat behavior *before* the owner's act on several occasions.

The situation should then be repeated, with the owner at increasingly greater distances behind the dog. When the dog fails to respond properly, the beanbag must be tossed again and the process repeated. This entire regimen must be continued for several days until the pet responds reliably when the owner is absent.

A deaf dog should never be placed in circumstances that are genuinely dangerous; this would be foolhardy and inhumane. Special treatment for the deaf dog should be the first consideration of the owners. With careful training, deaf dogs can enjoy a happy and rewarding life as family pets. This training also helps develop the patience and thoughtfulness of owners, especially family children, who take part in the program.

Incontinence

Incontinence is the inability to control urination and/or defecation. In this section, the term is also used to describe the *reduced control* sometimes apparent in geriatric animals. The condition can be upsetting to owners, as it warrants constant vigil to avoid cleanups. Many owners believe the affected animal is uncomfortable or in poor health. Some owners are revulsed and unable to cope with the problem.

I always recommend that incontinent dogs be carefully examined by a veterinarian to determine whether the problem is due to old age (lack of sphincter control) or a condition that can be treated. Urinary incontinence may be caused by conditions of the bladder and urethra. A relatively common cause in older spayed bitches is reduced estrogen levels; this may respond to hormone treatments.

Fecal incontinence has been associated with damaged anal sphincter muscles, which perhaps can be surgically repaired, or injuries to the lumbar or pelvic area, with resultant nerve damage. Nerve disorders usually are difficult to treat. Where loose stools associated with improper feeding are a part of the problem, dietary adjustments may be helpful (see Chapter 5).

The saddest situation is one in which the dog owner, unaware of possible corrective measures, believes that incontinence automatically warrants euthanasia. Even if the problem cannot be handled medically, some minor adjustments may make the incontinent dog easier to live with, and thus prevent the injustice of sending a faithful companion to its death.

A woman recently phoned me about her 13-year-old spayed bitch. The animal was healthy in all other respects, but had had urinary and fecal incontinence for about 2 months. As the conversation progressed, it became apparent that she was calling for advice on how to explain euthanasia to her children.

I told her flatly that the best approach was an honest one. "Just tell them its too much trouble for you and that you are going to take the dog down and have her killed."

This answer upset her. "They would never forgive me!" she said.

I explained the various things that a veterinarian might do for the dog, but she still could not overcome her own "problem." She was revulsed by feces and the odor of urine. The dog had been relegated to the back porch and winter was on its way.

I added a piece of common sense that has worked in similar cases. "I never recommend lying to a child about inevitable truths. And death is one of those. If you cannot face your children with the truth, I suggest you put diapers and plastic bloomers on the dog and let her into the house again. Treat her as she really is: not sick, but probably in the same boat you and I may be in one day: somewhat incontinent, but still useful to humanity."

Several days later the woman phoned to say that she had taken the dog in for a veterinary examination. With a diet change and medical treatment, the incontinence had been reduced to the point where the diapers and bloomers were working acceptably.

Other affected dogs have responded well to paper training or installation of a pet door.

Loss of Sight

The only problem I have encountered when an older dog began to lose its sight or when any dog became blind is convincing the owner that this does not necessitate euthanasia. Dogs can adjust to blindness and poor eyesight with little difficulty. Their senses of hearing and smell begin to function as directional indicators, even though they may occasionally bump into table and chair legs or stumble over objects (Figs 1-3).

The following steps may help a blind pet find its way about the house and yard more easily.

Figure 1. An aged Cocker Spaniel, blind for 5 years, exits the house through a pet door.

- *Mark upright obstacles*, such as chair legs and door jambs, with a light-scented cologne, spray or other scented substance. This helps the dog identify perpendicular objects.
- *Use a different scent on the floor* about 6 inches from steps or similar obstacles. Use a light scent to avoid the buildup

Figure 2. After eliminating in the preferred area, the blind pet is rewarded with petting.

Figure 3. Marking such obstacles as steps with a lightly scented substance helps the pet find its way back through the pet door.

of odors around the house, which has been the only owner complaint about this method.

- *Wear a small bell* or a bracelet that jingles. Visitors can also be equipped with such jewelry. This allows the dog to follow its owner's movements more easily. One owner I know hangs a small bell on his belt loop. His blind dog follows with amazing accuracy even on daily jogs.

Sightless dogs tend to adjust well to the problem, with little trouble to the owners. The suggestions above have been helpful in cases where the owner feels the need to do something to make the adjustment a little less difficult for the dog.

Older blind dogs may be handicapped, but they should be treated, as far as possible, as if they were normal. This means using the earned-petting routine regularly, and performing obedience routines learned before the onset of blindness. My own Dalmatian continued to go out every morning to sniff out and bring the morning newspaper until the day she died (Fig 4).

Senility

Dogs may become forgetful as they age. Signs of senility include unexplained housesoiling, and failure to recognize previously familiar people, animals, objects or places.

Figure 4. The author's Dalmatian, blind for 4 years, continued to fetch the bulky daily newspaper, and was rewarded with praise and petting.

Research in human and veterinary geriatrics has shown that certain nutritional supplements may benefit elderly dogs with forgetfulness and lethargy. Chief among these nutritional supplements is choline. Many geriatric animals are deficient in this neurotransmitter. Vet-A-Mix (Shenandoah, IA) manufactures choline tablets for dogs and cats, sold under the brand names of DynaLode and Cholodin. They are generally available through veterinary supply distributors.

We have used choline supplementation, along with house-training sessions, to treat housesoiling in older dogs. Choline also has been amazingly effective in combatting lethargy in several older dogs.

Physical Soreness and Irritability

It has always seemed sensible to me to treat the idiosyncrasies of old age with some consideration. It is reasonable to assume that the aches and pains of old age will cause some behavioral changes. However, some people do not *allow* their pet dogs the dignity of old age quirks.

"I always grabbed her by the rump and pulled her to me," said a client who was recently bitten by his 11-year-old Setter mix.

"She never bit me before. I think she's going balmy in her old age."

The solution to such problems, of course, is to have a little consideration for the pet's physical condition, and respect its needs. The following simple rules will help minimize problems.

- Let sleeping dogs lie.
- Feed a proper geriatric diet without tidbits or extras.
- Except when the pet solicits attention, do not bother it. When it does want to be petted, have the dog sit before petting. Then, be brief about it. This will avoid "spoiling" the dog in its old age.
- Never coddle the pet or act overly sympathetic when it seems to complain.
- Don't subject the dog to strenuous exercise if it invariably becomes sore afterward.

(This page intentionally left blank)

14

Introducing Babies and New Pets to Resident Dogs

The same general rules for introducing a new baby brother or sister to its older siblings apply to established household dogs. That is, the newcomer, whether a pup, adult dog, cat, baby or elderly relative, should mean *good times* for the dog. If the relationships with its owners are positive, the dog will feel good about the newcomer, showing good-natured interest.

Special Steps

If relationships are *not* positive, the learn-to-earn routine (Chapter 8) should be used at least 2 weeks before the newcomer's arrival. Also, if the resident dog has ongoing behavior problems, these must be corrected before the newcomer's arrival, so as to avoid linking the newcomer's arrival to the new behavioral regimen.

Four days before the newcomer is introduced, the amount of attention given the resident dog must be reduced to *below* the level of attention it will receive after the newcomer's arrival. Dogs are extremely sensitive to both the *quality* and the *quantity* of attention they get from their owners. Reducing the attention level before the newcomer arrives leads the dog to perceive an *increase* in attention it receives after the newcomer's arrival.

If the times for feeding babies or caring for other newcomers conflict with the times when the resident dog is accustomed to receiving attention, such as walks or play periods, these times must be adjusted to avoid conflict. When this is not possible, and "prime time" for the resident dog cannot be afforded, these customary activities should be eliminated at least a week before the newcomer arrives. Again, this avoids negative associations with the newcomer.

Personal Contact

When new puppies are brought home, the resident dog should be allowed free access to investigate while the owners offer plenty of jolly praise to the *resident* dog, not the puppy. Puppies adapt nicely and should be allowed to "fit in" with the resident dog's routine. In this way, the puppy will naturally assume a subordinate position to the resident dog, which will prevent rivalry as the puppy matures.

A new baby should be introduced with the Jolly Routine, and the dog should be allowed to sniff the infant. As to how *close* this contact should be, this is best left to the owner's discretion. Owners are more sensitive to their dogs' moods than outsiders. If the owner is nervous about putting the baby on the floor for the dog to freely investigate, this should be avoided, as the dog will sense the owner's anxiety and may perceive the baby and situation as "wrong."

If the dog's perception of the newcomer and its owners' response is upbeat and positive, the newcomer is usually readily accepted.

When Babies Cry, Crawl and Fall

Immobile, quiet babies are one thing, but a squalling infant is perceived as another kind of "animal" by a dog. Most dogs show concern when babies start their high-pitched complaining. This is normal canine behavior. However, when such crying begins, it is best to call the dog to Come, then "jolly" it so that it does not think the child is in pain. Then the baby can be attended to. In this way, most dogs will seek out the owners when the baby starts to cry, rather than rush to the baby. This can be life saving if the child is genuinely injured or ill, and the owners are asleep and out of earshot.

The first crawling by an infant may elicit extreme curiosity from the dog. As with other first-time experiences, the Jolly Routine should be used here, too. This also applies to the baby's first attempts at walking.

When the baby is actually walking, and tumbles or careens awkwardly toward the dog, "jollies" should be applied. If the child appears about to fall on or corner the dog, the *dog* should be shown by the owner's movement how to move *away* from the youngster. This should be continued until the dog moves away on its own.

When the baby falls, the owner should avoid rushing over and picking it up. Once again, a moment of jollies and a calm approach to righting the child will help avoid the idea that a fallen child warrants concern. Many parents whose dogs have developed negative relationships with babies tell me that the problem started when the dog was scolded or punished for rushing over to the fallen baby, an act which they *learned* from the parents!

Baby Investigates Dog

It is wise to allow a maturing baby to satisfy its interest in the dog. However, this should be done with supervision and lots of happy praise for the dog. It is *unwise* to scold a baby if it inadvertently steps on or sticks a finger in the dog's eye, pulls its hair, etc. The dog may believe the scolding is aimed at it or perceive the baby is being punished. Either way, there is the risk that the dog may later attempt to "discipline" the baby in the owner's absence. Rather, the dog should be jollied and the child should be calmly shown the proper way to pet the dog.

The foregoing steps help to ensure the most satisfactory integration of newcomers into the domain of a resident dog. If negative interaction is avoided and positive initial emotional experiences are accentuated, most dogs establish harmonious relationships with their new family members.

Adopting a Mature Dog

The tendency to get rid of a dog because of some minor inconvenience has created a vast pool of adoptable mature pets in animal shelters. Unlike inmates on death row, they have no right of appeal. Their lives are usually limited to the days until euthanasia. Many well-behaved mixed-breed and purebred dogs are in ample supply at shelters.

There are advantages and disadvantages of adopting a mature dog from a private party or a shelter.

Advantages

- The dog usually is already housetrained.
- The dog's behavior and personality tend to be stable, and not subject to the changes seen in maturing puppies.
- The dog is not subject to diseases of puppyhood.
- The dog's health record and behavioral history usually are available, and problems may be avoided.
- The dog's cost, if any, is usually lower than that for a puppy.

Disadvantages

- The dog has already "lost" its human family and may tend to be insecure. Therefore, it requires careful behavioral/emotional guidance.
- The dog may have behavior problems that are not evident until after several weeks in its new home.
- The new owners will not benefit from the optimum socialization periods of puppy development.

Fortunately, most humane society shelters evaluate all aspects of their dogs, from health to behavior and personality. Many shelters develop profiles of the home environments best suited to each dog and offer guidance in selecting an older dog. Once the choice is made, the following steps have proven most successful in helping the new dog settle in.

Introduction to a Resident Dog: If the owner has another dog, the program for introducing babies and new pets (see above) can be used.

The Ride Home: The dog should be picked up from the shelter and taken directly to the veterinarian for a general examination. This helps avoid bringing parasites or infectious organisms into the home. During the ride from the shelter, the dog should be in the passenger compartment of the vehicle, and the new owners should be friendly but calm. If the dog is restless or whines or drools, this should be ignored. In other words, overemotionality should be avoided.

At the New Home: Before the dog is brought into the house or apartment, it should be taken to the selected toilet area immediately. Urination or defecation in other areas should be stopped by distracting the dog. Its first memory of eliminating should be in the correct place, and the act reinforced with praise.

Once in the home, it should be offered a bowl of water in the place assigned permanently. If it drinks copiously, another trip to the outdoor toilet area is in order. Also, it may have to defecate soon after it eats.

The dog should then be allowed to investigate the *entire* home. It is vital that the new pet get to know the odors of its new home so as to feel secure about it. The owners should avoid following and talking to the dog.

However, an eye should be kept on it and a quick, single handclap used for distraction if it appears about to eliminate, pick up inappropriate objects, or get on furniture (if such will not be allowed generally).

Once they investigate their new home, most dogs turn their attentions to their new "family." The learn-to-earn regimen (Chapter 8) should be instituted by telling it to Sit before petting and praising. All family members capable of this must apply it consistently.

Housetraining: The housetraining program, as used for puppies, should be instituted. Mature dogs need guidance in a new home, just as new puppies do

Leaving the Dog Alone: Initially, the dog should not be left alone for at least 3 hours. Then, without speaking to the dog or making eye contact, the owners should quietly leave by the door generally used for routine out-of-home affairs. If, from outside the door, the dog can be heard fussing inside, the owners must not reenter until it has stopped for at least 4 minutes. Then the owners should go back in, avoiding excessive emotion, but speaking praise quietly, not at the door, but in an area the dog will be expected to occupy when left alone.

If the dog does *not* fuss, the owners should stay outside at least 15 minutes before reentry with quiet praise. Time away should then be doubled and redoubled until an hour passes with no unwanted behavior, such as barking, whining or pacing.

This program instills important *first impressions* regarding the owners' departures and arrivals. If these are unemotional and matter of fact, the dog will take them in stride.

Sleeping Arrangements: Given an opportunity, most dogs will sleep 16-18 hours a day. When the family sleeps, they do also. The dog should be encouraged to sleep in a bedroom where people sleep. If a dog bed is to be provided, it should be left in the bedroom so the dog can use it in the owners' absence. Most dogs tend to go there when left alone. If no dog bed is used, its sleeping spot should always be accessible.

Visitors: Visitors should be brought into the home as often as possible so the dog can learn to expect and greet them calmly.

Neighborhood Walks: Neighborhood walks should be avoided for the first few weeks. This "local quarantine" allows the dog to become firmly bonded to its new home and family. Neighborhood walks introduce distractions that may interfere with family relationships.

This plan will settle most dogs nicely in 2-4 days. However, in any social or learning situation, at least 6 weeks are needed before the newly adopted dog tends to retain its lessons permanently. As the dog gains more confidence about its social relationships, it may begin to "test" its place in the family regarding leadership and dominance. Depending on the nature of such actions (jumping up, etc), the appropriate correction program should be immediately instituted.

15

Training Systems and Professional Assistance

Dog owners have an ever-broadening variety of training and behavioral devices and professionals from which to choose. Likewise, veterinarians, groomers, breeders, dog trainers and pet shop proprietors face increasing numbers of requests from dog owners for recommendations on training devices and behavior consultants. This chapter briefly describes the various training devices and systems currently available, as well as trainers and behaviorists dog owners may consult.

Obedience Instructor Qualifications

Obedience instructors generally qualify through an apprenticeship program, first working as an assistant with an experienced instructor. Some areas have regional obedience instructor associations that have set standards for instructor qualification. The National Association of Dog Obedience Instructors (NADOI) has a program stressing humane treatment, along with an extensive apprenticeship program, after which practical and written examinations must be passed before certification. Certified NADOI instructors generally display the NADOI insignia in their literature.

Obedience Training Programs and Systems

Puppy Classes

Puppy kindergarten classes are growing in popularity and are generally conducted by obedience instructors. There is no standard format for these, nor am I sure there should be. This is because more information is needed before a well-balanced program can be devised, with systems flexible enough to deal with all types of puppies and people.

Puppy classes offer the owner an economical opportunity to socialize the puppy with other pups, dogs, adults and children at weekly meetings, often held indoors. Attending animals are in good health, which minimizes the danger of contracting disease.

Lessons concern health care, nutrition, exercise, grooming, and instruction to Sit, Stay and Come and, in some, leash walking. Food-bait reward systems are used in many classes, while others rely on praise and petting.

Some programs include housetraining. Many of these recommend crating puppies, a practice many owners take to extreme, crating puppies for over 9 hours during the day and all night.

Basic Obedience Programs

These vary so much in training methods, instructor competence and class size that the best advice is to personally investigate the instructors and techniques before enrolling. Basic obedience programs may have some of the following strengths and shortcomings:

Strengths:

- The classes afford an opportunity for socialization of attending dogs.
- The lessons may help control the dog on leash in distracting situations.
- Owners can meet other owners with similar breeds, problems or other common interests.
- "Graduating" dogs may progress to more advanced obedience training.

Shortcomings:

- Many classes are large, usually over 20 owner-dog pairs, affording little time for personal assistance.
- Courses often require 10 weeks, at 1 class per week, which some owners complain is too long.
- Some instructors are impatient and unsympathetic with individuals working with difficult dogs.
- Some instructors use apparently harsh measures, such as hanging an aggressive dog by its choke collar or kneeing a jumping dog in the chest, to demonstrate corrective measures on difficult dogs.
- The training methods may be rigid and mechanical, lacking variations that may benefit some dogs.
- The classes usually offer no advice on how to correct behavior problems at home.

Most disappointed owners say they wish they had met the instructors personally or first attended a class without their dogs so as to evaluate the program before enrolling. Most satisfied owners attended small classes, with fewer than 10 other students.

The owner with problems relative to on-leash behavior may receive assistance through basic obedience classes. However, those expecting personal assistance with behavior problems at home, unruly and/or aggressive dogs have been disappointed for the most part. Owners satisfied with basic obedience classes attended small classes that afforded personal attention from experienced instructors who displayed patience and understanding when problems were encountered with in-class or home behavior problems.

Private In-Home Obedience Programs

These vary widely in instructor experience and competence, techniques applied, course content and cost. The best advice to owners contemplating private obedience programs is to investigate *fully* the techniques to be applied, and speak with other owners, with similar problems and dogs, who have used that instructor. Both the instructor and the former clients should be asked about the harshest treatment techniques used during the program. If the dog owner wants assistance with behavior problems unrelated to training, this should be made clear at the initial interview, with special emphasis on the instructor's experience and techniques to be applied. Many owners who did not make inquiries complained that methods used on their dog were far more harsh than they anticipated, such as hanging, whipping and hitting unruly or aggressive dogs, or extensive hours of crating.

To avoid such problems, the screening procedure outlined later in this chapter can help select a trainer or behaviorist for correction of behavior problems.

Boarding Obedience Programs

Sending the dog away to a training facility for a few weeks is an appealing concept. However, it is expensive and still requires extensive followup work by the owners to be effective.

Boarding obedience programs are far longer than required in most cases, usually 6-12 weeks, after which the owner must still work with the dog almost daily to achieve the degree of obedience obtained by a professional trainer.

By contrast, in the early 1970s at our Sun Valley Ranch facility in Los Angeles, Peggy and I trained 5 dogs weekly in 4 1/2 *days*, both on- and off-leash to Come, Sit, Stay, Heel, Down, Go to a designated place, and Stay until released. This was combined with correcting behavior problems, from housetraining to fighting other dogs and biting. Our program was guaranteed to correct problem behavior and produce obedience *while in our charge*. This was easily demonstrated to our clients' satisfaction when they picked up their "instant good dogs" and put them through their ritual obedience routines.

The clients were thoroughly instructed on what to do at home, and were given a complete followup, in-home behavioral "prescription." Our program was immensely popular. However, when the dogs returned to their homes, the old environmental forces that had created the problems soon took their toll, as most owners (over 75%) lacked the motivation to change their *own* ways in living with their "new" dog. As a result, we were soon spending weekends in followup consultations to fulfill what we considered our ethical obligations to the clients and their pets.

Though the Los Angeles market of troubled dog owners would have supported it, we believed it was improper to continue our boarding obedience program, and abandoned it in favor of weekly meetings, for 6 weeks, with owners and their dogs. This proved remarkably effective in 96% of the cases treated during the following 7 years.

Most obedience trainers understand the value of the owners teaching their dog themselves or treating problems with the dog in its home environment. Many boarding kennels now offer weekly classes in which the *owners* are counseled and trained in obedience techniques. This is quicker, more effective and less expensive than adding the costs of boarding the dog for long periods, and still spending time on followup work at home.

Professional Behavior Consultants

Since the 1970s, the number of dog behavior consultants has grown from a handful to thousands. Their qualifications range from the self-taught to formally educated at universities. Some have undergone apprentice training with an experienced professional. Others have simply advertised their services and learned by experience.

The fact that training instructors, psychologists, animal behaviorists, zoologists and sociologists charge single consultation fees ranging from $15 to more than $250 is more an indication of a growing public *demand* than a measure of the competence of professionals attempting to meet it. After speaking with many dog owners and evaluating the entire spectrum of qualifications of dog trainers and behavior consultants, I developed guidelines that dog owners may use to locate the consultant best suited to that owner, their dog and its specific problems. These guidelines have been used by hundreds of dog owners, with excellent results.

How To Select a Dog Trainer or Behavior Consultant

The dog should first undergo a complete veterinary checkup to detect and, if possible, eliminate any medical condition related to the behavior problem. Ask the veterinarian to recommend at least 2 behavior consultants. If the doctor knows of other dog owners who have sought help from these professionals, these people should be called to relate their experiences with the behavior consultant. If the veterinarian cannot recommend 2 or more consultants, see the Yellow Pages or other sources (breeders, pet shops, dog clubs) for the names of other consultants.

Telephone the consultants. In this conversation, the consultant or the telephone receptionist should ask for the history of the dog to be seen. If the consultant or receptionist does not ask for this information, the owner should be aware that s/he may be required to pay a fee for a fact-finding consultation, after which the consultant may be found unsatisfactory to the owner or even unwilling to assist.

When the owner has related the dog's history during the telephone conversation, the consultant should be able to decide if s/he can assist. If so, the next step is in order. If not, other consultants should be called.

The owner should then ask the following questions about the program:

- Where and how long will the sessions be?
- Who must attend? (All people that interact with the dog should attend.)
- How many sessions will be required?
- Will special equipment be used? If so, what type and how will it be applied?
- What treatment may be required?
- If the program does not succeed, what is the next step?
- What is the fee?

Owners who follow this screening system report that its greatest benefit is that it helped them select a "compatible" consultant who uses methods the owner believes are humane and practical for their situation.

Devices for Training and Behavior Control

The devices described here are available to the public through retail stores, mail order houses and some veterinary practices. This review does not include all of the various products available, but presents an overview of significant innovations and modes of operation for those mentioned. Discussions on traditional neck collars, spike collars, reel-leashes and squirt guns are not included, as these devices are familiar to nearly all dog owners.

Anti-Bark Shock Collars

These have evolved from the early models, some of which could be triggered by sounds and extraneous radio waves. The new, sophisticated units can be adjusted for shock intensity, and triggered only by the dog's bark. Some have incorporated buzzers or vibrators that precede the shock, allowing the dog to avoid it by stopping its barking.

Remote-Control Shock Collars

Many models feature variable shock intensities, with buzzers or vibrators that precede the shock to allow the dog to stop the unwanted behavior and, hence, avoid the shock. Both short-range and long-range remote-control units are available. These are used by some trainers of field, field-trial and working dogs, as well as by some obedience trainers and behavior consultants.

Comment: Shock collars and their accompanying instructional literature fail to address the causes of problem behavior and, hence, merely attempt to suppress unwanted behavior. This may prompt the dog to substitute tension-relieving activities in place of the behavior problem in question.

Proponents of shock collars claim the variable shock intensity and preceding warning buzzer minimize or avoid pain. Opponents consider electric shock training as painful and unnatural. Many who oppose their use have tried the collars on themselves.

Invisible Fences

These are reviewed in Chapter 9 in the section on Fence Jumping.

Ultrasonic Devices

The hearing range of dogs is from about 20 cycles per second to over 50,000 cycles per second. While this range is similar, on the low end, to that of people, the upper range in dogs is more than twice as high as in people. Dogs can hear, but learn to ignore many of the sounds in the environment that are inaudible to people (ultrasound above about 20,000 cycles per second). However, most dogs react to a short burst of ultrasound.

Sounds above about 120 decibels, produced within 4-6 inches of the dog's ear, produce pain. The 2 ultrasonic devices mentioned here produce ultrasound below this threshold for pain. Their effectiveness revolves around momentarily interrupting, with a burst of ultrasound, the dog's attention to the undesirable behavioral activity.

Dog-Master Systems: Formerly called Hi-FiDo and Sound Rx, several different Dog-Master devices are now available through mail order houses, along with an accompanying manual and more than 30 audio tapes concerning use of the device to correct various behavioral problems. The devices consist of a chain of brass links (Fig 1). The burst of ultrasound (about 34,000 cycles per second) is produced by tossing the device at the dog's feet, or holding it in the hand and giving a single, quick shake, as if the user has a fistful of coins, none of which should be dropped. Both methods require considerable practice before the device can be used with the dog. Manual, vocal and visual timing skills must be practiced until the user's full attention can be devoted to the dog to detect its responses, often as subtle as the flick of an ear or a subtle change in gait or posture.

The Come command is initially taught with the aid of the Dog-Master device. When the dog obeys the Come command

Figure 1. The Dog-Master ultrasonic device consists of a chain of brass links.

without use of the ultrasound device, the device may then be used to correct undesirable behavior. The basic approach is to use the ultrasound device to get the dog's attention, especially when the dog is *anticipating* jumping up, running away, chewing, leash-pulling, etc.

Comment: The Dog-Master device is effective when used properly. We used it in many problem cases at our facility. Its only limitations are the skill of the user, and it requires dedicated practice to use it effectively. The "kits" now available include instructions sufficient for most dog owners to understand. However, as with any training technique, practice and forethought before application are required, or results can be disappointing.

Pet-Agree Transducer: Pet-Agree is a hand-held ultrasonic transducer powered by a 9-volt battery (Fig 2). It is manufactured by K-II Enterprises of Solvay, New York and currently marketed through mail order houses. A more powerful device is available to government agencies, utility companies and businesses, as a deterrent against aggressive dogs. When the device is pointed at the dog, pushing its button emits an ultrasonic frequency of about 22,000 cycles per second, along with an audible frequency. This startles most dogs. Instructions are limited to use of the device in gaining the dog's attention or interrupting its concentration on some other activity.

Comment: I tested the Pet-Agree device on 2 car chasers by pointing it at the dogs from my car as they were about to start

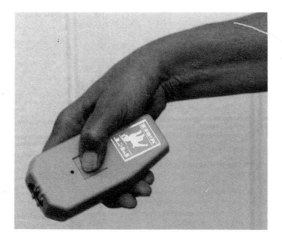

Figure 2. The Pet-Agree ultrasonic transducer is a hand-held battery-operated device.

the chase. Both stopped abruptly and retreated; they have not chased my car since. When the proprietor of a local kennel tested it with a constant barker, the dog stopped barking during the rest of its stay at the kennel.

This device may be useful if one combines with it other behavior-modifying techniques, such as the Jolly Routine (Chapter 7).

Cages and Travel Crates

Close confinement of puppies or older dogs in cages or crates to housetrain them or curtail unwanted behavior has received a great deal of support from many professionals. Esthetically, the idea does not appeal to most dog owners for humane reasons. However, proponents point out that dogs are naturally "den-seeking" animals because of their wolf ancestry. This, however, describes only the pregnant bitch; other wolves and dogs do not naturally seek burrows or dens. Thus, many misinformed owners lock up their puppies and adult dogs up to 18 hours a day while the owners work and sleep, so as to avoid problems.

The adaptability of dogs is illustrated by the fact that many of them tolerate these conditions. However, those that do not adapt to such ill treatment may attempt to chew or dig their way out of the cage or crate, causing serious injury to themselves. Others may salivate, defecate or urinate copiously.

Satisfied crate users often claim that their pets "enjoy" crating, citing the dog's happiness when the owner arrives home. There is no apparent evidence of stress or abuse. On the other hand, opponents perceive the dog's happy behavior as joy in anticipation of being freed.

Size Requirements: If crates or cages are used, it would seem prudent to afford the dog or puppy adequate space for standing, sitting and stretching. The National Institute of Health recommends the following:

1. Measure the dog from the tip of the nose to the tip of the outstretched tail.

2. Add 6 inches to this length.

3. Multiply that sum by *itself* to determine the floor area required (in square feet or square inches).

For example, a dog is 2 1/2 feet long (30 inches). Adding 6 inches yields a total of 3 feet (36 inches). Multiplying 3 x 3 results in a total of 9 square feet of floor space. If one is using inches in the calculation, one would multiply 36 x 36, resulting in a floor space of 1296 square inches. Divide this by 144 to arrive at the floor space in square feet.

Bedding and Water: Clean dry bedding, a few favorite toys, and fresh clean water should be provided to make the dog comfortable during confinement.

Location: Keeping the cage at the dog's regular sleeping spot may encourage it to sleep while the owner is away.

Duration of Confinement: Confinement should not exceed 3-4 hours.

Curtailing Cage Confinement: Even the most dedicated crate proponents suggest abandoning the practice if the puppy or dog displays anxiety behavior, such as whining, barking, pacing or self-mutilation, when confined in a crate.

Alternatives to Cage Confinement: Those who favor larger spaces for confinement suggest large play pens for puppies or baby gates across the doors of a den or kitchen area for pups and older dogs. As with confinement in a crate, water, toys and bedding should be provided in the area.

Comment: While confinement in cages and crates is often recommended to prevent some types of unwanted behavior, the frustrations underlying these problems remain untreated. For this reason, nearly all dog behaviorists consider cage confinement as inappropriate therapy. Misinformation and lack of owner education have led to many dogs being caged in enclosures smaller than those recommended for laboratory dogs, and for periods of up to 18 hours a day. This has led to serious injury of many dogs in their efforts to escape, in addition to marked neurotic behavior in some.

Halter-Style Collar Devices

Collars have been altered to include a muzzle component (Fig 3). Several variations of these halter-collars are available through retail stores, mail order houses and veterinarians. Some devices become muzzles when the handler pulls the leash, or can be adjusted to do so. The obvious advantage of the device lies in the handler's ability to control the direction of the dog's head with relatively little force, whereas the traditional neck collar requires great force. This is particularly true with unruly, highly active or biting dogs.

As compared with a traditional neck collar, halter-collars are quite obtrusive, at least to the dog. The nose band loops around the dog's muzzle, loosely if no tension is applied to the leash, and tightly if tension is applied to the leash. For this reason, some manufacturers suggest that the device initially should be placed on the dog without a leash for various periods to allow it to become accustomed to the halter-collar before its use in training sessions.

The devices are accompanied by excellent instructions. A toll-free telephone number is also available for additional advice to dog owners and suppliers. The veterinary version is called the Promise System, while obedience instructors and humane societies supply it under the label Gentle Leader. The device does not choke or muzzle the dog, but relies on pressure behind the ears and over the nose, which is comparable to the pressure applied to these areas of submissive dogs by dominant ones.

Figure 3. The halter-collar can be used with a standard leash during walks, or with a long lead for household behavior corrections.

Comment: The only negative comments I have heard about these devices has come from a few users who failed to follow instructions. On the other hand, when used according to instructions, behaviorists, trainers and dog owners have praised its effectiveness and humaneness.

(This page intentionally left blank)

Index

P, Q

R

S

T

(This page intentionally left blank)

(This page intentionally left blank)

(This page intentionally left blank)

(This page intentionally left blank)

(This page intentionally left blank)

(This page intentionally left blank)